Hounded - Truman's Story

CLIFFORD NEAL

HOUNDED - TRUMAN'S STORY

A HELLBENT SOUL PITTED AGAINST
THE GRACE OF GOD

2005

Hounded - Truman's Story

TABLE OF CONTENTS

To Kenny Cole, The Memory Of Truman Mahoney And To The Christ We Serve. (A Dedication Statement Is Furnished As A Part Of The Manuscript At It's Close.)

INTRODUCTION
Truman's Story

The world's supply of disposable friends is nowhere near as large as most people think. A true friendship deserves to be nurtured, guarded and shared.

The story that you are about to read came to be printed as a result of a friendship that developed between myself and a man by the name of Kenny Cole. I think it is important for you to know the circumstances of our getting to know one another.

I have for over three years now been involved in a project that has become a seemingly permanent hobby. The church that I serve as pastor gave me an old 1960 model GMC bus that had been the church bus for many years. I had expressed interest in converting the bus from a passenger bus to a motor home and offered to purchase it from the church. They had expressed interest in disposing of it because of its age and the fact that it was not being used enough to make it a viable ministry any longer. Instead of allowing me to purchase it, they wanted to make a gift of it to me. I was delighted with the gift.

So began a process of stripping the interior of the bus and making whatever repairs were needed to the interior. This was a long and tedious job but I enjoyed the work and found it to be a great developing means of exercise and mental relaxation.

After many months of work the interior of the bus was reconstructed into a very comfortable living quarters with everything needed to travel in style and comfort. It was basically intended to be a recreational and ministry vehicle to be utilized by my wife and I for several years into the future.

In the course of time however I found that there were always refinements that came to mind and I began to notice that other people had undertaken the same project. I happened one day to be looking for parts that were hard to come by due to the age of the bus and was launching a computer internet search. In the course of this search, I discovered that there were many groups of people involved in bus conversions that had formed information and assistance boards and would readily assist me in locating parts.

These groups were the most congenial and helpful folks I had run into anywhere in life outside the fellowship of a local church. I began to regularly involve myself in discussions of our hobby and exchanging photographs of our projects and ideas of ways and means of doing the job. These people became a real part of my life though I had never seen their faces except for an occasional photo posted with buses and such.

It was through one of these groups and the discussions of our hobby that I became acquainted with Kenneth Cole. He goes by the shortened name of Kenny and that is how I address him in the e-mail letters that make up this story. Kenny lives in California and I in Texas yet we seemed to immediately develop a strong bond. We discovered a common faith in Christ Jesus and I soon learned that Kenny had recently been diagnosed with cancer of the lung and brain.

He was involved in a bus project of his own with a bus similar to mine and we shared some information and expanded our knowledge of one another to the point that we soon felt ourselves fast friends, at least from my perspective. We shared and prayed for one another over the internet. Having been through an attack of cancer myself, I understood much that he was going through and this made the bond stronger.

I have come to care much for Kenny though we have never physically met. During the course of our exchanges, Kenny shared a very wonderful relationship that he had with our Lord and told me how he had been used of the Lord to bless others. He then asked me if I would share some of my experiences in ministry through the years.

While giving some thought to what I might share with him I remembered that buses had opened our contact with one another and from that I found my mind going back to an experience many years ago. There had been a time when I was serving a church as Associate Pastor and my ministry responsibility included a bus program where we canvassed neighborhoods in the area and made transportation available to any people who wished to attend our church.

Over the course of several years in this ministry, I met many hundreds of families and became involved with them in some wonderful experiences of life and faith. Through this program hundreds of people became a part of our church fellowship. Many joys, pains and sorrows were shared and my life was eternally enriched in learning to love and care for these people as they came to know and follow the teachings of Christ Jesus our Lord.

I could probably have chosen at least twenty people from those wonderful days out of which to share with Kenny but somehow one particular man and his family began to stand out in my mind. I decided to share the story of my meeting, involvement with and growing affectionate friendship with a man by the name of Truman Mahoney.

Truman's life, when looked at by most people, would have been judged one of total worthlessness. From early childhood and on through the major portion of his life, he was a pariah, a vagabond, a blemish upon society, a leech who lived upon the labors of others. He and his brother Harry set a course for themselves as teenagers to get what they wanted out of life by preying upon the good people of America. He was justifiably judged in the courts of our nation to be unworthy to live a free man in a free society. He spent much of his adult life in the prisons of America. He and those with whom he chose to associate struck fear in the hearts of the God fearing citizens of our land.

Truman was a man of superior intellect and courage and, given other circumstances, could have been a man to be admired and emulated. Yet to large extent, his was a wasted existence. It would seem that God made a mistake in allowing such a person to be born. But having said all of that and fully believing it to be true, I have learned that my judgement of the worth of a human being is severely flawed and shortsighted. I have also learned that only God is able to look into the heart of a person and know their true thoughts, intent and worth. And only He can know what possibilities lie ahead for every person to whom He has given life. I have also learned that what God sets out to do with a life, will get done. One way or another, He will bring that person to a desired end. There are some people who have the stamp of God upon their life, and that stamp cannot be erased.

God does and will allow that person all the possible leeway to find their own way into fellowship with their creator and, if they set out to do so early in life, they can do so. He will move heaven and earth to help them develop all the potential that He endowed them with. He has however chosen to allow every person the full freedom of choice in how they are to live out their lifetime. He will constantly endeavor to guide that person toward goodness, usefulness and an understanding of who they are in the scheme of the life that God has placed them in.

What I am wanting you to know is that God wants that person to live a life of God-likeness but will allow him to waste his life if he so chooses but in the end, He will bring that person unto Himself. He would prefer that a person use the reasoning power they were endowed with and choose to seek their creator early in life. But if they fail to do so, God will not and does not give up on them. If He must wait till the last day of that man's life to be reconciled with Him, He may do so. But reconciliation will happen. When, in His infinite wisdom, He knows there will come a day of reconciliation, He patiently and purposefully plods through life with that person and constantly holds out the branch of peace before them.

Sometimes the branch is used to sweep the feet from under the individual and is still not recognized for what it is. Sometimes it is used as a switch to lay a stripe upon the individual to gain their attention. Sometimes it is used to brush aside obstacles in order for the traveler to see his way more clearly toward God. It is used in many ways in the Hand of God but it is always before the face of the individual.

Because man has been given free will, God works with that handicap in His pursuit of relationship with man. This fact is fully evident in the terrible circumstances that mankind has created for himself in every area of his existence. Some men choose to never acknowledge God and in so doing, sink ever deeper and deeper into a self-centered existence of evil. In doing so, they affect everything around them, including the opportunity of life for others. They become a curse to those who would, under other influence, readily orient their lives toward their creator. Those people who will choose to live and die without God are foreknown by God for what and who they are and the choice they will make. He alone knows and must deal with such a man in His own way and He will.

One of the most difficult things for us as human beings to accept is the truth of this, our condition of existence. We would like to say it is not so but all our attempts to negate it will not change it.

Truman came into this world with several strikes against him that were not of his own making. He was led down a strife torn path and lost his way. He knew that God had a claim on his life but he did not see the way to acknowledge it for most of his life. When he did catch a glimmer of it, he chose to set it aside. As a result, his is a story of pitiful waste that was very tragic. At the same time however, he was in his own way making a statement for all who would come after him that is of earth shaking importance. His life is a solid example of the marvelous, wondrous, loving grace of our God.

Truman became a source of great joy to my heart as he came to know our Lord and was changed into one of the warmest, most gentle and loving children of our God that it has been my privilege to know. He affected many hundreds of people positively with his testimony of God's Grace.

Truman's full story has never been told. It will never be fully told because only Truman and God know all the details and God has sworn to forget all that was negative about it. I dare say that Truman himself would not want all the details spread before the public but he did want enough of it to be told to allow others to see his folly and set a different course for themselves. He made an attempt to share it with the world and died before finishing it. I know now that the timing of the story being told was one of those things that God controlled. Some part of it I have known for many years but could not tell all I knew for several reasons. Many lives could have been destroyed by the revelations contained in the telling. Truman did not live in a vacuum and several deaths needed to occur before many things recorded here could be spoken openly. I believe that the time has come for this story to be told. Some things will yet remain behind the curtain but enough will come to the front of the stage to be struck by the light of day. Hopefully enough light for the Olive Branch to bear fruit.

The following is a series of e-mail conversations between Kenny and myself in which Truman's Story is related to a friend whose life it is my pleasure to have touched. The exchanges have been edited and only small portions of our conversations have been left intact. I wanted to preserve the context without embarrassing Kenny by placing privileged information in the public eye so please forgive me for simply trying to show you the context of the telling of this story. I hope and pray that the story will be an encouragement to anyone who is not in a fellowship relation with almighty God. My experience with God has taught me that He loves people without reservations and, in His infinite knowledge and grace, seeks to establish a kinship relation with people everywhere. He is wonderfully gentle and patient and never gives up on us.

Truman's story is such a vivid example of what God can do with the worst and the best of us.

The telling of his story began in this case in December of 2003. It speaks for Truman and the God he came to know and it is my prayer that you will hear it.

Clifford Neal

CHAPTER 1
A DEVINE APPOINTMENT

Kenny,
I am not at all sure what I ought to share with you in the way of adventures in the Lord's service but after some thought, I think I will share one of the most memorable characters I have been involved with. There are so many but a few stand out from the crowd.

I REMEMBERED THAT BUS CONVERSION EXPERIENCES WAS RESPONSIBLE FOR THE TWO OF US BECOMING AQUAINTED. My experience with buses goes a long way back and involves using buses in the ministry. I decided to share a story from a time when I was serving a church as an Associate Pastor back in the late 1960's in Vidor, Texas.

I doubt that I can tell this story in one sitting so I will begin and go as far as time will allow tonight and then pick up later if it gets too wordy. I have never attempted to tell this story by writing it but here goes.

First let me say that my wife Donna and I have always been partners in ministry. I entered the ministry when I was 14 years old and have been preaching ever since. Donna and I were sweethearts in High School and married just after graduation at 18 years old. God sent us to Houston, Texas where we served for about 5 years before He moved us to the Golden Triangle area of Texas. (That's an area framed by three cities in

Southeast Texas: Beaumont, Port Arthur and Orange). Vidor is inside that area. In those days it was a growing bedroom community, somewhat rural, but with a rough reputation. It was famous nationally as a hot bed headquarters community for the Klu Klux Klan and generated many confrontations and opportunities for this humble preacher to face Satan and his handiwork with the love and Grace of our God. I labored there for Jesus for 16 years.

My responsibility in the church at the time I refer to, Pine Forest Baptist, was Outreach, Bus Ministry and Children's Church. This involved many hours of door to door visiting in the area in an attempt to enlist children and their families to ride buses to church. Particularly those unchurched families who were not in personal relationship with God. It was a very successful ministry resulting in hundreds of people being shone the way to faith in Jesus. Part of the visiting would involve taking members of the congregation with me to teach them the skills needed to share their faith. We met all kinds of folks and some of them still keep up with our ministry even to this day.

God has blessed us with many wonderful friends through the years who are closer than family in many ways.

I say all this to set the stage for you to perhaps begin to understand our lifestyle. I often find that many folks cannot identify with our experiences unless they share our faith and priorities in life.

Be that as it may, we were about our regular routine of visiting one day and my wife noticed a man and three children working in a small garden behind a tall cyclone fence that enclosed his home and yard covering a space of about 1 acre. The gate was locked and the people who lived next door had begun to ride our church bus and had recently become Christians. My wife asked the lady of the house, Mrs. Johnson, (the ones who rode our bus) about the man in the garden and received a retort ," Mrs. Donna, you don't want to have anything to do with that man, he is mean, has a foul mouth and will not let anyone on his property. They have been living there several months now and make no secret about the fact that they want to be left strictly alone."

Well the Spirit of God began to work on my wife about that family and for several weeks as we would pass the place we would always see the gate locked and a "keep out" sign on it. One Saturday as we were visiting the Johnson's next door, Donna noticed that the gate was open and saw the man and children working in the garden. She felt that the open gate was an invitation from God to enter and attempt to meet the family.

With some reservations, she walked into the garden and introduced herself and found a chilly reception. The man was not interested in church or our ministry but my wife has a way with children and these three seemed to immediately warm toward her. For several weeks as we would visit on Saturdays, we watched for the gate to be open and finally found it so. Donna entered the forbidden zone again and this time the children greeted her warmly and she felt free to explain to the father that we would have a bus passing by the next morning to take any interested children to church. She explained to him and the children what a children's church program involved. The children immediately began to ask their father to allow them to attend and ride the bus.

He said he would think about it and discuss it with their mother. The next morning as the bus pulled up to the Johnson home next door, those 3 children ran down the drive and climbed aboard the bus to go to church. The children responded wonderfully to the program we involved them in and began to learn about God and developed a hunger to know all they could. They came week after week and week after week Donna would visit their father in the garden, now finding the gate always open on Saturdays as we visited. Let me inject here that I also had ventured into the garden several Saturdays and had met the father. He introduced himself to me as Truman Mahoney and was always civil but reserved.

Eventually we met Mrs. Mahoney (Mary) and gradually developed a rapport with her to the point that we invited her to ride the bus with the children and attend church. After several weeks of "maybe one day", their oldest child made a commitment of her life to Christ in children's church and we were obligated to share this with the parents and seek their permission to baptize the child. This came to be acceptable after several consultations in the garden and on the day of the child's baptismal, the mother rode the bus with the children to church but Truman seemingly would not commit to attend the service. As the baptismal service began, who walked into the sanctuary but Truman.

From that day, Mary attended church and Bible Classes and occasionally rode the bus with her children. Truman refrained. Soon the other two children were saved and Truman attended their baptisms.

One Sunday Mary gave her heart to Christ and Truman attended her baptism. It became obvious that he loved his family but stoutly refused to become personally involved in church himself.

One day Truman was working on a project at their home and fell off a ladder. His leg was shattered and the bone protruding out of the flesh at the ankle, was driven into the ground by the force of his fall. Mary attended to it as best she could and got him to the hospital in Beaumont where Truman was employed.

After consulting with the doctors, Truman told them to take his leg off. He felt that the condition would create infection that could endanger his life and would rather live without the foot. His leg was removed just below the knee.

Truman cursed God and became very bitter and withdrawn.

One night a short while after he had been fitted with an artificial leg, he woke up and found their home ablaze. He struggled out of bed, crawled about the house collecting the wife and children and pushing them out a window and finally crawled out the window himself. Their home was a total loss. The garage only was spared. Our church responded by many folks coming to their aid in cleaning up and collecting what few small items survived the fire. Truman sat in the driveway and glared coldly. He cursed God openly. We found that the family had a small insurance policy but it would be insufficient to replace their home. They had no place to go and no funds to go with.

Our church provided a mobile home and had it moved on to their property for them to live in until they could make permanent arrangements and the day it was delivered, Truman broke down and wept openly. He was in church the next Sunday with his family. He made a commitment of his life to Christ at the close of the service and was a different man. The bitterness that had characterized his life was gone He became, almost immediately, an open and responsive person. God had finally caught up with Truman Mahoney.

His baptism was scheduled a few weeks later and was performed in an evening service . After the baptism, Truman came to me and said "Preacher, would you and Donna please come by the house after church tonight, I have something I must share with you." We agreed to go.

After a time of visiting and being served coffee and cake in their home, Truman said to me, "I have a long story to tell you that may take an hour or two, will you stay and hear it?"

I agreed and he went into another room and returned with a rather large box and sat it down on the floor in front of me.

The first item he removed and placed in my hands was a framed document. He said, "This box is one of the few things that survived the fire". The document was a Presidential Pardon signed by Lyndon Johnson freeing Truman from Federal Prison and stating that he had been released from Leavenworth Prison in Kansas several years earlier.

The story he began to tell me was his life story. It proved to be after one A.M. before we left their home that night. His story is a long one and it is still one that thrills my soul. It is a story of God's relentless pursuit of Truman Mahoney. The pursuit stretched over 50 years and is one of the most powerful statements of the patience, love and determination of our God to redeem one of his chosen ones that I have personally ever witnessed. I have heard our Lord referred to as "The Hound Of Heaven" and often thought that most folks do not understand the reference. Truman is an example of "The Hound" on the trail of its prey in a blessed chase.

Is this the sort of story that interests you? If so I will attempt to share it if you have the patience to hear it.

Bless you and Merry Christmas my brother,
Clifford

CHAPTER 2
HARD BEGINNINGS

Kenny,
We are back on line and I have some time to share another episode of our story so I will begin where we left off last time. Truman is sharing the story in his home.

Truman Mahoney begins at the beginning for him.

Truman was born the second son to a Methodist minister in Tarver Hill in the state of Illinois on January 2, 1911. He began by relating memories of a conflict in the congregation where his father was pastor and difficulties between his father and mother. Both parents were difficult for Truman and his brother Harry to please. It seemed that there were many wonderful families in the congregation who had loving family relationships and some of them were very affectionate toward Truman. Truman was envious.

He had been engaged in an on going discussion for about two years with his father and two other men in the congregation concerning his personal relationship with God. At about ten years of age he had decided that his life belonged to God but was not sure he wanted to place it in God's hands.

His struggle was based in his attempt to understand the seeming double standard his parents presented. His father's sermons and the instruction that he offered Truman made it appear that life with God was the very best possible for all people. Added to this, he saw the lives of the other two men as wonderful examples of joy and peace and purpose of life. Yet he had to deal with the reality that his own home life was filled with difficulties, anger, pain and confusion and constant strife. It seemed certain to him that someone was not being completely truthful with him and he resented it fiercely.

He did feel that his parents loved him but they did not love each other. He knew other people in the church who were married and had children who were very demonstrative in loving one another. The comparisons made him feel robbed in some way that he could not understand.

Somewhere around the age of eleven Truman's family was suddenly torn asunder with the forced resignation of his father by the congregation. It came to light that there was an affair between Truman's father and a lady in the church. The people whom he had idolized were now refusing to accept the kind of failure in his father that his father had accepted in them and had attempted to work through with them. He knew several men and women who were members of the church who had gone through all kind of family problems, including divorces and yet they were still loved by his father. They were still loved by the other church members. Why was his family so different? Why were they held to a different standard?

It seemed to Truman that everyone talked one set of principles but lived another. How could a God who loved him allow so much pain to come to him? Was this God real? If He was, then Truman could not believe that He was trustworthy. It was just too confusing. Perhaps he would be better off to just live his life and not need anyone, including God.

The strife between his parents soon led to a divorce and a total change in Truman's life. A short time later Truman's father married a woman with whom he had become involved in the church and the two of them moved to a neighboring town. Truman and Harry seldom saw him anymore.

The two boys lived with their mother for a time until she met and married another man. It became obvious that his mother did not want the children. They interfered with what she wanted to do with her life and when her husband began to show a fondness for the boys, she became insanely jealous. He made no secret of the fact that he did not like the way she treated the boys. She made all sorts of unreasonable demands of the boys and they began to rebel. Truman's sisters suffered a like fate.

Conflict grew in the new marriage and soon Truman's mother was demanding that the boys father take them into his home and assume responsibility for their up-bringing. He reluctantly took them in but his new wife was cruel to both boys and did not want them around either.

Harry was taking the whole thing worse than Truman was and began to run around with a group of boys older than himself. These boys often stayed out late at night and behaved themselves in ways that brought the attention of the local law enforcement personnel to be focused on Harry. Harry fought with his new step-mother and was a discipline problem for his father.

Truman seemed caught in the middle of everything. He loved Harry above everything and everyone in the world. He wanted to defend Harry against his father's new wife and failed to understand how his father could take her part against his own two sons. When he could, Truman would tag along with Harry and his friends. He began to feel accepted among them in spite of his father's warnings that they would lead him to ruin.

As it turned out, his father's warning became a prophecy for, a short time later, the brothers were carousing with this group of boys and looking for something to do. Someone suggested that they go over to a place where racehorses were raised and trained and there they could watch the training exercises. This sounded like fun so off they went.

After arriving and watching for some time, they found themselves fascinated with the whole process. They could not get over the fact that many of the jockeys who were working with the horses were no older than themselves and began to come back to the farm regularly to watch and learn. The young jockeys began to befriend the group of boys and soon all the time that could be garnered was spent there.

Soon the boys began to volunteer to help with the chores that the jockeys were involved with and became more and more familiar with the horses. They even managed to sneak off and go to a few actual races where they began to mix with a group of people who were interested in exploiting them for their youth.

In the course of a few weeks the boys were approached by some grown men with an offer to pay them to steal some particular horses for them. This seemed to be an exciting adventure so they agreed to do what was wanted and soon were deeply embroiled in a plot to steal horses from the very farm they had been visiting. An arrangement was made for them to steal the horses and take them to another nearby farm. When they arrived they would be met by some adults with enclosed trailers. The horses would be loaded into these trailers and taken elsewhere to be sold. The now professional thieves would be paid upon delivery of the horses to the nearby farm.

The band of boys chose a dark night to approach the horses they intended to steal and had no difficulty entering the barn where the animals were stabled. Because they had become fully acquainted with the horses, they were able to easily place ropes on the ones they wanted and lead them away from the farm. The problem developed when they were passed by several cars while leading the horses to the other farm and were recognized by the drivers of the automobiles.

The next day when the police were notified of the theft, it was an easy job for the police to locate these drivers who had witnessed the boys leading the horses down the road the night before. Before the day was over, the Mahoney boys had been arrested for the first time in their lives and so mark the beginning of a career of crime. In this manner the year 1923 became a year Truman Mahoney would never forget. His father was now totally convinced that he had to get the boys away from the group they were involved with.

A lengthy exchange of bargaining sessions between the local police and judge and Truman's dad produced an agreement that the two boys needed to be in a different environment. Several alternatives were explored and many arguments raged between Truman's dad and his new wife as to what should be done.

Finally a decision was made to place both boys in an orphanage located about thirty miles from either parent. His father told them that he did not know what else to do with them. He was afraid that they would wind up in serious trouble if he did not get them away from the influence of the boys they were running with. He thought a time away from everything and everyone would give them a chance to reorder their lives.

He also told them that he needed time to get his marriage on track and establish himself in a new career. He felt certain that after a while, he could bring them both back home to a different kind of life. They needed to be strong and stand up to life like men.

Upon packing a few belongings, Truman's father presented both boys with a small pocket New Testament and then took them to the orphanage and left them with a promise to come and visit regularly. He never did.

Days stretched into weeks and Truman found himself terribly homesick. He had hidden some of the clothing he brought from home and would not let the orphanage staff wash it because it carried the scent of home on it. He would lie in his bed at night with one of these pieces of clothing and think of home.

The small New Testament was a treasured item for the same reason but he did not read it at first. After several weeks however he began to look at the book and found that his father had written a short prayer in the flyleaf asking God to safeguard Truman. At first Truman only read that prayer each night but before too long he began to read the text of the Scriptures also. It seemed to comfort him. He did not understand a lot of what he read, but somehow he did not feel quite so alone when he read it. Memories of people who were happy and loving with one another would fill his thoughts and he would drift off to sleep.

Harry and Truman were so lonesome and began to think that the orphanage staff was keeping their parents from coming to visit with them. A plan began to form between them. They would run away and go home. There were no locks holding them in this place. They could easily slip out almost any night they chose. Harry was 14 years old and he knew how to do things. Truman trusted him completely and knew that he would be safe with him in any situation. He had asked if Harry knew how to get them home and this brought a belly laugh from him. "What do you think I am, a baby? Getting home will be simple. It will take us a while to make the trip but don't worry about it . We may need to steal some food to take with us when we go but that will be no problem either."

So they talked about the best way to get home and Harry said that the railroad tracks that ran through town was the same one that ran through the town where their dad lived. All they had to do was walk down the tracks until they got home. Harry asked questions and discovered that the distance was about thirty miles and he reckoned that it would take them about two days to get there.

They set a date for their escape and both of them slipped bits of food from meal tables and hid them in a syrup bucket that they had taken from the kitchen. They knew that if they left without telling even the other boys about it, they could be a long way toward home before it was even discovered that they were gone. It was an exciting adventure and Truman became so nervous that he could not sleep at all for the three nights before their "great escape".

Finally the time arrived and around midnight Harry came to Truman's bed and called his name very quietly. Nothing else needed to be said. Truman was up in an instant. He had gone to bed with his clothes on and they both took the blankets from their beds with them for use against the cold night air. They slipped out of the building without a sound and crept across the lawn to the street where they broke into a dead run and continued till both were completely out of breath.

True to his word, Harry knew where the railroad tracks were and, when they found themselves standing in the middle of the rails, Harry said, "If we go to the right, we could walk to mom's place. If we go to the left, the tracks will take us right to dad's house. I think we will be better off going to dad. At least I have friends there who will let us stay with them if dad is not at home when we get there. What do you think little brother?" Truman replied," I would really rather go to mom's but I think you are right, we better head for dad's house."

So away they went, down the tracks. There was enough light reflected in the sky from the city lights to let them see where they were walking for a short ways but when they outdistanced the glare, they were aware that the night was overcast and there was no moon. They had not even considered the need for a light and the first time that Truman stumbled and fell, he said," Harry, we better go back and get a light of some kind." Harry considered this for a while and said, "We better not risk going back little brother. We were really lucky to get away as it is and we might not be so lucky twice in one night. It is probably best that it is so dark because no one will be able to see us and if we had a light, we would get caught anyway. If we walk carefully, and stay between the rails, we won't get lost. We need to use the night to cover our getaway. We'll just keep going and when it gets daylight, we will find us a place to lie down and sleep all day. Tomorrow night, we should be able to make it to dad's house.

Walking through the dark night was an ordeal that Truman never forgot. A fog began to form around them and they found themselves holding one another's hand and stumbling along blindly. They seemed to fall every few minutes and soon both of them were hurting from having landed on the rocks that the rails were bedded upon. On several occasions they were startled and terrified by the sound of some animal in the bushes or trees that lined the railway and could hardly prevent themselves from breaking into a run in their terror.

Twice they stumbled and fell as they bolted in fear from a sudden sound and were so disoriented when they got back to their feet that they could not decide which direction to walk in. For the first time in many years, Truman heard Harry cry. This completely unnerved Truman. He sat down and refused to budge. Harry put his arms around him and they cried together.

After a while they began to laugh at themselves and in doing so gained a measure of composure. Harry made a decision, "I am sure we need to go this way" and he calmly pulled Truman to his feet and said, "You're too big for me to carry so lets go." Truman was not sure but he trusted Harry. His faith proved to be well founded for as morning began to dawn, and the sun light began to burn away the fog, they knew they were headed in the right direction.

They came to a small bridge over a little stream and went down the embankment and under the bridge. They had not thought to bring water with them so they were glad to discover that the little stream seemed cold and clear and they drank their fill. They were both starving so they sat down and opened their syrup bucket and ate from their stolen storehouse. They were exhausted so they rolled up together in the two blankets doubled together and slept like logs until they were awakened by a train rolling over the bridge above them. The two of them stuck their heads out from under the blankets like turtles and found the full light of day shining.

It was sometime in the evening hours and so they decided to risk being seen and set off down the tracks toward dad. Night soon overtook them and they were seemingly better able to make their way even though it was a dark night. There was mercifully no fog and they could see the stars and they seemed to give a glow to their railed pathway.

It was just after dawn when they arrived at their father's house. He was clearly shocked, not only that they were safe, but that their appearance was frightfully filthy. Their clothes were torn and they were covered with bruises from the many falls in the nights march. He had received a telephone call from the orphanage informing him that they had run away so he had been very worried about them he said. He seemed glad to see them and allowed them stay the day and spend the next night. A huge argument developed between their father and stepmother that lasted all night. In the morning their father drove them back to the orphanage and told them they would have to stay.

Another plan began to form in their minds. They would run away and go home to mother. They were able to sneak away and again walked two days to where their mother lived. She welcomed them into the house and prepared a meal for them. While they were eating, she telephoned the orphanage to come and pick them up.

Trapped. The two boys were very confused and angry and could not adjust to life in the home. They tried to forget their mother and father and in doing so grew closer and closer and the bond between them was stronger than iron. They were protective of one another to the point that the orphanage staff began to discipline them by threatening to send one of them to another home far away if they did not behave themselves. This proved to be a huge and constant fear for both of them.

After several months Truman was awakened one night by a member of the orphanage staff and led to the small apartment where this staff member lived. Once inside, Truman was sexually molested by the man and threatened with severe consequences if he told anyone.

He told Harry and was terrified at the anger and rage that filled Harry. They both had heard from the other boys how some had reported incidents in the past and had been ignored. After a few days, Harry came up with a plan. They would enlist the aid of several of the older boys and kill the offender. He wanted the man to pay for his offense but knew that the rest of the staff had covered up for the man and probably would continue to do so.

They had no problem getting six other boys to join with them but had to agree not to kill the man. They would beat him up and castrate him.

On the chosen night, the boys assembled and crept to the man's apartment and knocked on the door. When the man answered the door, they forced their way into the apartment and found that he had a young boy in the apartment with him. Each of the boys carried some sort of club and they began to beat the man into unconsciousness. They threw him on his bed and Harry took a knife from the kitchen and performed the surgical procedure on the man. They left him lying there and made their way outside. The two of them ran away again and told the other boys they would have to fend for themselves. They never knew what happened to the offender and the other boys.

This time they knew they would have to make it on their own so they walked for several days down a railroad track passing through Matoon and Champaigne,IL.. They were befriended by some tramps who treated them fairly well. They slept under bridges and learned to steal to provide food and clothing. At night around campfires Truman would reach into his pocket and remove his only item from home, the New Testament. When all others were asleep, he would read the scriptures and after a time began to feel a calling from God. He refused to heed that call and listened to Harry instead.

Harry and Truman, against the world, began to make friends with other young boys on the run. They became a self-supporting group and experimented with ways to provide for themselves. Stealing was the easiest and they became good at it. Months became years and they gravitated from small home robberies to more imaginative methods of conducting a criminal lifestyle.

The two of them began to wander over wider and wider areas and found themselves learning many different ways to turn a quick profit. The group usually worked together but on some occasions, individual members would engage in some enterprise by themselves.

Such was the case with the next brush with the law for Truman. On August 19, 1927 he was arrested and convicted of burglary in Terre Haute, Indiana and given a suspended sentence to the state reformatory because of his age. He was 16 years old. This did not seem to deter the boys from exercising their chosen profession because just four months later Truman was again arrested and tried for burglary in Pendleton, Indiana on December 4.

This offense brought a sentence of 1 to 10 years in the state reformatory and Truman found himself behind bars for the first time in his life. Being separated from Harry, he became a model prisoner and in a short period of time was released on parole. Rejoining the group, he was back up to the same pattern of behavior and was now learning to put into practice many new methods he had learned while keeping company with other boys of various backgrounds in the reformatory.

He was arrested again in Shreveport, Louisiana on February 5, 1930 on suspicion of burglary but was released for lack of evidence. Again in Shreveport on August 19, 1930 he was arrested and released. Leaving Louisiana, the group went back to Terre Haute, Indiana where they set up a semi-permanent base of operations. While there, Truman was again arrested for burglary on October 20, 1930 and returned to the reformatory for parole violations.

Upon his release, the group gravitated to the Chicago area where at the ages of 19 and 21, Truman and Harry were a part of a gang of thieves who were skilled felons. These were the prohibition years and the underworld in the Chicago area teemed with bootleggers. The two industrious teenagers discovered the perfect crime. They would hijack trucks filled with bootleg liquor and sell it to the competitors of the ones from whom they stole. It worked out wonderfully and profitably for them simply because the people from whom they stole could not report the crime to the police.

This went on for several months until they stole from the wrong people. They had stolen from Al Capone's organization and Big Al had some of his hit men sent to search them out and say to them, "Don't do that again." They were told that only their age prevented their immediate death and that there would be no second warning.

They decided that they had better change to a different style of work if they wanted to live so they did some research and decided that robbing banks in small towns would be an easy and profitable business.

They experimented with different means to rob banks and decided that the safest way to do so was to involve as little confrontation as possible. They would scope out a bank and learn its routine. Then, when they were ready, they would break into the bank during the wee hours of the night and lie in wait for the employees to come in to open the bank in the morning. As the employees arrived, they would capture them and tie them up and remain in the bank until the vault could be opened with the aid of the employees. They then would take whatever they chose and lock the employees in the vault and make an exit by simply walking out and locking the front door behind them leaving a "CLOSED FOR THE DAY" sign on the front door. This allowed them plenty of time to make a clean get-a-way. Small towns were perfect.

The long hours of waiting inside the banks called for a

silent vigil and Truman found himself using a small light and reading his New Testament. Very often he would hear the call of God saying, "Truman,I want you." or "Truman, you are a better person than this and I have a plan for your life." but he would shut his heart and listen to Harry.

It had become a practice for them to steal cars to use as get-a-way vehicles for the bank robberies and all of them became expert at this as well. This would allow them to leave a bank and drive to a location where one of their own cars would be stowed. Leaving the stolen car, they could then safely travel to wherever they chose.

One such theft of an automobile resulted in Truman being apprehended in the car and arrested. On October 1, 1934 he was charged with of a violation of the Dyer Act in taking a stolen vehicle across state lines and held for trial. On April 9, 1935 he was convicted and sentenced to three years in the Federal Prison in Atlanta, Georgia. He served his time there and was released on parole on July 13, 1937.

A BRIEF RETURN TO TRUMAN'S LIVING ROOM:

As Truman told his story on this late night visit, he would augment and substantiate his narrative by removing items from the box at my feet. Mostly in the form of newspaper articles from cities where they had carried off a robbery which would give details from law enforcement officials and employees who were captured and tied up as they came to work.

Occasionally things would go wrong as human plans are prone to do and they would have to resort to violence. Sometimes an employee would resist and be hit with a black jack or baseball bat or whatever weapon might be at hand. Sometimes a firearm would be used as a tool to beat an individual into submission and rarely someone would be shot. During the course of almost

3 years of robbing they had reached into many states and many banks and they had killed 8 people. Truman never disclosed to me who it was that did the actual killing and would not give a direct answer when I asked if he had done so himself. He said that some things were best left unsaid.

Some interesting and ingenious plans were often made to carry out a robbery. Some of these were extremely humorous and perhaps one would be worth taking the time to share in detail. They tried to avoid violence as much as possible.

Kenny, I think I will take another session to relate one such robbery as this post is getting far too long.

Let me tell you that I did not hear the complete story on that first night as we sat in Truman's home. Time would not have allowed it and, in retrospect, I don't think his family had ever heard the full disclosure. We were given an abbreviated version and in succeeding months Truman and I became involved in church and, as time proceeded, developed a close friendship.

One day we were discussing his past in relationship to the present circumstances of life and I commented that his life story would make interesting reading. I also suggested that he might be able to help many people find God by sharing his own experience.

A few days later, he called me and asked if I could come by the house as he had a matter he wanted to discuss with me. When I arrived, we talked about the idea of a book being written and possibly his appearing on a radio broadcast with me.

I was at that time involved in a weekly 30 minute broadcast over a station in Beaumont, Texas and he wanted me to consider with him the ramifications of his appearing on some of the broadcasts. After considerable discussion, we decided that it might be too dangerous for him and his family for some of this information to become public knowledge at this time. There were reasons that we will discuss later that seemed to dictate that we move slowly in any telling of his life's story. It was at this juncture that I realized his children did not know much of his past life in detail. It now appears that Mary also knew only bits and pieces. Upon asking him about this, he shared that some day he planned to sit down and make a full and complete disclosure to her. In the past he had been afraid to make her aware for her own protection.

He then asked me if I might be willing to assist him in the writing of a book, which could be published at some time in the future. After several discussions, over the next several weeks,we agreed to make the attempt.

We decided to first record as much of his life as possible on tape. I had the necessary recording equipment that I used in preparing for radio broadcasts so we began to sit down together as often as we could and he would talk and I would ask for clarification where I felt it was needed

As a result, we spent many hours sitting in front of microphones recording Truman's story. I found the sessions fascinating and we began to work on manuscripts separately and would compare notes occasionally. It was evident from the outset that we had widely differing opinions of how to present the material. We decided to work on a general outline and come to some agreement later as to final drafts. These sessions stretched over many months around 1970.

About this time, I was making a ministry decision myself that involved moving to a new church position with another church and we put the sessions aside for a season till I could relocate and establish some kind of schedule.

As it happened, many months slipped by before we were

able to resume our work. I was deeply involved in the new ministry where I was senior pastor and Truman was busy taking care of his family and working in his own church. Mary became pregnant with their forth child. She delivered a fine baby boy who was named Joseph. We could not know at the time that Truman would never live to finish the book or rear his newborn son. He died on June 7, 1977. Joseph was not yet one year old.

We had just before his death renewed our work on the book and I had left my hand written manuscript with him for examination. He was consulting another person to assist in a final draft of the book and I felt that I had gone about as far as I could carry the work. I lost interest without his enthusiasm to keep me going and not long afterward, I made a move to another church some distance away. The project died with Truman.

Mary remarried after some time and we drifted away from one another. I lost track of the family. I later learned that another person had been entrusted with the partial manuscripts and a lot of the documentation Truman had collected. He was going to attempt to finish the book. That person died and the material was lost to Mary, never to be seen again.

I never forgot Truman and through the years often used bits of his life as illustrations for sermons.

Many lives have been touched by Truman's life through the years in ways he would be delighted with if he knew. He continues to live in my heart and the Christ we both served is still using him to encourage folks to know that the "Hound Of Heaven" is searching out and calling to his own.

Till next time, May God bless you,
Clifford

CHAPTER 3
LEARNING TO PLAN AHEAD

K enny,
I have found a few minutes tonight to spend on our communication so I will attempt to share an episode from the life of Truman.

ON TO TRUMAN:

As I was saying about some of the robberies that the Mahoney Gang pulled off, they are down right funny if you can get past the horror of what they were doing.

It seems that the group was very intelligent but extremely naive for they planned their work in great detail and at the same time very often misunderstood their own limitations. Some things were not always what they judged them to be at all.

Let me share a particular bank job in a small town that was involved in an annual celebration where a parade was planned far in advance with considerable publicity concerning the schedule of the day's events.

The group had been looking at the town's bank for some time and had sent two of them in to study the situation carefully. While there, they became aware of the plans for the celebration and one of them was struck with what he considered a brilliant scheme to take advantage of the holiday festivities.

They had studied the town and its plans carefully. There was only one main highway that ran through the town so if they were detected and had to run, they could easily be caught for lack of escape routes. In studying the situation, they saw that there was a railroad that ran through the town that could be utilized as a possible means of escape. They also found that there was a stream that ran through the town with some street bridges over it inside the city. They realized that no one would expect bank robbers to make a get-away using either route. They knew that the bank was scheduled to close down at noon for the one P.M. parade and that the parade would pass in front of the bank as it made its way through the town.

They also found out that the bank would have a smaller than normal work force on that day because many of the employees were involved in the celebration and would be allowed to miss work for the day.

In studying the route that the parade would take, several ideas were tossed about. One particular plan developed as they found that about two blocks after passing the bank, the parade would take a turn on a cross street and pass over one of the bridges and proceed two more blocks and cross the railroad track as it continued through town. They discovered that a local shuttle passenger train was scheduled to depart shortly after the parade to return visitors back to their origins who had come to town for the parade. It was a fairly common practice in that day and time for a train to be utilized for such things. Few people had automobiles but many rode trains.

Further investigation found that a group of canoe enthusiasts kept several canoes beached along the stream under the bridge on the parade route. This was chosen to be an escape route for two of the gang who would steal one of these canoes and paddle out of town in the stream.

The railroad train would be used as an escape vehicle for two more of the members of the gang. As they looked and planned, they were sure that this was going to work out just fine. They found that tickets could be purchased after boarding the train from the conductor.

On a poster that was seen in several places around town, they discovered that a bicycle group was planning for a rather large group to ride together from town to a local lake for an evening picnic after the parade and had invited anyone interested to join them. They decided that this would be the means of the 5th member of the gang to escape town.

The newspaper was full of information about the various kinds of costumes that would be utilized by the local citizens in the parade and celebration. The planners read this with great interest and decided to lay out a most unusual and very bold plan to the other members of the gang.

After much discussion, the plan was put into action. It called for preparation on an unusual scale and would require nerves of steel.

During the night before the celebration, the gang hid a get-a-way car in a secluded spot a few miles outside the town. It was near a spot where the railroad passed over the stream flowing from the town. It was the same stream that emptied into a lake where the picnic was to be held by the bikers.

The designated driver dropped them off separately in town during the wee hours of the night. He then parked the car in the arranged spot and walked back to town. Each person had a particular set of assignments to carry out before meeting at the bank.

One man had obtained a bicycle that he had earlier hidden in an old shed. He found the shed and retrieved it. Taking care to avoid detection, he silently put it in a bike rack outside the bank. Another made sure the canoes were still in their usual place under the bridge and that paddles were hidden nearby.

They had obtained a wheelbarrow, which they had hidden in an old tool shed behind an abandoned house. It was brought out and this they took with them as they broke into the bank. Safely secured inside, they set themselves to await the coming of the morning and the arrival of the bank employees.

While they waited, they opened a couple of the bags that they had brought with them from the car and removed five costumes they had purchased for the occasion. After dressing themselves up as clowns and painting one another's faces, they settled down to wait.

Truman, in a secluded room, sat and read his New Testament. He wondered if God was aware of what they were doing. Was it possible? Somehow the thought was a comfort to him and helped him with his nervousness. He found himself drifting off to sleep.

As the employees came to work, they were ready for them but were not prepared for the reaction they got from them when they confronted them. They had to wave a gun at them to get them to take them seriously. Everyone thought as they were met at the door that the whole thing was a joke. At first this took the gang aback but it suddenly dawned upon them that the clown suits created this reaction from the employees. Even as they tied them up and made them sit on the floor, a couple of them broke out laughing and had to be struck hard enough to cause bleeding before they were convinced that this was serious business. They thought it was all a joke being played upon them.

When the last employee had arrived and had been tied up, they placed a sign on the front door stating that the bank was closed for the celebration and parade. After cleaning out all the cash they could stuff into two bags, which they had brought with them, they rechecked a third bag which contained candy and party favors. They then waited for the parade to begin which would pass directly in front of the bank.

As the parade came by the bank, the clowns exited the bank very casually. One of them was pushing a wheelbarrow upon which sat another clown who was holding a bag filled with cash. They leisurely locked the door behind them and thus left the employees closed up in the bank vault. Folks observing them thought that they were connected with the bank and were simply joining the festivities. Several even spoke to them warmly.

They stopped and took the bicycle from the rack and one clown mounted the bike and placed a prepared picnic basket in the carrying rack. The other two clowns danced out into the parade with bags on their backs where they were joined by the other three and thus became a part of the parade through town. They would take turns dipping into one of the bags, which contained candy and favors, and liberally tossed them to the crowd as they danced and biked and wheeled their way through town.

As the parade passed over the bridge spanning the stream, the wheelbarrow suddenly turned over and it appeared to those watching from the crowd that it was having trouble with the wheel. The two manning it dropped out of the parade at the end of the bridge and began to work on it. Attention from the bystanders was soon averted by the passing parade and, looking around to be sure no one was paying any attention to them, the two slipped into the bushes at the end of the bridge and down the creek bank. They dumped the wheelbarrow, threw the bag of money into a canoe and pushed it out into the stream and began to paddle away down the stream and away from town.

As the parade came to the railroad, the two carrying the other bags dropped out of the parade and very calmly entered the train and sat down in a seat to await the train's departure. The conductor came by and chatted with them. He had been watching the parade and had not seen them climb aboard the train. They told him that one of them had gotten sick while in the parade and felt that he could not make the rest of the route. The conductor offered to help in any way he could but was assured that they thought they would be alright after resting awhile. They asked if they could go ahead and purchase their tickets and he took their money and issued them each a ticket to the next town down the line. They asked if it would be O.K. for them to lie down and take a nap while they waited and were assured that it would be fine.

At the end of the parade, the clown on the bike continued to the gathering point for the picnic group and joined them for a leisure ride out of town. The picnic basket of course did not contain a picnic meal. It contained their weapons and the make-up kit they had used to paint their faces with. He had a lively discussion with members of the group as they pedaled along on their route toward the lake.

When he reached the bridge where the train would cross the stream, he told a person riding near him that he needed to answer the call of nature and the bridge appeared to be a place he could drop out of sight and relieve himself. He stopped and said he would catch up later and after they were out of sight, he went down the stream bank and under the bridge to await the arrival of the canoe and one bag of money.

The canoe was late in arriving and when it did, the two clowns were wet and the moneybag was missing. The miscalculation I spoke of earlier had expressed itself in that neither of the two passengers of the canoe had ever handled a canoe before. They found it to be very awkward and had struggled greatly to maneuver it down the stream. They were just now beginning to get the hang of handling the thing. They began to tell the story of their near-death experience of going over a waterfall and capsizing.

They now realized they had failed to check the course of the stream over the route they would have to travel and did not know that there were a series of rapids and waterfalls that they would have to navigate. Neither of them could swim either. The canoe had been swept over a waterfall with them aboard and turned over and the moneybag was dumped in a large pool of water.

They had barely escaped drowning. The bag was floating in the stream and was hung on a submerged tree that had limbs sticking out of the water's surface. They could see it but could not reach it. They had to leave it. After regaining the canoe from where it had been carried by the swift current down the stream and over some rapids, they found the paddles and continued down to the railroad bridge because they could not maneuver upstream past the rapids.

What to do? They discussed the situation with the newly arrived bike-riding bandit and all three decided to wait for the train to arrive bringing the other members of the gang.

The train could be heard approaching and soon arrived with two passengers who had decided to get a little fresh air to help with the illness one of them was still experiencing. They had made their way to the back of the last car on the train and were standing on the railed platform outside. As they approached the bridge the two clowns tossed the two bags they had been carrying off the train and into the bushes alongside the tracks. They then proceeded to jump off the back of the train, one after the other.

They rolled to a bruising halt in the bushes themselves and slowly got up and retrieved the bags and joined their buddies under the bridge. Here they opened the bag that had candy in it and emptied it on the ground under the bridge. In the bottom of it were the clothes they had worn into town the night before. They all changed out of the costumes they were wearing, stuffed the clown suits in the bag with several large rocks and threw it in the stream to sink from sight. They hurriedly washed the paint from their faces using the water from the stream.

A discussion was held about the other bag hanging on the tree in the middle of the stream at the waterfall. Both of the canoe operators were certain that neither of them could retrieve the bag. They had tried but the current was too swift and the water was too deep. They insisted that they would drown if they had to try. Time was beginning to worry them. Some of the bank employees could have been missed by now and an investigation started that would disclose their bold deed.

After a brief evaluation, it was decided that since Truman was the best swimmer, he would be sent back in an attempt to get it. He would keep the bicycle, hide it till he could retrace the route of the stream on foot to the falls, regain the bag and use the bike to make his way to an appointed place where they would meet him the next day if possible. If worse came to worse, he was to do whatever he though best but to take no unnecessary risks. Time was of the essence.

Truman hurried upstream to the falls and made several attempts to swim out to the bag but the stream was too swift. He finally decided to go over the waterfall and catch the limbs holding the bag as the current took him downstream past it. He was successful but when he released the water-soaked bag of money from the limb, he could not swim with it.

He nearly drowned but was able to hang on to it as he was swept over the rapids and down the stream to a place where he was finally able to drag it out and up the bank. It was too heavy to carry because it was waterlogged and he could not drag it through the heavy underbrush. He would have to put it back in the water and try to float down the stream to the bridge where his bike was hidden. This proved very difficult. He was beginning to be very concerned with time.

It took until after dark for him to accomplish the task and when he finally reached the bridge, he took most of the money out of the bag and stacked it on the bank of the stream. He got his bike and brought it to the stream where he put the bag in the metal carrier basket and made several trips up and down the bank carrying the cash in bundles and putting it back in the bag. Finally after an exhausting effort at pushing the bike back to the road. He mounted the bike and, thinking any moment that he would be discovered and arrested, traveled a fast as he could the rest of the night. Several times he had to fly off the road and into the bushes or trees to avoid being seen by passing motorist. At one point he was sure that he had identified one vehicle as a police car. At dawn, he found a place to hide in the forest and waited for dark to conceal the rest of his journey and escape.

He slept for a big part of the morning and then all afternoon he spread the money on the ground and dried it out. He was finally able to stuff it all back in the bag. When night fell he carefully made his way to the agreed place where he was to meet his gang. Several more times he had to move quickly to avoid being seen by several state troopers who seemed to be traveling both directions on the highway. The rest of the gang members had been about to give him up for lost or captured and leave without him. They would have too if Harry had not insisted that he would show up.

They decided that, what seemed like a perfect plan had taught them to spend more time in checking all escape routes thoroughly in the future. They never had this much trouble with get-a-ways again. At least not until one fateful day in Minden, Louisiana.

The gang would usually break up shortly after a robbery by splitting up the money among them and each going their separate ways. They all understood that if one was captured, he would lose his life if he ratted on the others. They had sworn this to one another early on in the organization of the group.

As for Truman and Harry, they remained together no matter what. They had determined that if one were caught, the other would do all that was possible to free him. They had even discussed the various means of breaking into jails if necessary to rescue one another. They had talked about possible scenarios of having to help with prison escapes if one of them were to remain free. They were certain that it could be done if necessary.

They had for some time been very concerned with long range planning. They knew that they could not continue this profession indefinitely. They had visited several states looking for a situation that would allow them to live to enjoy the fruit of their labors.

They had decided to use some of the money they gained to set themselves up as gentlemen horse ranchers. They purchased a large tract of land and built a farm to be used for raising horses in Grant County near Sheridan, Arkansas. They became part of the local citizenry there but continued to plan and rob banks. The largest portion of the money that the two of them were collecting was hidden in several places along the Mississippi River to be retrieved later and used in the future as they could launder it through their horse raising business. The plan was to bank it slowly and present it as the result of sales for their fine horses.

The ranch in Grant County developed as a joint venture between Harry and Truman until Truman decided to marry. Not long afterward, he decided to purchase a place of his own and so he and his wife Mabel began to shop around. He wanted to be close enough to remain involved with Harry but at the same time begin a family on his own.

They finally found two joining places for sale that they could purchase and combine into one in Perry County near Thornburg, Arkansas, which is about 70 miles from Harry's farm in Grant County. One of the places that they purchased had a nice house on it and was located in a beautiful valley. This adjoining place was a large tract of land, which they purchased, and the two together gave them the entire valley to themselves. This suited Truman perfectly and they immediately began to furnish the home in a style that suited both he and Mabel. Improvements were going to be a long- term project that they both looked forward to happily.

Harry's wife Bessie would have been happier to be closer to Truman and Mabel because she and Harry were rearing two children, Harry's son Johnny and Bessie's niece, who loved and idolized Mabel. They wanted to be able to visit at will but that would no longer be the norm.

In the meantime, life for these two gentlemen ranchers was very complicated. They explained their often absence from the farm as business trips to examine and purchase good breeding stock. Sometimes it was to attend seminars on horse ranching. Occasionally these were even legitimate and they would take friends or other ranchers with them for extended trips.

They thoroughly enjoyed these trips and were becoming quite knowledgeable as judges of fine horses. They made it a point to attend horse races and learn to communicate in the language of the industry. They even learned to bet on races and saw readily that this could be used as a means of explaining large sums of money coming into their possession.

They were rapidly expanding their circle of friends and business contacts across the country and reported to the rest of the gang members when they came across a bank that seemed to fit their particular requirements for what they began to term, "a withdrawal".

A representative would then be sent back into the town to study the situation from their unique business perspective. When enough information was gained that seemed to favor their involvement, a meeting of "The Board" would be called. It was not uncommon for these meetings to be held at the ranch. On some occasions, they would arrange for a meeting near the town in question and all of them would be utilized in checking out all the angles. They had become very proficient at what they were doing. They had learned how to collect all sorts of insider information as to the inner workings of a particular bank that they were interested in.

One of their favorite avenues of getting the information they wanted was to find an employee and develop a friendship or romantic relationship. It was amazing how gullible some ladies were when it came to romantic involvement with a handsome, eligible young man who was new in town and obviously able to spend considerable money at will.

It was also amazing how talkative a young bank employee could become with a group of friends while playing poker or some other casual activity. In some circumstances these employees could be persuaded to give up much needed information in exchange for cold cash.

They were constantly on the lookout for means and methods of gaining the skills they would need to carry out their goals. All sorts of new innovations were constantly cropping up that they would have to learn to overcome. Burglar alarms were becoming more and more sophisticated. Bank vaults were being improved constantly. They had to be sure that nothing would take them by surprise at any point in a job.

If things looked beyond the capabilities they possessed, then so be it. They would never try to push the envelope. There was always another bank in another town just suited to what they could do with practically no risk. They had come to know that the greatest asset they possessed was their ability to assess risk correctly. These were men who intended to become wealthy to the point that they did not need anyone at any time for anything.

Yes, these young enterprising businessmen were becoming very good at what they did. Crime was paying well. For now at least.

Perhaps a word about Harry's children might be advisable at this point Kenny. I know that Harry had been married before he married Bessie but the details of that union are a little unclear to me. I know that Johnny belonged to his first marriage. It appears that he was married when he was about 18 to his first wife. Bessie could not have children but was rearing her niece. That is about all I know of that situation but it does tell us something about the activities of these young men that may interest some who may take the time to hear this story.

Harry himself had many brushes with the law during those turbulent years from the orphanage to the development of his banking enterprises. As early as October 17,1929 he was charged with murder in Terre Haute, Indiana but was not convicted. He was arrested with Truman on February 5, 1930 in Shreveport, Louisiana but was released for lack of evidence

On March 14, 1930 he had been charged in the courts at Lafayette, Indiana for an offense that is not clear in the record and apparently was released on bond. He apparently left the jurisdiction of the area without permission and was later arrested in Shreveport, Louisiana and returned to jail in Terre Haute, Indiana where he was fined $100.00 and given six months in jail to be served on the State Farm.

It seems that he left the farm without permission and took a motor vehicle that did not belong to him in the process. He was arrested in Greencastle and taken into court and fined another $100.00 and court costs of $12.35 and given another six months in the farm. He served four months and 27 days and was released.

On December 21, 1932 he was tried in Lafayette, Indiana for manslaughter and found guilty by a jury and given 2 years and 21 days in the Indiana State Reformatory at Pendleton. It is obvious that he was developing into a very dangerous individual.

Well Kenny, I must close and send this off so, till next time my friend,

God bless you,
Clifford

CHAPTER 4
CONFLICT RESOLUTION

Kenny,

Well here it is Tuesday and I am just now getting around to posting an addition to Truman's Story. I pray all is well with you and that the cough you are experiencing will improve and your strength return. I for one will be happy to see winter move out and some warm, dry weather. I always feel trapped in winter.

But, on to TRUMAN:

As I have stated in the last episode, Truman and Harry enjoyed what seemed to be certain continued success and wealth from their bank robbing enterprise. They had several hundreds of thousands of dollars hidden away in buried caches along the Mississippi River in several states.

A lot of time, research and energy had gone into hiding these funds because they did recognize the possibility of being caught and having to spend some time in jail. They also knew that it was possible that someone could recognize one of them in some way and that they might have to go on the run. In either case, they would need to have resources available. If they could, of course continue in their present pursuit for a couple of years more, they planned to drop out of the banking business and live completely honest lives.

Serious problems began to surface that was probably inevitable. People never seem to be able to keep secrets for indefinite periods of time. It is just one of those quirks in the nature of some human beings. Some people are simply not able to maintain the expectations of others for very long if it is against what they consider to be their best self interest. Regardless of the risk or harm imposed upon others, some people are going to do what they want to do. Even if they have full knowledge that they are harming themselves, they will still continue down a path laden with danger. Such is the paradox of human intelligence.

Their gang began to have difficulty staying together because one of the individuals wanted to take unnecessary risks in spending money recklessly and drawing attention to him self. This created friction between the members and so the leader, Harry, began to look for a replacement for this troublesome member. He did not consult the rest of the group in doing so but it was impossible for this effort to remain unknown for long.

Bad blood began to flow when this became known to the difficult member. An uneasy tension began to rise closer and closer to the surface in every meeting where the group came together. This seriously slowed down all plans for new robberies.

They generally worked on several sets of plans at a time and would hold planning meetings near towns that had been scouted out by each member of the gang working as an individual. When a town and a bank were found that looked favorable, they would send in two members to study the situation. Their assignment was to learn as much as could be garnered over a period of time that could extend to as long as 8 months. When these two felt that they had all the information possible and were favorably impressed with the situation, a final planning meeting would be set. The entire group would then meet and go over the possibilities and determine whether to proceed with the robbery. Everyone had a full and equal vote in the decision. If anyone cast a negative vote, the operation would be placed on an indefinite hold. It would be revisited once more when Harry felt inclined to do so and, if there were still any negative votes, the plan would be dropped permanently.

This being the case, the member who was now being held in contempt by Harry, knew of plans that were being laid and the details involved. This tension was growing and would prove to be their downfall.

A bank had been chosen in Minden, Louisiana and given the green light to be put on their calendar. As time drew near for this job, the trouble came to a head and a decision was made by Harry. The offending member had to be cut out of the gang for all their safety. So a secret meeting of the whole group, except the offending member, was held and it centered around a decision of whether to cut the man out and let him go his way or kill him.

It was evident that he simply would not give up his dangerous actions and it was only a matter of time before he would be arrested. If that happened, they all felt that he would betray them. The decision was made to cut him loose.

The man was called to a meeting where he was told that he was out until such time as he was able to prove to them that he had reformed his ways. He was told that they had discussed killing him and did not want to do so but that if they felt that he continued to be a threat to them, he would die. He took the decision very badly but was given no alternative whether to remain a working part of the group. He was informed that a new member would be recruited to replace him.

Some of the gang thought that they should scrap all plans that the expelled member had knowledge of for fear he would be caught and made to disclose their plans to the police before they could stop him. After much discussion, it was decided that the Minden bank would be too lucrative to pass up and that all others would be scrapped. A whole new set of banks would be scouted after this one job.

This proved to be a fatal mistake in judgment.

AUTHOR'S NOTE

The offending member owned and operated a farm near the city of Minden and what made the matter even more difficult was the fact that he was related to Harry's wife. This brings me to the place that I feel it might be of interest to relate some of the details of the Minden robbery and this man's role in ending the career of this so far, successful operation. It might be that the identity of the other members of the gang would be of interest to the reader as well. As you know, I have deliberately left these people in the shadows up to this point in our story and there has been good reason for doing so.

As you may remember, I had stated before that Truman and I held several consultations about whether it was advisable to tell his story when we first began to think about it. The hesitation centered in the lives of other people who were still alive and might be affected by a telling of the story. It was very possible that not only Truman and Harry's families could suffer from a full disclosure of the facts but the other participants and their families as well. We both knew that while Truman was still alive, he could be putting those folks in untenable situations without even realizing that he was doing so. Many of them and their extended families could possibly be sent to jail if the whole matter was aired publicly. It was possible that law enforcement officers were still keeping some of the cases of robbery and murder under investigation actively. It was also possible that Truman himself might be rearrested and sent back to prison.

Now, many years afterward, this is still my concern and I have been severely handicapped by having no contact with anyone involved except Truman's wife Mary. I have therefore been doing some research in attempting to settle this question and after doing all I could to find these families and discuss their feelings on the matter, I think it is safe to proceed in a limited way.

I am therefore going to share as much detail as I can as it is revealed in the actual court records concerning the Minden bank robbery and augment that by what Truman told me personally. The story develops as follows.

Kenny, the hour is getting late so I will call it a day and pick up the story as soon as possible.

Blessings on you,
Clifford

CHAPTER 5
A TANGLED WEB

K enny,

THE RECORDS SHOW

Around June or July in the year of 1937, Harry was hosting one of the gang members, a man by the name of Dan Davis, at his place in Terre Haute, Indiana. (As I have stated before, Terre Haute was more or less a headquarters base for the operation of the Mahoney gang and both Harry and Truman owned homes there in addition to their ranches in Arkansas.) Dan was in the process of courting a lady by the name of Rosemary and they had decided to get married and wanted to use Harry's home for the wedding. This was arranged and sometime after the wedding, the newlyweds along with Harry, his wife Bessie and their son John Earnest Mahoney, took a vacation trip down to the Minden, Louisiana area where they would visit the A.R. Blake family. This was Bessie's father.

The visit lasted about thirty days and what Harry and Dan had not told their wives was that the real reason for the trip was to look at several banks and survey the area for escape routes in connection with possible future business engagements. They were absent from their wives a great deal of this time and told them and the rest of the extended family that they were squirrel and deer hunting with Bessie's dad, A. R. Blake. During this "vacation" the bank at Minden was singled out as a future target and the two families returned to Terre Haute.

Over the next several months, other trips were made to the Minden area by Harry to flesh out the details of the plans for the projected withdrawal from the bank. In the meantime, Harry had legitimized his dealings with the public in Terre Haute by operating a trucking business as a cover. He specialized in trucking gravel, coal and mining equipment over the entire area. One man with whom he became well acquainted was named J. C. Welch who lived at 111 South Second Street in Lafayette, Indiana. Mr. Welch was a prominent businessman who owned, among other things, the Riverside Country Club in Lafayette. What was not known about Mr. Welch was his connection with the underworld of crime in a big way. Here was a man with abilities to accomplish almost anything that needed to be done in laundering stolen property through his contacts in all the major cities across America. It made no difference what, where or with whom one might need to deal with among the gangsters of the world, this man could arrange it, for a fee. Harry and Truman had cultivated a strong tie with this man.

A general meeting of the gang was set for April of 1938 in Terre Haute and the fourth permanent member of the organization, Herbert Skaggs, was called to meet with Dan, Harry and Truman. During the course of the meeting, it was clear to everyone that they needed another person to fill the slot of the ousted member and it was decided that a man by the name of Frank Denmon who lived near Minden, Louisiana would be considered for the position.

The recruiting of Denmon would not need to take a lot of time as he would play a relatively minor role in the Minden job but it would be necessary to check him out personally with those who knew him better than any of the men present in the meeting. For this reason, it was decided that since Harry knew the area better than anyone else and had in-laws in the area, He would go down ahead of the others. He said he would take either Dan or Herbert with him and straws were drawn between the two to determine who would travel with Harry. Truman had other obligations in preparation for the up-coming job, which required his continued presence in Terre Haute.

Herbert Skaggs got the draw and plans were made for him to meet Harry on a train on the way down south. Herbert lived in Indianapolis, Indiana and, on a prearranged day, he wired a message to Harry that he would be passing through Terre Haute on the afternoon train and that Harry should purchase a ticket to St. Louis, Missouri and board the train in Terre Haute. This was accomplished and the two of them traveled to St. Louis together where they casually took a taxi to lunch and toured the city for a while before returning to the train station and boarding a train bound for Texarkana. Upon arriving in Texarkana, they found a rooming house and rented a room in which they paid for a week's occupancy in advance. The place did not require the giving of names and this was one of the reasons for selecting this particular room. They did not wish to be identified in any way as having been this close to Minden during these days.

This was done on about the last day of May in 1938 just over a week from the projected date of the up-coming withdrawal from the Minden bank. The two of them spent the night at the rooming house and got up early the next morning and took a bus to Shreveport, Louisiana, which was not very far from Texarkana. Their purpose in Shreveport was to purchase an automobile to use as one of the get-a-way cars during the robbery as well as get them around during preparations. After checking every used car lot in Shreveport looking for a particular kind of Ford automobile that they knew to be a very fast moving vehicle, they could not find one that suited them. Moving over to Bossier City, they finally found a Plymouth Sedan that seemed to be a reasonable substitute for what they wanted and purchased it for $85.00. They used a false identity that they were prepared for which changed Harry to T. R. Drake and gave his address as General Delivery in Shreveport for the registration of the car.

Taking possession of the Plymouth Sedan, they drove down to Minden and arrived about 8:00 O'clock at night. They had now established Texarkana as the temporary headquarters city while engaged in the business at hand. The next item on their agenda was to check out Frank Denmon as a possible new member of the organization. Harry had been to Mr. Denmon's home on one occasion but could not relocate it so he decided to go to his father-in-law, A. R. Blake who knew everyone in the area.

Upon discussing Frank Denmon with his father-in-law, Harry shared their interest in him as a possible member of his business partnership and asked him if Frank was a good man who could be trusted. A. R. assured Harry that Frank would be a good man if he decided to join the organization and that he would personally take them out to his place and discuss the matter with him. This suited Harry and Herbert fine so off they went to Frank's home where they met Frank's wife Ida and after offering them a brief outline of their needs and plans, the Denmons agreed to join ranks with the men.

A part of the Denmon involvement was the usage of their home as a safe house and base for the next several days before the robbery and as long as was necessary afterward. This was acceptable to both Frank and Ida. She was going to cook meals and provide lodging for the whole gang as the individual members arrived which would involve the purchase of supplies that would be needed.

Harry had her to sit down and make a list of what she needed and told her he would do the shopping necessary to purchase the items. This encounter took place on the night of June 1, 1938, which was a Wednesday just a week from the date scheduled for the robbery. This of course did not leave as much time to get to know the dependability of the Denmons as would normally have been demanded of a new member and Harry was a little uneasy about it. It could not be helped though because the member who had been voted out had been responsible for the establishing of a safe house for the job. The preparations he was supposed to make had not been completed so a new place had to be provided. The Denmon place would have to be it.

Herbert and Harry and A. R. soon left the Denmon farm and drove back to A.R.'s place where they left him and continued on to Texarkana. Once there, they spent the rest of the night and the next day loaded their belongings from the boarding house into the car and went across the street to the local A & P market where the bill of groceries and other items that Ida had ordered were purchased. Placing the supplies along with everything else in the Plymouth, they set out to return to the Denmon home located in a rural swampy area some distance from Minden. They arrived and spent Thursday night there and worked on Frank's car, an old Model T Ford, in an attempt to get it running. It had been disabled for several months and was not even registered. It was thought that the vehicle might be needed before the job was completed so they replaced the battery, some wiring and the coil along with some headlights before it could be registered and roadworthy. Finally, the vehicle was usable again and on Friday night Harry, Herb the two Denmons and their son all took a ride around the area to make last minute checks on the roads they planned to use in leaving the bank. It was essential that they know if there was any kind of construction or other problems that had developed since the roads were last checked. All look well.

The five of them returned to the Denmon place and they remained there until about 10 o'clock on Sunday morning. At that time Harry and Herb took the Plymouth and went back to Texarkana to meet Truman and Dan Davis at Union Station according to a schedule that had been worked out before any of them had left Terre Haute.

Kenny, this seems like a breaking point in the story so I will close for today and write more as time will allow.

Bless you,

Clifford

CHAPTER 6
AN INSIDE VIEW

Kenny,

It seems that I have time to share another episode in Truman's story with you tonight so I hope the two of you are faring well enough to do a little reading. We left off last time with Harry and Herb meeting Truman and Dan in Texarkana.

To bring everything into perspective, I need to back up and explain what was transpiring back in Terre Haute involving Truman and Dan while Harry and the rest of the gang were in Louisiana.

When Truman left Harry at the railway depot in Terre Haute where he would board the train and join Herbert on the way to Louisiana, he went to Harry's home and spent the night there. The next day Dan Davis came to the house and brought the guns and ammunition that were to be used in the job in Minden. These guns had been carefully selected over a period of years and were entrusted to the care of Dan. The practice had been that once a gun had been fired in the course of a robbery, it was destroyed and never used again. This required a replacement and Dan was the expert in securing untraceable weapons and making certain that they were maintained in excellent condition.

Dan lived in Terre Haute and was very good at what he did. They had never had a failure in the use of the weapons he provided. Today, he brought them to Truman along with his suitcase containing the clothes and travel items he would need for the trip to Minden. These items would be stored at Harry's home till they were ready to leave.

Truman, in the meantime, was responsible for collecting the other items needed for the job, which included handcuffs to be placed on the employees of the bank as they came to work. These he purchased from several different sources in cities as far away as 200 miles from home. He always wore a disguise when making these purchases and used false identification to safeguard the planned usage of the materials. Clothes to be worn by each individual were also purchased by Truman from many sources and all the labels removed from them so as to be untraceable when discarded after the job. All these items were to be a part of the luggage being assembled for Truman and Dan to take to the safe house that Harry and Herb were arranging for.

Truman and Harry had studied methods of disguising the members of the group so that the law officers who investigated the robberies they were responsible for would be confused. They deliberately studied the methods of other gangs and tried to make their work appear to be the work of others. This included disguises and role reversals from one job to another that would cause witnesses to seemingly be describing someone other than the Mahoney gang. They were always very careful in preparing for this deception and Truman was the planner of these disguises. If masks were not used, then various wigs or make-up schemes were employed. This fact alone is probably responsible for the group being able to evade capture long before they actually were. It was a stroke of genius. The plan often went so far as to have each member verbally call one another by assumed names while dealing with employees of the bank being robbed. They even practiced changing the sound of their voices and would occasionally assume accents in their speech so as to cause witnesses to believe them of foreign nationalities. Different members of the gang would perform differing tasks from job to job to further confuse those seeking to track them down.

A method of warning Truman and Dan not to come to Minden if things did not develop according to plan had been worked out also. It called for a telegram to be sent to the local Western Union by Harry and addressed to T. R. Drake, the same name used to purchase the Plymouth, which would declare Louisiana's work to be at an end. If it came, they would not go.

On Saturday June 4th Truman checked and found that no telegram had arrived so he set off to meet Dan at the Union Depot. Truman brought all the luggage and they purchased their tickets and boarded the train to St. Louis, Missouri where they disembarked and had a several hour layover awaiting the train to Texarkana. They boarded the train about midnight and arrived in Texarkana the afternoon of June 5th where Harry and Herb were waiting for them. Loading all the luggage in the Plymouth, the four partners made their way back to the Denmon place. There seemed to be some confusion in the records as to the exact location of the Denmon place as Truman told me that it was nearer Haughton, Louisiana than it was to Minden. Whatever the reality was, it was within easy driving distance of Minden but in a rural setting. I tend to believe that the Haughton area is correct.

During the time of their absence, a guest had arrived at the Denmon home. Ida had gotten a message from A. R. Blake that he wanted to come and visit a couple of days and asked Frank to meet him at Fillmore where the bus stop was.

Fillmore is a small community between Minden and Haughton and Frank had gone and picked him up and brought him out to the place.

Upon arriving at the Denmon place around dusk dark on that same day, they were all very tired and soon retired for the night. After a good night's sleep, all four of them got up early took a bath and went fishing to relax and go over the details of the events that were to lie ahead in the next few days. On several occasions during the course of the next several hours, trips were made around the area rechecking the escape route roads to prevent any last minute trip-ups. The Denmon Model T Ford was most often used in these trips because they wanted folks who would see it to think nothing out of the ordinary was happening. Everyone knew the car and its owners. All four members of the gang and Frank Denmon would participate in these detail checklist preparations.

On Monday night, all five of them traveled to Minden in the Plymouth where they stopped at a creek bridge just outside town and left Herb and Frank to await their return. This was done as a precaution against their being recognized together because both of them had been in the town earlier and were seen by many folks. It would not have been a good thing for folks to remember having seen Frank in the company of four strangers. He was well known in Minden and after the robbery, it would certainly have been remembered.

This trip was made as a last minute recheck of the bank. The three drove on into town and parked the Plymouth about 2 blocks from the bank and walked to an alleyway that ran behind the bank. They made a quick check to see that everything was as it had been and to be certain that they would not need to bring some specialized tools to gain entry. The premises were as they expected and they now felt very sure of themselves that they had covered all the bases completely. The only unusual element recognized was the presence of someone working late in the bank. The lights were on in one area of the building and in looking through a window they saw a man sitting at a desk doing paperwork. This gave them no pause because they would return at a much later time of night than on this trip.

They returned to the car and went immediately to the bridge and picked up Herb and Frank. The time was now about 10:00 P.M. on Monday night and they returned to the Denmon place by a back road that took them through the little town of Doyline. They were all tired but wanted to double-check the weapons that Truman and Dan had brought down. There were three revolvers and one automatic pistol and after satisfying themselves that all were in good order, they went to bed.

The next morning, as they were down at the spring taking their baths, Mr. Blake left. They were surprised to find that he was gone when they returned to the house and were a little upset that he had left without saying goodbye. It seemed strange and Truman and Harry both commented that it was not like him to leave that way. It was also odd that no explanation was offered by the Denmon family of the means he had used in leaving.

Well Kenny, the hour is getting late once more and my mind is beginning to be a little fuzzy so I am going to shut down the press for the day and wish you a good night. I know it is two hours earlier where you are so maybe you will get this in time to share a bedtime reading with your dear wife. I will attempt to give you a look at a real life bank robbery pulled off by real professionals in the next post.

Bless you,

Clifford

CHAPTER 7
BANK ROBBERY IN MINDEN

Kenny,
    It has been several days since I last posted a letter to you and I am beginning to feel that the story is getting cold. So I will sit myself down and try to put my mind back into the proper mode to share another chapter in our continuing saga. Hope this is a welcome addition.

We last left the gang making last minute checks of the bank building in Minden on a late night trip into town. On the next day:

The day was Tuesday and was spent mostly in bed. They knew that they might not have another opportunity to sleep for several days if anything went wrong so they all tried to get as much rest as possible. They also knew that the night ahead would call for them to be at their very best ability to be alert. As dusk began to fall that evening, Harry, Truman, Herb and Dan got in the Plymouth and drove to Shreveport to find and steal a fast car that could be used as a first line of defense get-a-way vehicle. They needed one that could in no way be traced to them and was large enough to handle all of them and the loot they planned to take out of the bank. It needed to have been stolen recently enough that the police would not yet be looking for it in Minden. This would allow them not to have to worry about an accidental discovery by some local patrolman as the car would be seen so late at night in a strange town.

They did not find what they were looking for in Shreveport so they expanded their search to Mansfield, a small town a few miles from Shreveport. Parking the Plymouth on the edge of town beside and old repair shop, Dan and Harry got out and walked around town looking for what they needed. The need was for a car that could be discarded very soon after leaving the bank. If it had been seen by anyone and reported, they would no longer be in it but in the Plymouth instead as they would switch to it a short way out of town. A quick switch here was essential.

They found a Ford Agency that had a Ford coach inside a garage area and returned to the car where Truman and Herb were waiting. They told them to head toward Shreveport and to stop at the city limits and wait for them.

Returning to the Ford agency, they entered the garage by a side window, opened the door from the inside and drove the coach out the door and headed toward Shreveport. They passed Truman and Herb where they had stopped by the roadside awaiting them and traveled on ahead of them to a service station where they stopped and filled the Ford's gas tank and then went their separate ways. Harry and Dan went back to the Denmon place and picked up the guns and all the other materials they would need and then headed out to a place on the Cotton Valley road to meet back up with Truman and Herb.

They had chosen this spot to hide the Plymouth while the four of them got in the Ford and drove into Minden to the area of the bank. They parked the Ford about two blocks from the bank and all four walked to the rear of the bank in the alleyway. Truman was to remain across the alley from the bank as a lookout until the other three could get inside the building. As he watched, the three other men entered the bank through a window and once inside, replaced the screen and then prepared to wait for the employees to come and open the bank. It was about 3 O'clock in the morning of June 8, 1938, a Wednesday.

When the three men entered the bank building, Truman remained hidden in the alley for about twenty minutes to be sure that they had not been observed and were in no danger of being detected. He then returned to the Ford and found that it would not start. He worked with it and finally rolled it backward and downhill out of the place where it was parked and jumping in, popped the clutch with the car in reverse and luckily, it started. He drove out of town. His part in the plan was to stay away until the next morning so as not to draw attention to a strange car parked in town and then return to town about 8:15 A.M and park the car about three blocks from the bank.

He drove out on a county lane near Gibsland, a neighboring community, and parked in a deserted area, being very careful to stop the car on an inclined place. He had learned not to trust the Ford back in town. After being there some time, he decided to start the car and found that once more it would not start. He got out and worked with everything he could but had to again push it to get it rolling down the incline and repeat the clutch popping procedure to get it running. He was now afraid to kill the engine so he decided to drive around the rest of the night and in so doing hopefully charge up the battery.

He made it to the appointed parking place at 8:15 back in Minden and as the plan had called for, at exactly 8:30 A. M. he turned the car out into the street and drove into the alleyway behind the bank and stopped across from the rear door.

While Truman was holding up his end of the plan, the other three men were in the bank. The first of the employees to arrive at the bank were an black man and small white man together and as they entered the building, they were captured and the black man was tied up. They were questioned as to when the rest of the employees would show up and readily gave the asked for information. This was about 7:30 A. M. and the next two who showed up were women who entered as the two before them, through the front door. These two were tied up along with the white male and all three were placed beside the black in the rear of the building.

The next man to show up was a heavy-set fellow and he was captured and questioned as to when the vault would open up. This man proved to be a Mr. Harper and was the president of the bank and was not happy about being tied up like a pig. A few minutes later two more girls came in and were tied up and placed with the others. The next two who came in were together and were blacks and were called to the back by the president and there captured and tied up as well. They did not use the handcuffs they had brought but decided to use lengths of strong cord instead. Mr. Harper had managed to work his hands free at one point and was in the process of trying to get his feet free when Harry noticed what was happening. A quick cuff to the back of the head produced a string of profanity from Mr. Harper so Harry took a handkerchief from the man's pocket and stuffed it in his mouth and told him to stay quiet or he would crack his head.

About this time the vault time lock opened and the little man who had been captured at first was brought out of the back to finish the job of opening it. Dan and Herb began to clean out the money that was exposed in the first compartment of the vault but the rear of the vault could not be opened without a key. Harry asked for the key and the little man said he did not know where it was but one of the girls would know.

The two of them went to the back and asked for the key and she told them it was in a desk drawer up front. Going to the desk, Harry could not find the key so he went back and got the girl and brought her up to get the key. She readily found it and unlocked the door inside the vault for them. They filled a large sack with whatever looked like it might be useful which included a large quantity of bonds and stocks that appeared to be of a negotiable type.

They then went to the back and got all the employees and brought them into the vault. Harry brought in chairs for all the white people and made them sit down and then placed all the black folks in the back compartment of the vault by themselves. The white folks were tied to the chairs and the blacks were tied together with their heads facing one another and their hands behind them. Their feet were tied together and then a cord was looped around each one's neck and tied. It was then looped over to the next one in the circle and looped and tied around that neck and so around the entire circle. This was done so that none could get up on their feet or untie one another. It was about this time that Dan, who was somewhat of a jokester, took a large purse, which looked like a suitcase, belonging to one of the girls and filled it with nickels and sat it down beside her. He laughed and told her to take a vacation on him.

The bank President, relieved of the handkerchief, spoke up and said, "You are not going to lock us up in this vault are you?" and Harry looked at him and said, "Not if you will give us time to make our get-a-way." To which the man responded, "How long might that be?" and Harry responded, "About eight to ten days." And everyone laughed. The president then said, "The money is insured, take it and get out. We will keep quiet for the rest of the day." To this Harry replied, "That does make me feel better and I thank you for your cooperation." The vault door was closed and locked and the three of them went to the back door and looked out to see Truman in the Ford sitting across the alleyway. Herb checked to be sure that the front door was still locked and the closed sign in the glass.

Harry walked out the back door and over to the driver's side of the Ford and opening the door slipped in behind the wheel. He swung the car around and over by the back door of the bank and Dan and Herb stepped out, locking the door behind them, and tossed the bags of loot into the car and got in them selves. Harry turned the car out into the street and moved calmly through the morning traffic out to the highway toward Cotton Valley. As they rode away from town, Truman and the other two men were changing clothes and stuffing the ones they were wearing into a bag. They stopped about five miles out where the Plymouth was hidden and left the Ford. Transferring everything and everyone to the Plymouth, Truman took the wheel and headed back toward Minden to the road that wound through the backwoods toward Doyline. He took this road and leisurely drove through Doyline and on toward the Denmon place. While they made this trip, Harry also changed his clothes and the bag was now ready for disposal. Herb reached into one of the loot sacks and fished out a handful of bills and handed Truman $125.00 for expenses to be used in getting everything done that would be required of him in the hours ahead.

When they approached the Denmon farm, Frank was out plowing by the road, which was a prearranged signal that there was no cause for alarm and the coast was clear for them to return to the house when ready. A short way down the road Truman stopped and Harry, Herb and Dan got out and took all the loot and guns, and whatever else that had been used in the robbery, off into the swamp. They took it all about a half a mile and hid it where Frank had shown them a secluded area that would not be traveled by anyone. Truman then turned the Plymouth back out and drove off toward Coushatta, Louisiana.

His plans were to get rid of the car in a way that it would never be connected to the hold up. He intended to drive it as fast as he could after getting many miles away from Minden and overheat the engine enough to ruin it and then sell it to a junkyard dealer.

He drove across the river at Coushatta and turned back toward Shreveport. It began to rain and in stopping to get gasoline, he got soaking wet. Once in Shreveport, he stopped at a dry goods store and bought a new suit of khakis and then drove on toward Kilgore, Texas. The car finally gave up the ghost near Longview and he sold it there at a junkyard for $10.00.

He hurriedly made his way to the local bus station and caught a bus to Kilgore where he arrived about four O'clock in the evening and boarded a Limited train for St. Louis, Missouri. From St. Louis he caught a train for Terre Haute, Indiana where he arrived the next day, June 9, 1938.

It was to be his job to establish alibis for himself and Harry by making purchases in Terre Haute upon arrival. This would make it appear that they were far away from Minden, Louisiana when the bank was robbed. He did this by renting a car in Harry's name from the Deming Garage, passing himself off as Harry. He then took Bessie's car to Mace's Tire Shop and bought new tires for it in his name and thus left a record that he and Harry both had been in Terre Haute about the time of the robbery down in Minden.

Truman then went to Harry's house and spent the night with Bessie and Mabel, telling them that he and Bessie would need to go to Louisiana the next morning to get Harry. The plan had called for them to use Bessie's car, which was a Terraplane, made by Hudson. He and Bessie got up early the next day and drove to Little Rock, Arkansas and arrived there a little after noon on June 10. Truman did not want to arrive in the area of the robbery during daylight hours so they amused themselves there until about an hour before sundown and then headed out toward Texarkana. He did not have to hurry as he had plans to arrive at the Denmon home around two in the morning and that was the time Harry would be expecting him.

Kenny, the hour is getting late and I need to get a little rest so I will end the session here for tonight. As you can see, these gentlemen tried to cover all the bases in seeing that no trace of their ever being in Minden was left. Next time we will see what was happening back at the Denmon farm.

Bless you,

Clifford

CHAPTER 8
GET-A-WAY?

Kenny,

We left off in the middle of the escape of the gang from Minden after the robbery with Truman and Bessie driving from Terre Haute down to the Denmon farm to pick up the three partners. You will be interested to find what was happening there in the meantime, I believe.

While Truman was burning up time and arranging alibis for himself and Harry, the rest of the gang had remained in the swamp with the money till dark on the day of the robbery. Frank had brought a sandwich lunch out in the swamp to them and after dark they made their way to the house through the swamp. They had wanted to be sure that no policemen had come looking for them before approaching the house.

The three of them spent the night in the house and next morning they returned to the swamp to bring the loot and weapons and handcuffs to the house. Everything else had been buried in the swamp.

They dumped the loot on the kitchen table and as they divided up the cash, they were very disappointed in the total. Apparently one of two things had gone wrong. Either the reports they had gotten on the wealth of this particular bank had been exaggerated or they had somehow missed out on finding it in the vault. The total only came to about $18,000.00. They then began to examine the bonds more closely and discovered that a lot of them were of a negotiable type. They did not take the time to try and determine the value of the bonds but instead decided to entrust them to Harry's keeping. Harry had connections and hiding places for such instruments and said he would get them sold and they would divide the proceeds up at a later date. Some of the non-negotiable bonds were then burned in the kitchen stove.

Each of the four main partners were taking an equal share of the cash and Frank and Ida were given about $500.00 in paper money and another $400.00 in coins. The Denmons said they were happy with this division and so everyone placed their share in leather satchels that belonged to each of them. These satchels, along with their suitcases were taken out and placed in the barn.

The group was waiting now for Truman and Bessie to come and pick them up for the return to Terre Haute and, after dark had fallen, Harry, Herb and Dan went down to the Spring to take a bath. This spring was in the woods some distance from the house and was the source of drinking water for the Denmon family as well as a bathing place. In the times of the events of this part of the story, there were many people who had no plumbing in their homes, especially in the rural areas of America. So this arrangement of bathing facilities being built next to outdoor springs was very common. As was also common, the Denmon family washed their clothes in large pots over open fires adjacent to the spring. This being the case, these three men had taken towels and fresh underwear and clothes with them to the spring and left their suitcases in the barn. The night was very hot and the cold water was a refreshing relief.

While they were bathing, Frank came down to the spring and said that there seemed to be some kind of activity going on down the road a ways that had him a little worried. He seemed very nervous and told them that Ida was going to remain alert and would make a loud noise of some sort if anyone came to the house. It seemed a prudent thing for them to remain at the spring until the matter could be checked out. As they finished their baths, Frank said he would go up to the house and check to see if anyone had showed up there. If so he would step out on the porch and call his dogs. This would be a signal for the gang to stay in the woods till they left. At that time he would blow his dog calling horn as a signal that the coast was clear and they could return.

After what seemed a long time but was probably only a few minutes, there was no call to the dogs so the three of them came warily back to the barn to leave their used towels and underclothing. Upon entering the barn, they noticed immediately that their suitcases seemed to be in different arrangement than when they left them to go to the spring. They began to check to see if anything was missing and it appeared everything was there, including the money. Herb was sure someone had gone through his things so he sat down and counted his money. It was all there. This seemed to satisfy them that maybe they were just imagining things so they went on in the house. The disturbance down the road went unexplained and seemed to mystify the Denmons.

They all stayed up until Truman and Bessie arrived in the Terraplane about 2;00 A. M.. It was Saturday June 11th. No time was wasted in leaving the Denmon place. The loading up of the car and quick farewells had them on the road before 3:00 A. M.. Just a few minutes before their departure, Truman took Frank Denmon aside and stressed to him the importance of the care he should be giving to keeping his normal routine in the weeks and months ahead. He warned him not to spend money recklessly and if he made purchases at all out of the ordinary, to go to one of the larger cities where he was unknown to do so. Frank had already expressed to Truman that he needed a new car and so Truman took this last opportunity to advise him not to purchase a new car but a used one instead. This would seem more normal to the people who knew him and would therefore draw no unnecessary attention to him. He reminded Frank that the local police department would be joined and augmented by federal investigators. These people would be skilled in hunting down bank robbers. Frank should consider every move he made carefully and if he proved himself to be trustworthy, the group would be considering the possibility of including him in future business arrangements. This exchange finished, he shook Frank's hand and went to Ida, gave her a warm hug and stepped to the Terraplane door. A wave and they were all aboard and gone.

Herb and Dan were dropped off in West Monroe, Louisiana about 3:30 on that morning to make separate trips to their homes by rail and bus through a long irregular route requiring several changes of trains and buses. Harry, Bessie and Truman then drove from Monroe to the Mississippi River near Tallulah, Louisiana where they deposited the bonds in a place of safekeeping that had been carefully and strategically prepared for. Then taking a ferry across the river, the Terraplane's nose was turned north to Memphis, Tennessee and on through Cairo, Illinois, into Terre Haute and home to Harry's place. Mabel was there with Harry's two children and all of them went to bed. The travelers slept around the clock and woke to Mabel's call for breakfast.

That morning, both Truman and Harry counted their money and found it to be considerably short of what had been placed there. It now dawned upon them that Ida had probably gone through their luggage in the barn while they bathed and had taken some of their money while Frank was with them at the spring. This would be dealt with at a later date they decided.

That evening Dan Davis came to Harry's home and stated that his money was short also. A glaring question loomed before them, "Why was Herb's share not short when he had counted it?" The dependability of their new partner was now in serious jeopardy. Herb's honesty was never in question so it was assumed that the Denmons had left his share untouched in an attempt to cast suspicion on him. Harry spat out a long string of expletives that made the air smell of brimstone and slapped the breakfast table they were seated at and ended with," If there's anything I hate in this world, it's a thief." Truman and Dan looked at one another and fell out of their chairs on the floor laughing. His hasty judgement to accept Frank and Ida would eat at Harry the rest of his life.

A discussion resulted in a decision to leave the area for a vacation and in the course of getting ready, Truman said he had really come to like the Terraplane car of Bessie's and offered to buy it from her. Hudson automobiles were a favorite of Harry and he had one at the farm in Arkansas that was newer than the Terraplane along with a new Chevrolet pickup. She agreed to sell it to him for $700.00 and he went and had the title changed to his name before leaving town. He and Mabel were planning to go to Arkansas to the farm at Thornburg and then prepare for an extended vacation in Texas with her relatives.

Harry and Bessie and their two children, packed luggage into a new pickup truck that he had purchased and headed toward Arkansas as well on July 3rd. While traveling to Arkansas they ran into Truman and Mabel by accident about 100 miles out of St. Louis on the Poplar Bluff, Missouri road.

They visited a while and decided to travel together for a while and stayed overnight in Poplar Bluff where Harry put his pickup truck in storage. He and Truman had a building there that was used to keep various supplies and tools of their trade in and Harry had decided that he wanted the truck to be there for emergency use if the occasion should ever arrive that they needed it. This seemed as good a time as any to place it there and would save him a trip back later. That settled, all of them got in the Terraplane and they drove on to Clinton, Arkansas together. They stayed at a tourist camp two nights and then drove Harry and Bessie on to the farm near Sheridan. Truman and Mabel journeyed on to their farm near Thornburg.

From Thornburg Truman and Mabel went down to Benton, Louisiana and visited with Mabel's mother for a couple of days. Taking her mother and a sister and brother, they made a trip over to Kilgore, Texas and visited with another sister of Mabels then on to Houston, Texas where they visited with other relatives of Mabel for two weeks. They spent time in Galveston and several other places of amusement and finally returned to Benton where they dropped off her mother, sister and brother. From there, they returned to the farm at Thornburg.

Kenny, the events reflected here give some insight to the fact that both of these men wanted to live lives very different than what they were involved in. It says to me that given a different start in life, they would not be in the pickle they were about to face.

I often think of my own family upbringing and realize that I could have gone this way myself very easily. There is much in Truman's background that I suspect most people could identify with in one way or another. I myself come from a broken home and know what it is to struggle to find my place in the world. Had it not been for the Grace of God, there was a time in my life when I was headed down the same path that Truman trod.

It may not have led to bank robbery and murder but I have no doubt that it would have taken me toward prison. But God knew my steps and raced ahead to split the trail and offer me a different route. I have much to thank God for.

I do know my friend that you are in a valley and on a trail that looks frightful but please know that God is measuring your every step.

Praying for you tonight,
Clifford

CHAPTER 9
END OF THE LINE

Kenny,

As I recall, our last post left Truman at home in Thornburg with not a clue that his life was about to be irrevocably changed. So I hope you will be able to see the Hand of God reaching out to him as I see it. I know most folks would not think so but since I know the end of the story, I can say for certain, "It is so". The Hound Of Heaven is on his trail and is forcing him to choose between possible directions at almost every curve in the path. In retrospect Truman saw this clearly but at the time it was happening, he chose to reject all that seemed to lead away from his goals.

Let me return to our narrative:

On Monday July 25th the State Police came to the Thornburg farm and arrested Truman and took him to jail. When he arrived at the jail in Pine Bluff, he found that Harry and Bessie were already in the jail and their two children were being held also. He was able to arrange for the police to let Mabel come and pick up the children and take them back to his farm in Thornburg. Harry and Truman were told they were being charged with bank robbery in Minden, Louisiana and would be transferred there soon to answer the charges.

This transfer took place within hours and the two brothers were taken, along with Bessie to the Caddo Parish Jail in Shreveport, Louisiana for interrogation by the authorities from Minden and Federal Bureau of Investigation's Special Agent James O. Peyronnin of the New Orleans Office of the Department of Justice.

On July 26th charges were filed before U.S. Commissioner Albert E. Bryson for the U.S. Western District of Louisiana in Shreveport by Agent Peyronnin. This information is on record in the National Archives and clearly states that charges were filed against Frank Denmon, Mrs. Ida (Frank) Denmon , Harry Mahoney, Truman Mahoney, Herbert Skaggs, alias Herb and Dan Davis, alias Dan O. Davis. The document is stamped with the seal of U. S. District Court, Western District of Louisiana and Filed as Evidence that had been used in court hearings and action on November 9, 1938.

This document clearly demonstrates that the names of all the participants in the robbery were known to the investigating officers before Harry and Truman were arrested. In the course of researching court documents, it became clear that the Denmons were in custody in Minden and had given the names to the investigators before the Mahoneys were arrested. It is further revealed that the Denmons also possessed some of the negotiable bonds from the robbery and it is plainly stated that an unnamed individual who also had some of the bonds and cash from the robbery had given evidence against the whole gang. **It is the opinion of the author that this person was none other than the ousted member of the gang and is almost certainly A. R. Blake, Harry's father-in-law.** Research has led the author to believe that Mr. Blake made a deal with the investigators to reveal what information he had concerning the Minden robbery in exchange for immunity from prosecution and that his name never be revealed to the participants as an informer. The author also believes that Mr. Blake was a part of the theft that took place on the last night of the gang's presence at the Denmon farm along with the Denmons. The unexplained (so called) disturbance that night down the road that was reported, was created by Mr. Blake in conspiring with the Denmons to steal a share of the loot. It is the authors contention that it was Mr. Blake who went through the bags containing money and bonds while the gang was at the spring bathing and removed what he considered to be his rightful share as a participating member of the planning stages of the robbery.

It is also plain that Dan Davis and Herbert Skaggs were not apprehended until several weeks after the Mahoneys and Denmons.

Evidence shows that Frank Denmon was the person who gave the gang up to the Sheriff of Webster Parish and F.B.I. Agent Peyronnin in July of 1938.

It is to be remembered at this point that Truman was suspicious of the man early on in their involvement with him. As he told the author, the man was not the most brilliant person he had run across and so he had carefully told him that he would have to be very careful how he spent the money they gave him. The man was careful for a period of time but after two or three weeks, he began to feel that it was safe for him to begin to purchase a few things. He began to make some rather large purchases of items that his neighbors knew he did not have the money for. Attention began to be drawn to him and word began to circulate that the man must be doing something illegal. He had traded his Model T in on a much newer automobile.

The man was stopped for a traffic violation by a deputy sheriff from the area who made the comment to him that he was really coming up in the world in being able to drive a new automobile. He jokingly questioned the man about his newfound wealth. In doing so, he observed that the man became very frightened and gave him a story about having recently inherited a sizeable sum of money from a wealthy relative's estate.

The deputy knew the man's relatives and immediately knew the man was lying. He became suspicious and decided to take the man into custody in charging him with the traffic violation and in that way, take him to jail briefly. The deputy knew that many people could be persuaded to talk a lot more freely while sitting in the police station. He knew this man and his reputation and it did not take long for the truth to come to the surface.

Frank told the officers, while being held in the jail, that he had been given the money by some men who had stayed at his place for a while. It was a kind of rent money. Further probing soon brought out the fact that the men were bank robbers and that they were involved in robbing the Minden Bank. The man told them that the men were related to A. R. Blake and that Mr. Blake had brought them out to his place. What he did not tell them was that his wife was related to Harry's wife Bessie.

The Police Chief and the High Sheriff had a consultation and decided to check this story out. They made a trip out to the Blake farm and, sure enough, they discovered a drunken individual with a large amount of cash on him. A search of his home revealed some of the stolen securities in a dresser drawer in a bedroom. The man would not cooperate with them so they took him into custody and carried him to the Minden jail.

The man was a hard nut to crack but the sheriff was a man who could be pretty persuasive with a piece of rubber hose applied to usage for which it was not designed. The man attempted to buy his way out of custody by revealing the plans for the Minden robbery and that Harry and Truman were involved. What Mr. Blake did not tell the authorities was that there had been many, many robberies that these men had been involved in over a period of many years. He led them to believe that this was the very first such endeavor entered upon by the whole group, himself included. The Denmons of course could honestly state that this was true for the two of them.

For this reason, the investigators never were able to tie this gang with any other bank robberies until much later. There were many bank robberies that had not been solved in many states and law officers across the nation were aware of conflicting information as to who was responsible. Most thought that there were several gangs active and at large who were more or less copying each other's methods. Some few investigators saw a lot of similarities in the work and were saying that it all could be one group of men.

It was known that there were at least five members of the group, if it was just one gang, but the bank employees who had dealt with them in past robberies gave conflicting accounts of their appearance and demeanor. Some had said they were kindly disposed and treated bank employees with respect. Others reported them to be ruthless and violent when opposed in any way. All reports from one robbery had stated that the employees believed only one of the men carried a gun. Only one had been displayed in their presence. These varied reports caused many small town law enforcement personnel to vie with one another for the honor of cracking these cases and arresting those responsible.

Truman shared with me that on one particular occasion some information had come to a local Sheriff that a robbery was going to take place at the City Bank and Trust of a small county seat town on a particular night. He later came to know that this was the result of a member of the gang talking in a bar room under the influence of alcohol.

These conflicting reports caused confusion among the law enforcement agencies as to the danger to be faced in dealing with them and so the police chief of this city was feeling over confident in the ability of his force to meet and deal with the robbers. The information given by their informant led them to believe that the men would not violently resist arrest.

So, the chief and the Sheriff and some of his deputies, acting on this information, surrounded the bank and attempted to arrest the gang just before daybreak. When his men were in place as he had stationed them, the chief called out loudly to the men he supposed to be in the bank to come out with their hands up. He had seriously underestimated the men he was confronting and was taken completely by surprise when gunshots rang out from behind his men.

He had no idea of the precautions and planning that this group put into the work they did. In any job they worked on, there always was a contingent plan and since the early days of making mistakes, they had always had a guard posted outside each bank. They had foreseen the possibility of being taken by surprise and had practiced escape methods extensively. Any approach by law enforcement would be detected and in any confrontation, the outside lookout was prepared to fire from cover upon the lawmen. This was to create confusion and divert the attention of the lawmen long enough for the members inside to make a break for it. Each member already knew what to do and what route of exit to take. So, instead of the robbers being taken by surprise, it was the lawmen who found themselves on the defensive.

There was a brief gun battle resulting in total confusion allowing the man who had fired from behind to escape as well as the other four. What the local Chief and Sheriff did not know was that the Mahoney gang could be very dangerous and knew how to plan their work with great precision.

This particular brush with the law, along with several others had taught them what to expect from most small town policemen. Truman shared with me that every encounter had added to their expertise and caused them to plan more and more carefully. So they were not surprised to find that some of their careful planning was paying off for them.

As I have related already, they had learned to approach their work with all the dedication of a brain surgeon. Every possible effort had always been made to mask their true identities while involved in the implementation of each and every robbery. They had always made sure that there was enough variation in their dealing with bank employees so that descriptions given after a robbery would differ. This would lead those doing any investigation to great difficulty in connecting them with every job.

Back in the jail at Shreveport, the painful fact was that now both of their wives were in custody and when most of the interrogations took place, all four were present in the same room. This room was really a cell that was used to fingerprint prisoners and question them. Most of the time the sheriff or his deputy from Minden was present when they were questioned but generally only listened. It was Agent Peyronnin who was the chief interrogator.

It was soon very clear to the men that they were not suspects in most of the robberies they had committed. Several states where they had operated had charged other gangs with many of the jobs actually carried out by them. In the final analysis, only a few of their operations were ever even brought up by those who questioned them. They were delighted and relieved to find that some of their most violent encounters had been pinned on other groups.

There was plenty enough evidence available for both Federal and State charges to be brought against the whole group however. The knowledge that they were not connected to other banks they had robbed worked to Truman and Harry's advantage in dealing with Agent Peyronnin and the U. S. District Attorney J. Fair Hardin. Seemingly they convinced these men that they were new to the profession of Bank Robbing and in confessions that they made there was a carefully coordinated effort to support the lie.

When they were first interrogated, they denied all knowledge of the robbery and attempted to use the alibis that Truman had taken such great pains to establish. This was rebuffed by Agent Peyronnin and they were told that they had witnesses who had already confessed and implicated both brothers. Agent Peyronnin also threatened to charge both of their wives as conspirators and with violations of possessing stolen money and several other things. The wives were going to jail.

This was more pressure than Truman and Harry could deal with so they agreed to cut a deal with the Agent and the U. S. District Attorney. They would confess and return all the loot they still had in exchange for a promise not to charge their wives. This deal was worked out and they changed their "not guilty" pleas to "guilty.

They were being held in Shreveport, Louisiana for trial and after being housed there in the jail, newspaper reports in the city of Shreveport carried headline accounts of the whole affair. It was reported that the gang that had been responsible for terrorizing the city of Minden in robbing its bank was caught and would be tried here. This report seems ridiculous in light of the actual court records.

An amusing story was related to me by Truman of how that

at night in the jail, a bunch of rats kept running through their cells. Truman hated rats and he found a garbage can lid and began to chase them and tried to kill them by hitting at them with the lid. The noise of striking the concrete floor with the lid sounded like gunfire. The next day the local paper carried a headline article of an escape attempt by the Mahoney gang from the Shreveport jail in which gunshots were exchanged inside the jail. It seems that some guard had jokingly started the yarn in jest and it had been retold and exaggerated and told as fact to a reporter.

SUCH WAS THE NEWFOUND REPUTATION OF THE MAHONEY GANG AND THEIR EXAGGERATED PROPENSITY TO VIOLENCE.

This exaggerated reputation was not entirely off the mark however for later, as they were awaiting trial in Shreveport, a real escape was planned and carried out. It involved both Bessie and Mabel Mahoney and is a very interesting story within itself. It seems that around August 15, 1938, a plan was carefully worked out by the wives. These enterprising ladies were able to find a young boy by the name of Wilma David Cotton from Lubbock, Texas who was working on a remodeling job at the Shreveport jail where Truman and Harry were being held. They convinced him to help them by paying him to smuggle 12 hacksaw blades in to their husbands. He also placed a rope on the roof of the jail under the third story window located in the cell where Truman and Harry were being held.

On September 17, 1938 the metal working brothers were able to saw through the bars of the jail and use the rope to lower themselves to the ground and make good their escape. They did not last long on the outside however and were soon apprehended and returned to the jail.

Wilma David Cotton left Shreveport and went home to

Lubbock but was traced there and arrested on October the 15th and returned to Shreveport to face the court.

The two wives and the Cotton boy, who was a juvenile, were charged as conspirators and after trial were sentenced to prison. The Cotton boy was sent to Reformatory for two years in the U. S. Southwestern Reformatory in El Reno, Oklahoma and then released on 3 more years of probation. Bessie and Mabel were sent to the Federal Reformatory for Women at Alderson, West Virginia for two years each on the 10th of November of 1938. Harry and Truman were brought before a judge and they plead guilty to escaping and were given a three year sentence to be tacked on to any other sentence they might serve.

This might be a good place to let you know that I found a good bit of information on the women's trials and jail time in the National Archives. I am not certain about Mabel's background and Truman had little to say about her but it was recorded in the files that she had been arrested for prostitution before she married him and that Bessie had been the proprietor of a Shreveport, Louisiana bordello before marrying Harry. It seems that both Truman and Harry were often found in such establishments from early teenage days.

The Minden bank robbery was confessed to by the brothers and brought terms of 14 to 28 years in Angola Penitentiary for Truman and Harry. They were not charged with murder in Louisiana but the District Attorney did place in the record of the court that both Truman and Harry had previously been convicted of manslaughter in another state. For this reason the judge felt the punishment should fit the bank robbery charges committed by a dangerous person. This plea bargain was accepted by the court in Webster Parish, Louisiana with Judge J. F. McInnis presiding, and on October 11, 1938 they were condemned and sentenced. On October 26 they were taken into Federal court and again plead guilty to the charges of bank robbery and were given 15 year sentences in Federal Prison.

They were sent to Angola Prison where they were assigned Prisoner Number 29571 for Harry and Number 29572 for Truman. While they were housed there, Truman told me of the treatment he had suffered at the hands of a particular boss among the guards. This man would beat prisoners with glee and was a sexual sadist who would be sexually gratified in beatings. Truman suffered several such assaults. In later years, Truman would return to Angola. But that is another chapter for another day.

Kenny, this saga is turning out to be a rival for "The Longest Day" and I hope it is not getting laborious for you. Please feel free to ask questions if you have any and I will attempt to address them in the text of the material.

I know you are sharing the story with others and I would appreciate any feed back from them as well. I want the story to honor our Lord and if it is not doing so, I need to address that.

Bless you my brother,
Clifford

CHAPTER 10
LOSING CONTROL

Kenny

Well, I am ready to resume the tale so I hope you are prepared to read another chapter.

After Harry and Truman had spent several months in Angola Prison at Camp E, they were in mortal fear of their lives from the guard in question and decided that they had to find a way to get out of Angola. They had tried to escape and found it too difficult and the punishment too harsh when caught in the attempt. So after discussing all the possibilities, they wrote a letter to F.B.I Agent James Peyronnin asking him to come and visit them. They offered to confess to other bank robberies if he could have them sent to a Federal Prison to serve out their sentences.

The author found this letter reproduced in several communications in the National Archives and was amazed to find the original handwritten letter still in existence and in the files as well. It was on a small lined page from a tablet common in that day. I was so struck by this that I made a photocopy of the letter for my files. I thought it might be of interest to the reader to read in its actual wording. I am therefore presenting it in its whole content, including the spelling and grammatical errors. The letter was hand written by the inmates. It is as follows:

***

March 19, 1939
H. A. & T. R. Mahoney
Angola, Louisiana
Camp E.
Mr. Perrinon
Federal Bureau of Investigation
Department of Justice
New Orleans, Louisiana
Dear Sir,

At your earliest convience, if possible, we would like to have a visit with you, concerning possible arrangements for a release from the State of Louisiana to the Federal Government. Subsquent to such a transfere we disire to come clean regarding other Federal insured bank robberies in which other participants are yet untried and at large. We believe this will safeguard ourselfs against the possibility of prosicution at the time and when we are finally released.

We are incarcirated with others involved and unless assured of removal we shall not disclose what will surely point to us. We are sincerely,

Very Respectfully yours
H. A. & T. R. Mahoney
Angola, Louisiana
Camp E

***

Agent Peyronnin did go to see the brothers and was taken into the warden's office for an interview with both of them. The letter's contents were confirmed and they discussed the fact that the sentences they were under included 15 years in a Federal Prison which was to run concurrently with the 14 to 28 years they were serving in Louisiana. They felt they would not live to complete their sentence in Angola but refused to talk unless they had a guarantee of a transfer.

Mr. Peyronnin stated in a document that is in the National Archives that the warden, who was listening to the conversation, called him aside and told him that the prison of Angola was severely overcrowded and he was in the process of transferring some 28 prisoners to the Federal Prisons. He offered to release the Mahoneys to the Federal Authorities on a "reprieve" from the governor if Mr. Peyronnin wanted to cooperate with the brothers. Agent Peyronnin and the warden assured Harry and Truman that they would be released to the Federal Authorities and transferred if they would talk. This they did and confessed to several small bank robberies in the states of Indiana and Illinois, which had not been solved, along with several burglaries.

The above interview took place in April and on May 2, 1939 the Mahoney brothers were taken from Angola and placed in the New Orleans jail on May 5th . On May 19th they were taken from New Orleans and on May 22nd were delivered to the Federal Penitentiary at Leavenworth, Kansas.

In the course of time they were taken to other states for Federal trials where they had not hurt people in the process of robberies. These incidents had been carefully chosen by Harry and Truman before confessing to them with full knowledge that any sentences resulting would probably never be served. They were given sentences in Federal courts that would have to be served before finishing their sentences in Louisiana but would run concurrently.

During this whole time frame, Truman was able to keep his little New Testament and would almost nightly find himself reading it and would always hear the call of God to repentance and salvation. He always resisted and delayed any decision to respond and often vowed not to read the book any more. HE ALWAYS WENT BACK TO IT FOR COMFORT HOWEVER AND WOULD KNOW THAT GOD WAS CALLING OUT TO HIM THROUGH THE TEXT.

Truman became incorrigible and attempted several escapes. As a result of this and other federal convictions for more serious charges than robbery, Truman was eventually transferred to Alcatraz Prison. This was the most formidable place in the Federal Prison System, an island in San Francisco Bay in California where he was to serve the rest of his federal sentence. It was a place especially designed to house the most dangerous and escape prone men in the federal system.

Here Truman found himself in the same cellblock with some noteworthy individuals. Bob Stroud, (The Birdman of Alcatraz) was across the way from Truman, Machine Gun Kelly bunked next to him for a short while and at one time Al Capone had occupied the cell Truman was housed in. Years were spent here and many difficulties arose and were related by Truman. Truman was not one to sit idle and decided to continue his education. He was a very intelligent person and soon became fairly well educated and learned several trades.

I think that this might be a good place for me to take time to share with you the real day-to-day life that was lived by the men who occupied Alcatraz Island. I have debated a means to accomplish this and have decided that of all the possibilities that have occurred to me, one seems to fill the bill better than any other.

I think that no measure of existence for those condemned to live behind the walls of prisons can better speak of the pain and drudgery and deprivation felt by those who reside there than a real look at the daily imposed rigid schedule of their lives. For one to understand what prisons can do to an individual, one would have to share the experience.

So my friend I am going to attempt to impose that existence upon you by asking you to imagine yourself being processed into the population of Alcatraz Prison.

Begin on the ferryboat landing across the bay from Alcatraz and among a group of prisoners being transferred there. Feel the chains locked around your ankles and wrists as you are stiffly shuffled aboard a ferry that gives you a commanding view of a small, fortress appearing little island that seems to be solid rock. From this vantage point the place seems too small to be a federal prison. It is over a mile out to the island from your present position but it appears much further.

As you slowly draw closer to the place, a fear and dread that you can taste rises up like bile in your throat. You know the history of the place because every inmate of every federal unit in the whole United States has been indoctrinated with and threatened by the stories of those who have been there. You have been encouraged to read all the printed material you could get your hands on by then because they have told you that the only thing that will occupy your mind while there is escape. Check it out now because you will need the information when you get there.

You know that Alcatraz was the brain child of F. B. I. Director J. Edgar Hoover who conceived it as a deliberate threat to the criminal world that was growing across America. He collaborated with Attorney General Homer Cummings and the Director of the Bureau of Prisons, Sanford Bates to construct such a place as a public statement that criminals would be made to be sorry for their crimes.

The place had been a military prison before being chosen to take the status of America's Devil's Island. It was created to house kidnapers, racketeers and individuals guilty of predatory crimes and those deemed too dangerous to live among lesser criminals. It was classified as a concentration model, an experiment in isolation and segregation such as Americans had never seen before.

When you arrive and are directed off the ferry and onto the dock, you find that everything is uphill from here and you are placed aboard a van that takes you to the top of the hill. You are instructed to follow the guard into the basement receiving area where the chains are removed because escape is no longer considered possible. You are told this very unwelcome fact by the guard who met you at the dock and are ordered to form a line for a briefing.

The warden has made it a point to be on hand for your arrival and you are herded into a small receiving area behind at least three steel doors that have clanged shut behind you on the way to it. You are given a brief indoctrination and a matter of fact lecture by the warden who lets you know that he is sitting in for God for the duration of your visit to his kingdom. He will see all, know all and control all of your life until you leave. There are rules, which cannot be violated in any shape, form or fashion at any time. You will be given a written copy of them and you will memorize them and you will live by them every minute of every day. These rules will govern your thinking and actions. You will no longer need to make decisions except as outlined in these rules. It is not a matter of "if" you will obey the rules, there is no other choice left to you. You are told to make your stay as pleasant as you can within these rules.

You are told that there are two ways to leave the island, dead or alive, and he will make the decision whether it is alive. The other is up to you.

From this little welcome you are then processed through the

intricate system of physical examination, housing assignment, clothing and essential issues of personal items furnished and the feeling of being more and more swallowed up by a monster that threatens to digest you into nothingness. The bowels of the place seem to stretch onward without end.

The rulebook that the warden spoke of is a part of the essentials that have been issued to you and as you sit in your newly assigned cell, you are told to begin now and read it through carefully. Be sure that you understand every item and term. If you have questions, ask your neighbor for clarification. You open the booklet and begin to read:

Author's Note

The following material has been collected from official government documents posted on the internet. It has been altered to fit the format of this story only in that it has been slightly edited by the author. No details have been changed. Spelling has been corrected except where the author thought that misspelled words were intended to be as they appear in the text.

It is the opinion of the author that this booklet does a better job of describing life in Alcatraz in a clearer and more coherent manner than it was presented to him by Truman.

One small notation should be added to let the reader know that there was a different rule of silence enforced at Alcatraz for the greater part of Truman's time there. This rule was one of the most difficult for Truman to adjust to and he expressed great relief to the author over the lifting of some of the tension and fear that the rigidity of it imposed upon everyone.

The author realizes that nothing short of actually being incarcerated on the island of Alcatraz could possibly convey the horror of life there. Truman gave such graphic expression to the constant state of mind of those who lived there that the author decided not to try to attempt a recreation of it in this work. He does however feel that most people never stop to consider the depths of depravity in the human soul that prisons have to deal with. Most people are never involved intimately enough with the criminal element of our society to understand that rules not imposed are rules that do not exist for them. The standards that most of society imposes upon itself do not exist in the minds of most career criminals. If they are confronted with any rule in life that is optional and is not forced upon them, they consider it not applicable to them personally. Such rules do not touch the conscious for them therefore they can disregard them with complete ease of mind. Most such career criminals consider the rest of society stupid and weak and placed in the world to be victimized in any way that their needs dictate.

Truman had degenerated to this level of animalistic thinking in his life and therefore had more trouble with the imposed regulations than any other part of prison life. He still had a small part of his being, that he was aware of, that made him different from those around him but at the time kept it hidden and revealed it to no one. Something deep inside him would not let him feel that he was truly a part of what life was for those around him. He could not express it in words but he knew it was there. Something in him longed for a different kind of existence but he seemed helpless to move toward it. Circumstances, in some way he could not define, had ruled his life to this point. What to do to change directions he could not seem to grasp. It was easier to let others make decisions for him and to go with the flow. Harry knew what was best for both of them. Harry had always relieved him of the burden of decision but what would he do without Harry?

He did not know.

His developing mind was beginning to be influenced by the books he was reading and the rules imposed upon him. He was beginning to have to think for himself. He found himself feeling that he was two different people inside the same body and did not yet know which one was the real one.

Some day, somewhere, he knew he would have to face both of these and make a decision on how to deal with them. Somewhere down deep inside, he knew that God was a part of what he was going to have to face.

Harry had preceded Truman several months in taking up residence on the Island. This was a place that seemed to the brothers to be escapable. Communication with one another here was going to be very difficult but it was a comfort to Truman to know that Harry was at least nearby physically. There was no contact from the outside for either of them so the tie between them only grew stronger.

As we have repeatedly shared, these two men were of a superior intellect and when they looked the situation over on the island, several possibilities began to form in their minds that made escape something to explore. They had learned to use other people more effectively to run risks for them during their years of imprisonment.

As they found a possibility that seemed worthwhile, they would leak the information to certain inmates who would in turn share with others and before too long a real plan would materialize. They would encourage this deliberately to test the capabilities of the prison staff to resist becoming out smarted.

If someone else could make it off the island, they knew that it was then possible and they could work from that knowledge for themselves. Several of the plans that they hatched were tried by others with complete failure and they soon knew that the only way to succeed was with help from outside. You could get off the island but you would have to have someone pick you up out of the water. There was no such person to whom they could appeal for help. Only an act of God could get Truman out of this place.

Kenny, I have decided to break the text at this juncture because of the volume of the material contained in the booklet that follows. Some readers may not want to take the time to digest these detailed rules for life so I am deliberately setting them off in a chapter to stand alone.

Bless you my brother,
Clifford

Truman (left) and Harry (right) Mahoney photographed upon entering Alcatraz in 1940. Harry arrived on January 7 and Truman on June 9.

CHAPTER 11
A STRUCTURED LIFE
Alcatraz: Inmate Regulations

These "Institution Rules & Regulations" were in effect at the United States Penitentiary, Alcatraz, during Warden Paul J. Madigan's administration (1955-1961). They were issued to all inmates in the form of a typewritten booklet to be kept in the cell. Earlier regulations were somewhat more rigid but copies are not available.

REGULATIONS FOR INMATES

U.S.P., ALCATRAZ

REVISED 1956

INMATE REG. NUMBER, ___532_____

This set of Institution Regulations is issued to you as Institutional Equipment. You are required to keep it in your cell at all times.

INDEX

1. GOOD CONDUCT
2. GOOD WORK RECORD
3. GOOD CONDUCT RECORD & GOOD WORK RECORD
4. STATUTORY GOOD TIME, MERITORIOUS GOOD TIME AND INDUSTRIAL GOOD TIME
5. PRIVILEGES
6. DISCIPLINARY ACTION

7. TREATMENT UNIT

8. PROSECUTION IN THE U.S. DISTRICT COURT

9. FORFEITURE OR WITHHOLDING OF EARNED GOOD TIME, STATUTORY GOOD TIME OR INDUSTRIAL GOOD TIME

10. RESTORATION OF FORFEITED OR WITHHELD GOOD TIME

11. TRANSFER TO OTHER FEDERAL INSTITUTIONS

12. RECOMMENDATION FOR CLEMENCY FOR MILITARY PRISONERS

13. YOUR COMMITTED NAME & REGISTER NUMBER

14. COMMENDATORY REPORTS

15. DISCIPLINARY REPORTS

16. CONTRABAND

17. ATTEMPTING TO BRIBE EMPLOYEES

18. THREATENING, RIDICULING, OR ATTEMPTING TO INTIMIDATE OR ASSAULT OFFICERS, OFFICIALS, EMPLOYEES OR VISITORS

19. TRADING, GAMBLING, SELLING, GIVING OR LOANING

20. RECREATION

21. WORK

22. LOAFING, LOITERING, VISITING OR UNAUTHORIZED ABSENCE FROM WORK

23. YOUR CONSTRUCTIVE SUGGESTIONS OR LEGITIMATE COMPLAINTS

24. INTERVIEW REQUEST SLIPS

25. MONEY

26. PRISONER'S TRUST FUND

27. THE PRISONER'S MAIL BOX

28. DAILY ROUTINES

29. BATH ROOM RULES

REGULATIONS FOR INMATES
U.S.P., ALCATRAZ

This booklet is issued for the information and guidance of inmates of the U.S. Penitentiary, Alcatraz, California. It outlines the Institution's routines and explains what is expected of you in the matter of conduct and work. You are expected to learn and obey the rules and to perform your assigned work to the best of your ability.

1. **GOOD CONDUCT** means conducting yourself in a quiet and orderly manner and keeping your cell neat, clean and free from contraband. It means obeying the rules of the Institution and displaying a co-operative attitude. It also means obeying orders of Officials, Officers and other employees without delay or argument.

2. **GOOD WORK RECORD** means the reputation you establish as a willing, capable workman, doing your best at whatever work you are told to do.

3. **YOUR GOOD CONDUCT RECORD AND YOUR GOOD WORK RECORD** will be reviewed every time you are considered for work assignments, cell changes, and disciplinary action.

4. **STATUTORY GOOD TIME, MERITORIOUS GOOD TIME AND INDUSTRIAL GOOD TIME** are types of reduction in sentence which can be earned only by inmates who establish and keep a good conduct record and a good work record.

5. **PRIVILEGES.** You are entitled to food, clothing, shelter and medical attention. Anything else that you get is a privilege. You earn your privileges by conducting yourself properly. "Good Standing" is a term applied to inmates who have a good conduct record and a good work record and who are not undergoing disciplinary restrictions.

6. **DISCIPLINARY ACTION** may result in loss of some or all of your privileges and/or confinement in the Treatment Unit.

7. **TREATMENT UNIT** is the segregation section of the Institution where privileges may be restricted to a minimum.

8. **PROSECUTION IN THE U.S. DISTRICT COURT**

in addition to Institutional disciplinary action may result if you commit any serious offense such as assault, escape, attempt to escape, rioting, destruction of government property, etc.

9. **FORFEITURE OR WITHHOLDING OF EARNED GOOD TIME, STATUTORY OR INDUSTRIAL,** in addition to disciplinary action and/or prosecution in the District Court, may result if you become involved in any serious misconduct.

10. **RESTORATION OF FORFEITED OR WITHHELD GOOD TIME** will not be recommended unless you can show at least one year of better than average good conduct and good work when you are called for your annual Classification Hearing.

11. **TRANSFER TO OTHER FEDERAL INSTITUTIONS** will not be recommended unless you can show a better than average good conduct record for several years at this Institution.

12. **RECOMMENDATION FOR CLEMENCY FOR MILITARY PRISONERS** will not be made unless they can show better than average good conduct and good work records for several years at this Institution.

13. **YOUR COMMITTED NAME AND REGISTER NUMBER** are used as a means of identification. You will be addressed by your surname (last name) only. Your register. number is also used as the laundry mark on your Institutional Clothing.

14. **COMMENDATORY REPORTS** may be submitted by Officers who observe your behavior and find it better than average. Such reports are filed and help you to establish a good record.

15. **DISCIPLINARY REPORTS** may be submitted by Officers who observe your behavior

and detect violations of the Institutional regulations. If you are interested in keeping a good record, you should conduct yourself according to the rules.

16. **CONTRABAND.** Anything found on your person, or in your cell, or at your work place, which was not Officially issued to you, or Officially approved and purchased by you, and Officially listed on your property card, will be classed as contraband. Possession of contraband of any sort is a serious offense and will result in disciplinary action. If you steal anything from other inmates or from employees, or from the Institution, you will be punished.

17. **ATTEMPTING TO BRIBE EMPLOYEES** by giving, or promising to give them anything, is a serious offense. You must not give or sell or receive or buy anything except through the Official channels.

18. **THREATENING, RIDICULING, OR ATTEMPTING TO INTIMIDATE OR ASSAULT OFFICERS, OFFICIALS, EMPLOYEES OR VISITORS** is a very serious offense.

19. **TRADING, GAMBLING, SELLING, GIVING, OR LOANING** your personal property or your government issue items or services, or contraband of any kind is a serious offense. You are expected to keep the things that are legitimately in your possession. If they are found in another inmate's possession, disciplinary action will result for both parties. If anything is stolen from you, report the loss to the Officials as soon as possible.

20. **RECREATION.** As a general rule, you will work eight hours a day, five days a week, with Saturdays, Sundays and Holidays devoted to recreation. Movies are shown twice each month. Exercise Yard activities include baseball, handball and various table games. Newly arrived inmates are kept in

Quarantine Status for 30 days and are not allowed recreation during that period.

21. **WORK.** You are required to work at whatever you are told to do. Usually your first assignment will be to temporary maintenance jobs around the cellhouse. Other maintenance jobs include the Culinary Unit, the Clothing and Bath Room, the Library, and the Yard Detail. By doing good work on your maintenance assignment you earn Statutory Good Time. You may also qualify for additional Meritorious Good Time and/or pay, if your work and behavior are outstandingly good and are of outstanding value to the Institution. If you make a better than average work and conduct record while on your maintenance job, you may be considered for an assignment to a Federal Prison Industry Shop where you may earn Industrial Good Time and pay in addition to your Statutory Good Time.

22. **LOAFING, LOITERING, VISITING, OR UNAUTHORIZED ABSENCE FROM WORK** will result in disciplinary action, and may result in loss of your job, and withholding of, or forfeiture of, good time.

23. **YOUR CONSTRUCTIVE SUGGESTIONS OR LEGITIMATE COMPLAINTS** if made by you to the proper Officials, will receive careful consideration. However, if you make groundless complaints for the purpose of creating dissatisfaction and/or stirring up trouble; or if you agitate' or rib' yourself or others into trouble, you will be subject to disciplinary action.

24. **INTERVIEW REQUEST SLIPS** may be obtained from the Cellhouse Officer. When you wish to ask an Official for information, for an interview to request some service or when you want to make a constructive suggestion or a legitimate complaint—use an interview slip. Instructions are printed on the slips

25. **MONEY.** You are not allowed to have money of any kind in your possession while in this institution. Use of cigarettes or other items as jail money' is forbidden. Your earnings and whatever funds you brought with you, or which may be sent to you by approved correspondents, will be kept on deposit for you in the Prisoner's Trust Fund.

26. **PRISONER'S TRUST FUND** is operated like a savings account in a bank, except that it does not draw interest. With the approval of the Associate Warden, you may authorize the withdrawal of funds from your account for legitimate purposes such as the payment of attorney's fees and/or purchase of textbooks and educational materials. You are required to save a part of what you earn, and may contribute part of your earnings to dependents.

27. **THE PRISONER'S MAIL BOX** in each Institution is designed to provide any inmate an opportunity to write directly, without inspection by institutional authorities, to the Director of the Bureau of Prisons, the Attorney General, the Parole Board, the Surgeon General, Federal Judges, Department of Justice Officials, and in the case of military prisoners to the Secretary of War or Navy, or the Judge Advocate General, or the Adjutant General, regarding any matter of importance to the individual, to the inmate group as a whole, or any matter of importance affecting the institution and its personnel or Officials. The Prisoner's Mail Box is open to all inmates regardless of their status. See Section #41.

28. **DAILY ROUTINE:** 7:00 A.M. Weekdays...7:15 A.M. Saturdays, Sundays & Holidays: Morning wake-up bell. See Section 30 for instructions in making bed, policing cell, etc.7:20 A.M. Weekdays...7:50 A.M. Saturdays, Sundays & Holidays: Count Bell. Stand up by your cell door, facing out, remain there until the bell signal sounds again, indicating

the count is correct. Absolute silence must prevail during all counts.7:30 A.M. Weekdays...7:50 A.M. Saturdays, Sundays & Holidays: Breakfast. When your door opens come out promptly and proceed in single file to the Dining Room in a quiet orderly manner. Do not change places in line by moving forward or backward. You may carry books and magazines to the library exchange table but do not carry books or anything else to exchange with other inmates nor put anything in other inmates' cells. The Officer at the tray-dispenser cart will direct you to file past the steam table to the right or left, as he sees fit, to balance the lines. You must Follow his instructions without question. See Section #33 for other Dining Room Rules.

Upon returning to your cell after breakfast, tidy up your cell, placing all trash in your wastebasket. Place this basket outside the cell door at the first opportunity so that orderlies may empty it. If you leave the building for work or recreational activity, put on appropriate clothing. Caps are not worn inside The cellhouse at any time.

8:00 A.M. Weekdays: Outside Work Call. Industries and other outside details will proceed in single file through the rear cellhouse door to the yard.

In rainy weather, all outside workers are called out by details. Remain in your cell until your detail is called, then proceed promptly to the West End of the cellhouse. Your detail officer will escort you as quickly as possible to your place of work.

In fair weather, or when it is not raining too hard, details will remain on the Yard until the Lieutenant gives the signal to line up. You will have a few minutes to smoke and converse. When the line-up bell rings, move promptly to your proper place in your detail and face the South wall. Smoking is not permitted between the Yard and your place of work. Your detail officer will give the signal to proceed through the rear gate to the Work Area. Move in single file.

Laundry workers will turn right at the ramp and enter the Laundry. Gardeners and incinerator operator will wait at the Garden Area Gate. If you work in a lower-level' shop or outside', proceed to the lower level and stop at the designated lines. Form a column of Twos and await the signal from your detail Officer to proceed.

When you reach your place of work, change in to your work clothes and go about your work as directed by your detail Officer or Foreman. Smoking is permitted in the shops except where there is some hazardous condition. Smoking is a privilege. Be very careful about putting matches and butts in the butt-cans.

8:25 A.M. Count Bell on Saturdays, Sundays & Holidays.

8:30 A.M. Saturdays—Main Line Bath. (See Section #29)

9:25 A.M. Saturdays—Count Bell.

9:30 A.M. Saturdays—Yard. (See Sections #37 & #42)

8:30 A.M. Sundays—Religious Services. (See Sections #40 & #48)

8:40 A.M. Sundays—Yard.

8:30 A.M. Holidays—Yard.

8:40 A.M. Weekdays: Inside details will proceed directly and quietly to their places of work. They will confine their activities strictly to their assigned duties and upon satisfactory completion of these duties will return directly and quietly to their cells.

Culinary Detail inmates have a special schedule of work and recreation hours.11:35 A.M. Weekdays: Outside details will stop work, check in tools, wash, change clothing and prepare for return to the cellhouse.

11:45 A.M. Weekdays: Outside details leave shops on signal and proceed in column of twos to the cellhouse. Do not carry on loud and boisterous conversations. Do not jostle or indulge in horseplay with others.

YOU MAY BE STOPPED AND SEARCHED AT ANY TIME. DO NOT ATTEMPT TO CARRY CONTRABAND.

11:50 A.M. Weekdays: COUNT BELL.

12:00 Noon. Saturdays, Sundays & Holidays—Return to cellhouse from recreation Yard. Line up in Yard according to cell block and gallery area and proceed to the cellhouse on signal.

12:00 Noon. Weekdays: Dinner.

12:10 P.M. Saturdays, Sundays & Holidays: COUNT BELL.

12:15 P.M. Saturdays, Sundays & Holidays: Dinner.

12:30 P.M. COUNT BELL.

12:35 P.M. SICK CALL. See Section #36.

INTERVIEWS: You will be notified if you are scheduled for an interview with any Official. See Section #24.

1:00 P.M. Weekdays: Outside Work Call. Same as A.M. Routine.

1:00 P.M. Saturdays, Sundays & Holidays: COUNT BELL.

3:10 P.M. (TUESDAYS ONLY): Return to cellhouse for Tuesday bath line.

3:25 P.M. COUNT BELL. (Tuesday only).

3:30 P.M. Bath lines—Tuesday Only.

3:30 P.M. Weekdays. (Other than Tuesday) Yard recreation period ends. Return from recreation area.

4:10 P.M. Stop work on outside details.

4:20 P.M. Outside details leave shops to cellhouse.

4:35 P.M. COUNT BELL.

4:40 P.M. Supper.

5:30 P.M. COUNT BELL. Final Lock-up Count.

SATURDAYS, SUNDAYS & HOLIDAYS:

3:45 P.M. Return from Yard.

3:55 P.M. COUNT BELL.

4:00 P.M. Supper.

4:40 P.M. COUNT BELL. Final Lock-up Count.

RECREATION PERIODS: Saturdays: 9:30 A.M. to 12:00 Noon: 1:15 P.M. to 3:40 P.M.

Sundays: 8:40 A.M. to 12:00 Noon: 1:15 P.M. to 3:40 P.M.

Holidays : 8:30 A.M. to 12:00 Noon: 1:15 P.M. to 3:40 P.M.

Movies are shown twice monthly on Sundays and Holidays in the afternoon.

29. BATH ROOM RULES: Bathing and laundry exchange are scheduled for mainline bath inmates every Tuesday afternoon and Saturday morning. Items of clothing will be exchanged as follows:

TUESDAY:

1 handkerchief

3 pairs of socks

1 face towel

1 sheet

1 pillow case

1 lt. undershirt

1 shorts or drawers

SATURDAY:

1 handkerchief

3 pairs of socks

1 face towel

1 B & W pants

1 blue shirt

1 lt. undershirt

1 shorts or drawers

When you go to the bathroom you will display all items of soiled clothing before the inspecting Officer. You will then deposit this clothing in the proper hampers and take your bath. You are expected to bathe in a reasonable length of time. Go to the issue window and draw your clean clothing. Check each item.

Minor repairs and replacements will be made immediately, if possible. If this cannot be done, the Clothing Room Officer will take your name and number and place you "on call."Special issues of' clothing and equipment will not be handled during bath line.

Give your name and number to the Clothing Room Officer and he will place you "on call" for these special items.

Do not carry blankets, coats, shoes or other articles to the bath room. Special arrangements are made for collection and laundering of woolen articles and for the repair of shoes.

CULINARY DETAIL BATH LINES: The culinary details will bathe on Mondays,

Wednesdays & Fridays, in two groups as designated by the Steward. Each group

will go to and from the bathroom in a body. When the first group has finished

bathing and returned to the Culinary department or to their cells, the second

group will proceed to the bathroom. Exchange items and days will be as follows:

MONDAYS:

1 Face towel

1 pr shorts

2 pairs of socks

1 lt undershirt

1 white pants

1 white pants

1 handkerchief

WEDNESDAYS :

1 face towel

1 pr shorts

2 pair socks

1 lt. undershirt

1 white pants

1 white shirt

1 handkerchief

1 sheet

1 pillowcase

FRIDAYS:

1 face towel

1 pr shorts

2 pair socks

1 B & W pants

1 blue shirt

1 heavy undershirt

1 lt. undershirt

1 white pants

1 white shirt

1 handkerchief

On Wednesdays and Fridays, Culinary inmates will draw those other supplies which are issued to the Mainline on Tuesdays & Saturdays.

30. CELLHOUSE RULES. Caps are never worn in the cellhouse. You may smoke in your cell, in the Library or in A-

Block, but not elsewhere in the cellhouse. DO NOT SMOKE OR CARRY LIGHTED CIGARETTES OR PIPES ON THE GALLERIES OR FLATS IN THE CELLHOUSE AT ANY TIME. WALK—DO NOT RUN when moving from one place to another.

Upon entering the cellhouse, remove your cap and walk directly and quietly to your cell. Loud talking, loitering or visiting on the galleries, stairs or aisles is not permitted. Don't enter any other inmate's cell at any time.

When you talk in the cellhouse, talk quietly. Don't create a disturbance. Keep your cell neat and clean and free from trash and contraband. Keep your property neatly arranged on your shelves, as shown in the cell diagram on Page #8 [not included here]. Don't leave things stacked on the bars or on your folding table and seat. Don't paste or tack anything on the walls or shelves in your cell.

Keep the floor and the bars of the cell-front free from dust and dirt. The only articles permitted on the cell floor are shoes, slippers, trash baskets, drawing boards and musical instruments.

Your cell is subject to search at any time. Contraband items found in your cell will be confiscated and a disciplinary report will be placed against you for possession of same.

Any dangerous articles such as money, narcotics, intoxicants, weapons, or tools, found in your cell or on your person, that could be used to inflict injury, destroy property, or aid in escape attempts will result in disciplinary action and possibly U.S. District Court action. The presence of articles of this nature on your person or in your cell will be considered evidence of intent to use them for unlawful purposes. "Extra" razor blades are classed as dangerous weapons.

At the wake-up bell in the morning you must get out of

bed and put on your clothes. Make up your bed properly (as shown in the diagram on Page #8) with your pillow at the end near the bars, blankets tucked neatly under the mattress, and extra blankets folded neatly at the foot of the bed. Sweep your cell and place the trash in the trash basket. Don't attempt to flush trash down the

toilet. Don't sweep trash or dirt out onto the gallery or off the gallery.

At 9:30 P.M. lights out, retire promptly. All conversations and other noises must cease immediately.

Keep your person, clothing, bedding, cell equipment, toilet articles, personal property, library books, etc., clean and in good order at all times. You must not mark or deface your cell, library books, furniture, equipment or fittings of the institution. Do not throw anything from your cell at any time.

Advise the cellhouse Officer when you need hot water and a mop to clean your cell. You will be required to remain in your cell and clean it whenever it is reported for being dirty.

Loud talking, shouting, whistling, singing or other unnecessary noises are not permitted. You are permitted to hold QUIET conversations and to play games QUIETLY with your adjoining neighbors ONLY.

Do not tamper with the electric outlets or radio fixtures in your cell. If they do not operate properly, notify the Cellhouse Officer.

Your cell light must be turned out when you leave your cell except when you go to meals. LEAVE YOUR CELL LIGHT BURNING WHEN YOU GO TO MEALS.

[a cell diagram for the individual is displayed at this point in the booklet]

A—12 Books (Maximum)

B—Personal Papers

C—Paint Box etc.

D—Radio Headphones

E—Ash Tray & Tobacco

F—Extra Soap

G—Mirror

H—Toothpowder

I—Razor & Blades

J—Shaving Brush

K—Shaving Mug

L—Drinking Cup

M—Face Towel

N—Bathrobe

O—Raincoat

P—Calendar

Q—Coat & Cap

R—Soap

S—Sink Stopper

T—Cleaning Powder

U—Toilet Tissue

V—Extra Shoes & Slippers

W- Musical Instrument/Case

X—Broom

Y—Trash Basket

Z—Extra Blankets

N.B. Extra Blanket is to be folded neatly at foot of bed. Pillow at the head of the bed toward the bars. Blankets are to be tucked in under the mattress. Shoes, slippers and musical instruments & cases are to be under the bed with the shoes or slippers under the leading edge of the bed.

No fires are permitted in the cell for any purpose whatsoever. Do not attempt to heat water in your cell.

Cell changes are made only on the approval of the Associate Warden. Submit a written request to the Cellhouse Officer who will forward it to the Associate Warden for consideration.

Each inmate is given a property card on which the cellhouse Officer has listed all his personal property. UNLISTED articles which are found in your cell will be confiscated and considered as contraband. At no time will you change or alter your property card. The cellhouse Officer will list any authorized additions to your card. In addition to the personal property listed on your property card, you are allowed the following articles in your cell:

CELL ISSUE EQUIPMENT

2 shelves
2 sheets stationary
2 envelopes
1 can cleanser
3 pencils
1 Radio Headset
1 sink stopper
1 75-watt light bulb
4 wall pegs
1 whisk broom
1 lamp shade
1 set INSTITUTION REGULATIONS
1 « rolls toilet tissue
1 drinking cup
1 ash tray
2 cleaning rags
1 wastebasket

NO SPECIAL SHELVES, BOXES, DESKS OR PICTURE FRAMES WILL BE ALLOWED

BEDDING

2 Mattresses (Maximum)

2 sheets

2 pillows

1 to 4 blankets

2 pillow cases (if 2 pillows]

TOILET ARTICLES

1 shaving cup

2 razor blades

1 safety razor

1 cake soap

1 comb

1 shaving brush

1 pair nail clippers

1 mirror

1 can toothpowder

1 face towel

1 toothbrush

1 cake shaving soap

You will keep your property card listing your personal property, above your cell door behind the locking mechanism.

31. CLASSIFICATION, PAROLE, EDUCATION AND SOCIAL MATTERS: At this institution, these functions center in the Parole Office and you are free to request an interview with the Parole Officer when problems arise concerning these matters.

CLASSIFICATION: You will be reclassified each year shortly before or during the month of your parole eligibility date (except military prisoners who are reclassified just prior to their military annual review dates) and you will be given an opportunity to appear at the Classification Committee meeting to present any problems you may wish to discuss with the Committee.

PAROLE: A few months before your Parole Eligibility Date, you may file an application for a parole hearing. If you do not choose to file at that time, you may sign a waiver. This waiver will not interfere with your right to file for a hearing at a later date.

EDUCATION: Although there are no school classes at this institution, limited facilities are provided for cell study of books available from the library or from correspondence schools. Library rules are listed in Section #45.

SOCIAL MATTERS: If you have social problems outside the institution, such as correspondence problems, you are free to request an interview with the Parole Officer. The Parole Officer will also help you with the development of your release plans.

32. CLOTHING: The standard inmate uniform for all normal activities inside the cellhouse consists of: blue chambray shirt, Blue & White (B&W) trousers, web waist belt and issue shoes. This uniform is worn at visits, interviews, meals, movies, etc. Your shirt will be buttoned except for the top collar button. The sleeves will be rolled down and buttoned. Your belt will be worn with your register number in plain view, at the center of your back.

You are required to wear this standard uniform to and from outside work or the Recreation Yard, but you may add to it your cap, jacket, coat or raincoat. You may wear tennis shoes to the Recreation Yard only.

You will wear your robe and slippers or shoes when going to and from bath. You are not allowed to change or alter any of your issue clothing. Keep your clothing neat, clean and in good repair at all times.

Special work clothing is issued for work details. This special clothing will be kept at the place of work and will not be brought to the Yard or cellhouse. Culinary inmates wear a special work uniform consisting of white cap, white shirt and white pants. This uniform is issued for work only but is worn between the cell and Culinary Unit. Culinary workers are cautioned to be wearing their complete uniform with all buttons except the top collar button fastened before leaving their cells to go to work.

INMATES WILL BE ISSUED ON ARRIVAL:

1 B & W Pants

1 Cap

1 wool coat

1 Blue shirt

1 belt

1 pr shorts

1 bathrobe

3 pairs socks

2 handkerchief

1 Rain coat

2 pairs shoes

1 wool undershirt (on request)

1 pair slippers

1 lt undershirt

AUTHORIZED EXTRA CLOTHING ISSUE:

Culinary workers: 1 white shirt: 1 white cap: 1 white pants.

Barbers: 1 white shirt.

Office Orderlies: 1 white shirt.

Passmen: 1 white shirt: 1 white pants.

Hosp. Orderlies: 1 white shirt: 1 white pants.

When they are available, heavy undershirts may be issued upon request to the Clothing Room Officer. They are issued on the call-out list after the Saturday bath. Heavy undershirts are worn for a full week and are not exchanged on Tuesday bath line.

Clothing issue, replacement and repair are scheduled during Saturday bath line. Inspect your issue clothing when you receive it. Make certain that you have your own clothing and that all of it is in the lot. Report immediately any discrepancies to the Clothing Room Officer and tell him of your needs for replacement or repairs. If the service cannot be provided immediately, you will be recalled after the bath line for attention.

If you damage your clothing accidentally during the week, notify the Cellhouse Officer and you may be permitted to go to the Clothing Room for repairs or an emergency issue.

33. DINING ROOM RULES: Meals are served three times a day in the dining room. Do not exceed the ration. Do not waste food. Do not carry food from the dining room.

Wear standard uniform. (See Section #32).

Conduct yourself in a quiet, orderly manner. You may converse in normal tones with persons near you. Boisterous conduct will not be tolerated in the dining room.

Observe the ration posted on the menu board and take all that you wish to eat within the allotted amounts, but you must eat all that you take.

You may go to the coffee urn on your side of the dining room only when no other inmate is there. Do not go to the urn for the purpose of visiting with others.

Do not pass or exchange food, cigarettes, notes or any other items anywhere in the dining room.

You will be given ample time to eat but no loitering will be permitted.

Shortages of silverware at the table must be reported to the Officer immediately before beginning to eat.

After you have finished eating, place your silverware in the right hand compartment of your tray. Empty bread, cake or pie trays and pitchers will be passed to the end of the table toward the center of the Dining Room. Inmates seated at that end of the table will arrange them for inspection by the officer assigned to the table.

When all inmates on a table have finished eating, the inspecting Officer will give the signal to rise and leave the dining room. Proceed in single file directly to your cell. Enter your cell without delay. Do not loiter or visit on the galleries. Do not enter another inmate's cell at any time. Cell door will be locked as soon as you enter your cell.

34. **HAIRCUTS AND SHAVES:** Haircuts will be of regulation type. You are not permitted to wear your hair in an unusual manner or have any special haircut except as authorized by the Associate Warden.

You will be placed on call for a haircut approximately every three weeks. You will be told when you are scheduled for it.

You may be allowed to go to the Recreation Yard after your haircut if you are in good standing.

You will shave in your cell. Razor blades are exchanged each Saturday by the Evening Watch Officer. Two new blades are issued in exchange for your two old blades. Failure to account for both of your blades at any time will result in a disciplinary report. Loss of a razor blade must be reported to the Cellhouse Officer immediately. Do not wait until issue night to report the loss.

You must be clean shaven at all times. No special beards, mustaches or goatees are allowed.

35. **INTERVIEWS:** If you wish an interview with the Warden, Associate

Warden,Captain,or other Official, submit a written request slip stating briefly what

you wish to discuss and give the request slip to the Cellhouse Officer.

You will be notified when to remain in your cell for the interview.

36. **MEDICAL ATTENTION:** Medical attention is available to all inmates. A member of the Hospital Staff conducts a daily Sick-Call line in the Cellhouse at about 12:30 P.M.

To attend sickcall, proceed directly to the West End of the Cellhouse and stand quietly in line until called. After consultation, return directly to your cell.

Do not loiter or visit on the gallery.

If you become ill at any time, notify an Officer and you will receive medical attention. Do not make unnecessary disturbances.

When you receive a medical lay-in, you will remain in your cell except for religious services, meals and movies.

If you are notified by the Medical Officer at sick-call to remain in your cell for Hospital call-out, you must do so.

You are allowed to keep in your cell only those medications issued to you by the Hospital Staff. Empty and unused bottles are to be returned to the West End desk. No medications will be kept in your cell longer than 30 days.

37. **MOVEMENT OF INMATES:** All inmate movements will be by block and galleries, to yard, work, meals, sick-line,

band room and bath line. Movements will be from cells to West End of the Cellhouse and then to destination.

Movements to picture shows and Religious Services will be from cells to East End of cellhouse and then to Auditorium.

All movements from yard will be by galleries. Inmates will line up by cellblocks and galleries in the designated areas on the yard and proceed to the cellhouse as called by the Yard Officer. While awaiting the signal for your gallery to come in, do not wander around in other gallery lines, or indulge in scuffling or jostling with others. Industries and other "outside" details will return to the cellhouse without lining-up in the yard.

38. SUPPLIES: Toilet tissue, matches, soap, cleanser, etc., will be issued on Tuesdays and Saturdays during bath lines. Writing paper and envelopes are issued only on Tuesdays. Toothpowder will be issued on either of the bath days in exchange for your empty container.

Toothbrushes, combs and fingernail clippers will be issued by the Clothing Room Officer, after a proper request slip has been submitted. Your old item must be exchanged for the new item.

39. WORK REGULATIONS: If you are assigned to an Industries shop, go to your place of work as stated in Section #28. Do not leave your assigned station in the shop without permission from your Foreman or Officer.

Work assignments are made by the Associate Warden. If you wish a work assignment or re-assignment, send a request slip to the Associate Warden and state your experience in the type of work you are requesting. Send a separate slip with this information for each job application.

Work changes will not be made for trivial reasons. Your request will be considered only on the basis of merit, and then only when a vacancy exists.

When in need of advice regarding your work or work assignment, consult the Associate Warden by interview slip.

The regular work-reports submitted by your superiors, supervisors, foremen, shop Officer or other Official are taken into consideration at all hearings for other matters. Special attention is paid to work reports at your hearings before Board meetings for consideration of restoration of forfeited good-time, transfer, parole reports, clemency and/or work changes.

Do not take issue with an Officer, foreman, supervisor or civilian employee on account of any order he may issue to you. If it should seem to you that such person is exceeding his authority or abusing his office, do not argue. Follow his instructions and report the matter to the Associate Warden after the duty is performed.

Smoking is permitted in designated areas. If in doubt, ask your foreman or Officer.

Do not carry any unauthorized articles to or from your place of work.

Do not carry work clothing from the work area to the cellhouse.

Removing tools or other articles from your work area is forbidden. Do not loan any tools or other work material to any inmate without the express approval of your superiors.

Immediately report any injury received while at work. If you become ill, report to your foreman.

Do not manufacture any unauthorized or contraband article, nor perform any unauthorized service for yourself or for any other inmate. Do not assist or interfere with another inmate's work except as directed by an Officer or foreman.

40. **AUDITORIUM RULES:** When preparing to attend religious services or movies, in the Auditorium, you must remove everything from your pockets except your handkerchief and

eyeglasses and eyeglass case. All other items will be classed as contraband. There is no smoking permitted in the Auditorium and you are not allowed to wear or carry, caps, coats, jackets, cushions, blankets or pillows.

Use the East-End cellhouse stairs when going to and from the Auditorium. Walk quietly and be co-operative if and when you are searched for contraband. Upon arrival at the Auditorium, take the seat assigned. If you have poor vision, and wish to sit in the front seats tell the Officer who is directing the seating. After being seated, remain in your seat until the Officer directs you to leave.

Loud talking, pushing or boisterous conduct is forbidden.

In general, you are expected to conduct yourself in an orderly manner, with proper consideration for the rights of others.

Leaving the Auditorium before the end of the program is permitted only in emergencies. Quietly notify the Officer in charge and he will permit you to leave. You will not be able to return to the Auditorium.

The privilege of attending Religious Services and movies is important to you. This privilege may be withdrawn for violation of the rules.

41. **CORRESPONDENCE:** Upon entrance to the institution, each inmate will be given a form to fill out, listing the persons with whom he wishes permission to correspond. After approval of the list, inmates may correspond only with the approved correspondents. You will refrain from discussing other inmates or institutional affairs. Violent or abusive letters will not be mailed.

Correspondence is limited to two (2) outgoing and seven (7) incoming letters a week. All regular inmate mail will be collected by the evening watch Officer in the cellhouse. Writing materials are issued during the Tuesday P.M. bath line, at the supply table in the clothing room.

SEALED CORRESPONDENCE: As stated in Section 27, sealed correspondence may be addressed to certain Officials. Such letters may be sealed and placed in the special mail box which is located at the West End of the Cellhouse. You are not required to place any identifying information on the envelope and it will be forwarded to the Bureau without inspection.

SPECIAL HOLIDAY MAIL: In addition to your regular mail privileges you will be allowed to send your Mother an extra letter on Mother's Day. At Christmas time you will be allowed to mail (4) Christmas Cards. You may receive greeting cards only on the following occasions: Christmas, Easter, Father's Day and your birthday.

Inmates will not ask Officers, Officials or civilians to write or post letters for them or receive mail through Officers, Civilians or Officials except when acting in their official capacity.

42. **YARD PRIVILEGES:** Exercise yard rules: All inmates in good standing are allowed the yard privilege on Saturdays, Sundays, and Holidays, if the weather permits. In addition, inmates who have completed their assigned tasks, or who have been "laid in" by detail foremen, or who have been "held in" for haircut, medical attention, interview or other Official business, may be allowed the yard privilege on weekday afternoons if they are otherwise eligible.

Inmates who are "restricted" or who are in "idle" status because they have quit a job, or refused a job, or were removed from a job for disciplinary reasons, are not eligible for weekday afternoon yard.

Inmates held in for dental or hospital call may have yard after their appointments, subject to the Doctor's approval.

Inmates using cushions, tables or other institutional athletic equipment must return the same to the metal detector when recreation period is over.

No gambling is allowed. You may play chess, checkers or backgammon. Authorized card games are Hearts, Cribbage, and dominoes. No card game will be allowed if it is a "draw" type of game or does not use the full deck on the deal.

All card tables will be set up behind the screens at the West-End of the yard.

All games will cease immediately when the bell rings for the termination of the yard period. No loitering will be permitted to finish uncompleted hands or games.

43. USE OF TYPEWRITERS: You are permitted to work on your own case or to hire a lawyer to represent you. A typewriter is available if you are able to type.

Apply to the Associate Warden for permission. You are not permitted to work on another inmate's case or to give another innate legal advice or instructions.

After you obtain permission to use the typewriter, you will be notified when a machine is available. You will bring all materials to "A" Block where they will be inspected. All typing material, books, papers, etc., will remain in "A" Block until the typing has been completed. All papers will be signed and labeled. One copy of all papers typed shall be made for the Institution records. After the papers have been inspected by the Associate Warden, your copy will be returned to you.

44. LIBRARY RULES: Each cell contains a catalog which lists all of the books contained in the library. If you do not have a library catalog or library card, address a request to the Librarian to obtain one. Fill out this card with your name, register number and cell location.

(1) To request delivery of library books to your cell, refer

to the catalog for the "Call" or identification number of the book you want and place that number on your library card. Place the card on the table at the entrance to the dining room on your way to breakfast. Return books in the same manner.

(2) The library books you request are checked out to you and must be returned within the time limit shown on the DATE-DUE slip inside the back cover of the book. Failure to return the book to the library prior to or on the date due, may result in forfeiture of library privileges.

(3) You are permitted to have not more than three CIRCULATING library books in your cell at one time. Keep your books and magazines neatly arranged on the shelf in the cell when they are not being read.

(4) In addition to the circulating books, you are permitted to have a Bible, Dictionary and study books up to a maximum of twelve (12) in your cell at one time. This includes all books, personal, library and study course books. Books beyond the maximum of 12 will be confiscated. A maximum of 24 pamphlets may be kept in your cell at one time. Pamphlets beyond this maximum will be confiscated.

(5) Handle library books carefully. Many of the worn out books, especially fiction books, cannot be replaced since they are out of print. You are cautioned not to loan or exchange books with other inmates or to toss books to other tiers or the flag. Defacement, mutilation or destruction of books will be cause for disciplinary action even to the extent of forfeiture of good time.

MAGAZINES: The library subscribes to a few magazines such as the National Geographic and these magazines can be obtained from the library, not by using the library card, but by submitting a request form. Library magazines must be handled with care and promptly returned to the library for redistribution. Do not remove articles or pictures.

You are permitted to purchase (by subscription) not more than eight (8) magazines from the approved list. Requests for the purchase of magazines are submitted to the Mail Censor using the regular request slip. When magazines arrive at the institution, the mail Censor marks your number on them and forwards them to the Library for distribution. Magazines are withdrawn from circulation 30 days after delivery.

45. **MOVIES:** Movies are shown twice monthly for inmates in good standing. See the AUDITORIUM RULES in Section #40.

46. **MUSIC RULES:** Musical instruments may be purchased if approved by the Associate Warden.

Guitars and other stringed instruments may be played in the cellhouse in a QUIET manner only between the hours of 5:30 P.M. and 7:00 P.M. No singing or whistling accompaniments will be tolerated. Any instrument which is played in an unauthorized place, manner, or time will be confiscated and the inmate placed on a disciplinary report.

Wind instruments, drums and pianos will be played in the band or Orchestra Rooms on Saturdays, Sundays and Holidays. At no time will you play any wind instrument in the cellhouse.

Permission to play instruments in the Band, Orchestra or bathrooms may be granted by the Associate Warden to inmates in good standing. The Band room is a privilege and permission to play there must be requested from the Associate Warden.

A limited number of inmates may be allowed to take musical instruments to and from the recreation yard. Permission must first be obtained from the Associate Warden.

No inmate on "idle" status or on "report" or restricted will be allowed to use the Band Room, Orchestra Room or to take instruments to the yard.

An inmate whose musical privileges have been restricted or revoked shall be removed from all musical lists, and his instrument stored in "A" Block until otherwise authorized by the Associate Warden.

No inmate is allowed to give, sell, trade, exchange, gamble, loan or otherwise dispose of his personal or institutional instrument or to receive such from another inmate.

Institutional instruments may be loaned to inmates in good standing upon the approval of the Associate Warden.

All instruments will be listed on personal property cards. Institutional instruments shall be listed as "On Loan" from the institution, together with the date of the loan and the identification number of the instrument. Surplus parts for musical instruments together with and including extra sets of guitar strings shall be kept in "A" Block. Guitar strings shall be purchased in the regular manner and stored in "A" Block until needed. An old set of strings must be turned in to the cellhouse Officer to draw a new set.

47. **RADIO:** Radio programs are carefully selected for the enjoyment of all concerned. Protect your radio privileges by conducting yourself properly with consideration for the rights of other inmates during broadcasts.

You are issued a radio headset on the signing of a receipt for the same. Do not tamper with your radio outlets, phones, or other equipment. If they do not work properly, notify the cellhouse Officer quietly. Your headsets are of a "tamper-proof" type. Evidence of tampering with any part of your radio equipment will result in a disciplinary report.

The operator of the radio is not in the cellhouse. Do not shout any instructions, advice or abuse.

Programs are scheduled for the following hours:
Weekdays: 6:00 PM to 9:30 PM

SATURDAYS, SUNDAYS & HOLIDAYS: 1:00 PM to 9:30 PM Loud laughter, yelling, cheering or clapping will not be tolerated. Your headset must be kept at the rear of the cell when you are out. Do not leave your headset plugged-in when you leave the cell. Headsets found plugged-in or hanging on the outlet box will be picked up.

48. **RELIGIOUS SERVICES:** Catholic and Protestant Services are held regularly on Sundays in the Chapel. Jewish Services are held on appropriate occasions.

Religious advice and counsel are available by sending a request slip to the Chaplain. The menu board in the dining room will indicate the schedule of the Religious Services.

Regular Auditorium Rules will be observed during all Services. See Section #40 for Auditorium Rules.

49. **SPECIAL PURCHASES:** There is no commissary at Alcatraz. The institution supplies all your needs. You are not allowed to have anything sent to you from home, friends or relatives. You may be allowed to purchase certain items such as textbooks, correspondence courses, musical instruments, or magazine subscriptions. All such purchases must be listed on your property card by the cellhouse Officer.

After your purchase request is approved, you must sign a withdrawal slip and return it to the cellhouse Officer. If you receive only a part of what was signed for on this withdrawal slip, the balance of the money will be returned to your account. Only those items actually received are charged to you.

All purchases will be entered on your property card. No bartering, trading or giving as a gift of any purchase is allowed. You are not permitted to loan any items to any other inmate nor to borrow from another inmate.

50. **TOBACCO AND SMOKING REGULATIONS:** Pipe and cigarette tobacco is available from the dispensers

at the West-End of the cellhouse. Take what you need for immediate use, not to exceed six packs altogether. Don't hoard tobacco. Don't waste tobacco.

Cigarettes: One pack of cigarettes may be issued to each inmate in good standing, each Monday, Wednesday and Friday evening. Inmates who are restricted or on report will not receive cigarettes. You are not permitted to have more than 3 packs (60 cigarettes) at any one time. If you are found to have in excess of 60 cigarettes at any one time, all will be confiscated and you will be placed on a disciplinary report.

Matches: Matches and cigarette papers are distributed during bathlines. Do not accumulate more than 10 books of matches nor more than two of the 150-paper size books of cigarette papers.

Smoking: Smoking regulations vary for different areas. If in doubt, ask your foreman or Officer. No smoking is permitted in the Cellhouse at any time except within the cells, library or "A" Block. Smoking is not permitted in the dining room or kitchen except for certain areas assigned for kitchen workers. Smoking is permitted in the yard but not between the yard and your place of work.

51. VISITS: You are allowed to receive one visit each month from members of your immediate family or other persons approved by the Warden. Visiting hours are approximately 1:30 PM to 3:10 PM weekdays.

In all personal visits you will confine your talk to personal matters and refrain from discussing other inmates, Institutional matters, etc.

Visits with your Attorney of record may be arranged through the office of the Associate Warden.

52. THE GOOD TIME LAW: Revised Title 18 of the

United States Code, effective September 1, 1948, provides in Section 4161 as follows:

"Each prisoner convicted of an offense against the United States and confined in a penal or correctional institution for a definite term other than for life, whose record of conduct shows that he has faithfully observed all the rules and has not been subjected to punishment, shall be entitled to a deduction from the term of his sentence beginning with the day on which the sentence commences to run, to be credited as earned and computed monthly as follows:

Five days for each month, if the sentence is not less than six months and not more than one year.

Six days for each month, if the sentence is more than one year and less than three years.

Seven days for each month, if the sentence is not less than three years and less than five years.

Eight days for each month, if the sentence is not less than five years and less than ten years.

Ten days for each month, if the sentence is ten years or more.

When two or more consecutive sentences are to be served, the aggregate of the several sentences shall be the basis upon which the deduction shall be computed."

Section 4165 provides as follows:

"If during the term of imprisonment a prisoner commits any offense or violates the rules of the institution, all or any part of his earned good time may be forfeited. "Section 4166 provides as follows: "The Attorney General may restore any forfeited or lost good time or such portion thereof as he deems proper upon recommendation of the Director of the Bureau of Prisons."

53. GENERAL RULE: Though not mentioned in these

rules, any disorder, act or neglect to the prejudice of good order and discipline, and any conduct which disturbs the orderly routine of the institution shall be taken cognizance of by the Warden or his representative, according to the nature and degree of the offense, and punished at the discretion of the Warden or other lawful authority.

This is a lot of reading and writing for one session Kenny so I expect that you will have to take a day or two to digest it. I would like to be able to have everyone know the two Truman Mahoneys that I knew and be able to see what a miraculous work God performed in him. The transformation was full and complete. It was as if one man died and another moved into the same body. I was made to marvel that the man I am describing here could change so drastically.

I never cease to be amazed at the work of God.

But I need to close for now so I will share another episode when time will allow. Perhaps I will share Truman's experience with Bob Stroud. We will see.

Bless you my brother,
Clifford Neal

CHAPTER 12
DESPAIR AND HOPE

Kenny,

Hope you are having a good day. I am this afternoon returning from an overnight camping and hunting trip in my coach, which was a very pleasant experience. We are blessed here in my area with access to several National Forests that have excellent camping facilities and we enjoy the facilities as often as we can.

I am trying to answer e-mails and thought I would try to begin a new episode of Truman's Story for you. I seem to remember that I left him in Alcatraz and intended to look at some of his rooming companions.

One that I was interested to hear Truman share about was Robert (Bob) Stroud, The Birdman of Alcatraz, whose colorful story has been immortalized by many writers and more than one movie. Truman reported that the movies were about as far off target as one could be in portraying the real Bob Stroud. I suppose he would be in an excellent position to know as he was housed across the isle from Mr. Stroud for some time in Alcatraz.

Truman had a man in the cell next to him on both sides most of the time that he was in this cellblock and Bob Stroud, as I understood it, was directly across from Truman.

He indicated that Mr. Stroud did get some very favorable treatment from the Warden but was reluctant to share the details of why this was so. He indicated that some things were better left unsaid. I do not know why he shared what he did and how he made the decision as to what was allowable and what not. He did indicate however that Mr. Stroud was a very evil person who was totally void of any expression of compassion for any human except himself. He was a depraved individual who delighted in inflicting pain and would go to any length to inflict it on anyone who was available.

Truman and his neighbors were often the target of his depraved amusements. One of the things constantly repeated was that Mr. Stroud would roll toilet tissue into balls and set them on fire whenever he could catch Truman asleep. He would utilize an improvised catapult to shoot them across the isle and into Truman's cell and set his blankets or sheets on fire. This was an extremely funny thing to Mr. Stroud, especially when Truman or other men were burned in the process. Truman hated him and swore that the man was so depraved that he would have sex with his own mother through the bars of his cell when she was allowed to visit with him. He seemed to delight in doing so in full view of the other members of the cellblock and would roar with laughter at their reactions. It seems that the man's mother was allowed to visit him on some kind of regular basis in this manner. I do not know how this kind of visit came to be allowed but it was not the normal thing for a prisoner to be allowed visitors in the cellblock. Truman could never understand how the man came to be treated so kindly by the folks who wrote about him. Well, enough about The Birdman. Truman had many such stories to relate about the man.

One other amusing incident involved Truman and George "Machine Gun" Kelly who shared the cellblock with Truman for some time. Kelly often bragged about his exploits in the cellblock and Truman, at one point, reiterated to him that he and Harry had appreciated The Capone Organization. He shared how they had made a living robbing it of its assets for a period of time by hi-jacking their moonshine delivery trucks in and around Chicago.

Kelly looked at him with great contempt for a full minute and then broke out laughing as he remembered hearing of the incident when Capone had ordered his underlings to go and warn Harry and Truman to cease and desist in their operations or lose their lives. He came over and shook Truman's hand and said he was glad to have the opportunity to meet him. He remembered that he had been impressed by the ingenuity of the young hoodlums in the operations they were involved in back in Chicago. He remembered that they were just kids and that Capone had reportedly told his people to go easy on them unless they refused to leave his operations alone.

During the course of the time that followed, Kelly questioned Truman about the bank robbing business that he and Harry had gotten involved in. He was particularly interested to learn how they had avoided detection and arrest for as long as they were reported to have done. He also was very interested to learn why and how they had been caught. It seemed that Kelly had given some thought to his own career as a bank robber and wanted to know the ins-and-outs of the trade from another expert. He told Truman that he would not be in prison very long and when he got out he wanted to approach the business in a different way than he had in the past. He said he intended to break out of Alcatraz and if they ever met on the outside, he would like to work with the Mahoney brothers. Truman never took any of this seriously and knew Harry would never work with Kelly.

I want to emphasize that even in Alcatraz, Truman was

able to keep the little New Testament that his father had given him as a child and would still read it, at night mostly. He related how that God never let up in calling out to him to repent and turn to Christ. He continued to resist until an incident occurred that is recorded in several books and movies that, once more, do not tell the full story.

The incident was connected to a riot that took place in the prison, in which several hostages were seized by the inmates. Truman was not a part of the rioting group and had no part in the hostage taking but nevertheless was in the center of it. He decided, along with his neighbor in the next cell, that there could be no good end to the matter so they would remain in their cells and refuse to participate in any active way in the events.

A stand-off was maintained for some time and negotiations were getting nowhere when the officials in charge decided to put the whole matter down in a way that would be a lesson to any who would choose to consider such actions in the future.

At a given signal, an elite group of guards and a contingent of special trained forces stormed into and through the area where the rioters were holding hostages. With Tommy guns blazing they laid down a lethal wall of bullets into every cell till all the rioters were dealt with. Several were killed and many wounded. Truman related that as the men ran down the isle outside his cell, he and his neighbor who was visiting in Truman's cell at that exact time, dived under the bunk in his cell in an attempt to avoid the bullets being sprayed through the bars of every cell.

Truman was the first under the bunk and his neighbor was behind and to the outside of him so that when the bullets flew through the cell and all around them, Truman felt his cellmate stiffen and moan pitifully as he felt the jolt of bullets striking flesh. Truman did not know if he had been hit or not for sure but thought that both of them had been hit. He began to feel blood soaking his clothing and the floor as he continued to lie still and wait for things to calm down enough for him to move and examine their condition. Truman felt something wet all over his face and when reaching carefully to wipe it away he found the substance to be the splattered brains of his neighbor who had been hit in the head and other places.

Truman was sickened to his stomach by the revelation and began to throw up all over himself and the body of his neighbor. He lay there for what seemed like forever, afraid to move. He was aware that any sudden movement could bring a new round of gunfire flying his way. He could not tell if he had been hit himself and was trying to fight down the rising panic from within himself. He forced himself to breathe deeply and mentally take stock of every member of his body for damage.

He felt no pain but he knew that gunshot wounds sometimes created such shock that one would not feel the pain of it for some time afterward. He had seen a man walk around for over 30 minutes with a very serious gunshot wound without ever realizing he was hurt. For some reason his mind began to convulse with that image as clearly as if he were looking at the man that very moment. A sudden noise brought him to the recollection that this was a different time and a different situation. As he lay there trying to take stock of himself, he decided that he was not seriously hurt and the knowledge of that caused him to suddenly begin to shake uncontrollably.

His companion's body was still twitching and making slight gurgling noises but he told himself that there was nothing he could do for him. Everything in him wanted to shove the body away from him and run but he knew it would be the wrong thing to do. All he could do was to wait. Then it occurred to him that he could at least yell out. He opened his mouth to scream but nothing would come out. It was as if his vocal cords were gone and his throat was one giant locked muscle. He continued to convulse violently. After what seemed like hours, the jerking of his body began to subside and became a nervous tremor that would not stop. It was as if he were freezing to death.

As if out of a fog, he began to hear a human voice wailing. The wailing started in a soft muffled whine and rose steadily in volume and pitch until it seemed it would rupture his ears. His mind would not help him locate the origin of the wailing. He struggled to get control of his mind and suddenly, as if a bright light had been flashed inside his head, he knew that he was the origin of the sound. He found that knowledge somehow funny and before he knew what was happening he was pushing the body of his companion away from him and now found himself beginning to convulse with uncontrollable laughter. His intestines began to contract and his stomach muscles locked in pain but still he could not make himself stop laughing. He somehow became aware that he was urinating in his pants and the thought only added to the volume and force of his laughter.

Finally the storm troops came back and tried to yell him into silence but to no avail. Someone grabbed him by the arm and pulled him out from under the bunk and as he was trying to get to his knees, he felt something fall out of his shirt pocket. He looked down and saw lying in the blood and vomit and brain matter, his little New Testament and he heard God say, "**Truman I love you and have protected you and I am calling you**". With a suddenness that felt like someone had physically hit him, the laughter stopped. In its place, he felt himself begin to cry. He was vaguely aware of several men congregating around him. One of them bent down and slapped his face very roughly and he looked up at the man and cried out uncontrollably "God, if you will get me out of this place, I will give anything you want". With that statement, reality and sanity flowed back into his wounded brain.

Two sleepless days later, Truman was taken to the Warden's office in what he thought would be an interrogation. When he entered the office, the warden told him to have a seat and after looking at Truman for several minutes, he said very calmly to Truman, "How would you like to get out of this place?" Truman could not believe his ears and asked him to repeat the question. To which the warden replied, "I said, how would you like to get out of this place?"

Truman considered a response very carefully and after a long minute he asked the warden, with all the conviction he could put in the question, "Who do you want me to kill?" The Warden began to snicker and broke into a belly laugh. After a few minutes of wiping his eyes and blowing his nose the warden had composed himself. In a tone that could leave absolutely no doubt of his sincerity, he told Truman, "I have an offer to make you and it may well entail the losing of your own life and possibly that of some others as well". Without hesitation, Truman said, "You name it, I'll do it."

The warden then went on to tell Truman that there was a drug smuggling operation going on in Leavenworth Federal Prison in the state of Kansas that the officials had been trying to stop for many years and that it was about to become public knowledge. The threat of public ridicule to the prison officials had brought about a plan that was being put into effect to uncover those involved in the drug smuggling and put a stop to it.

The plan involved sending someone into the prison

(undercover) who could infiltrate the system and disclose the complete operation. Truman was being offered the opportunity to be that person and if he were successful and lived to finish the task, he would be given a Presidential Pardon and released from prison. Truman thought about it for about 5 minutes and made a counter offer. "If you will release my brother Harry as well, I will do it." Such was his love for Harry. The warden thought this over for a few minutes and responded that it might be possible.

Before he could give a positive answer he would have to clear it with those planning the operation and had the authority to make such a decision. He dismissed Truman with a warning that if a word of the operation were leaked, he would hold Truman personally responsible and see that the rest of his life was spent in solitary confinement. After about a week, the warden summoned him for another session on the matter and informed him that he had checked out this possibility with the Federal Prison Officials and that his terms would be met. Harry would go free as well.

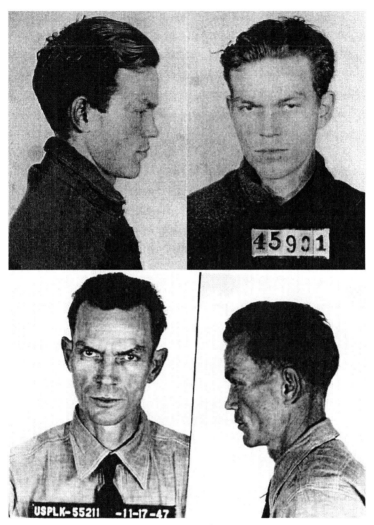

Truman Mahoney at age 24 entering Federal Prison in Atlanta, Georgia on April 9,1935 (top) and Leavenworth Prison in Kansas on Novermber 17, 1947 at age 46.

The story of this work would make a book in and of itself but to keep this one from becoming hopelessly bogged down, let me say that Truman was successful and through his efforts, the whole smuggling operation was broken up and several inmates were dealt with appropriately. In addition, a whole organization of people outside in the free world lost their freedom.

If it became known that Truman was responsible for the betrayal of the ring leaders, he would be branded as a snitch and marked for death from inside the walls of the prison and by the associates of those from without as well. All possible care was extended by the authorities to prevent any leakage of this information but one could never be absolutely certain that his life would ever be safe.

But there was a bitter pill that Truman was going to have to swallow connected to the completion of his assignment at Leavenworth. When he should have been released, he was called into the warden's office and informed that he still had to face the sentence imposed upon him by the State of Louisiana. He was going to be transferred to Angola Prison to serve the time required by Louisiana. Anger rose up within his chest and he fought with all the control he could muster. "I was promised a full pardon and that I would be released when I finished the job I agreed to do. How can you send me back to that place? I'll die there, you know it as well as I do. Sooner or later the word will get out on what I have done here and when it does, orders will be given and I will die. You know that the people I have put in prison will see to it. You are giving me a death sentence."

The warden seemed truly sorry and admitted that this was a real possibility and told Truman that the matter was out of his hands. The Federal Prison officials had no control over the State Prison System. They would keep their promise and he would receive a pardon from the president for the crimes he was convicted of in Federal Courts but the State of Louisiana would not agree to co-operate. He would have to finish his time there. The claims upon him for Federal Prisons would be set aside and that was all they could do.

He was told that everything possible would be done to prevent his involvement in the affair at Leavenworth from being discovered. He needed to become a model prisoner at Angola and they would do everything they could to see that he was released on parole at his first hearing.

With a rage in his heart against the system that had used him and lied to him, he was returned to Angola with the resolve that he would live through what seemed a certain death sentence. He knew the kind of place that Angola was.

Months became years and Angola lived up to every particle of its reputation as a place that destroyed men's souls. Truman hardened his resolve and was able to maintain a near perfect record during his time there. The parole board finally said, "Enough". He had met his goal.

Truman was finally released with a full Presidential Pardon signed by Lyndon Johnson. On that day he was told that he would have protective cover for one week and would thereafter be on his own. He was very afraid that word was already out that he had been the person to rat on the smugglers and that his life would be worthless if he were caught. He was taken to a hotel for the night and there began to unpack his belongings and there fell out of his bag and onto the bed, his LITTLE NEW TESTAMENT.

He heard God say, "**Do you remember your cry from the riot strewn cell?**" He sat down on his bed and cried for over an hour before he could control himself and then said to God, "We'll see what happens."

Next episode: Truman and Harry reunited with great plans for their future. How do we deal with the friends of the drug smugglers on the outside? How can we find out if anyone knows and is going to be after us? And what are we going to do with our lives?

Well Kenny, as you can see, the plot is thickening. I am struggling somewhat to know how to share the rest of this story. It has never been publicly revealed how all this came about so I am trying to be as careful and yet as open as possible. Pray that I do nothing to hurt anyone.

I must close and get some other things out.

Praying for you my brother.

Clifford

CHAPTER 13
FREEDOM'S PLAN

Kenny,

I appreciated the photos of you and Jackie. It really helps to be able to know what a person looks like when praying for them. I pray that you will regain your weight and strength and will be remembering your son and his family as well.

This has been a busy day for me but it is winding down and I will attempt to share some of Truman's Story for you.

As Truman was released from the prison, he was in touch with Harry and arranged to meet him in Indiana where they would make plans together.

Both of them have been in jail many years and are now getting on in years. They are both single and are interested in looking for wives as they both have longed for companionship and dreamed of rearing families but both think it may be too late for them. They also want to give every appearance of two reformed men who are going to be model citizens.

This might be a proper place to share that both of them had entered prison with severe cases of venereal diseases. In fact the prison records from Alcatraz show that Truman was given 100 injections of experimental drugs in an attempt to kill the infection of syphilis in his system. This was before the days of penicillin and Truman told me that he had volunteered to receive the injections as a means of obtaining money. It seems that some prisoners were offered such an arrangement through a drug-testing program sponsored by the government and drug companies. The drugs had some adverse effect on Truman that he suffered from the rest of his life.

All that considered, both Truman and Harry knew that their days of debauchery and bordello hoping had cost a heavy price. They both wanted to find wives.

Harry finds a wife first and then Truman. I don't know a lot about Harry's wife as I never met her but as you know, I did get to know Truman's wife, Mary. She was over thirty years younger than Truman and he met her through Lillian, Harry's wife, who is Mary's sister. Mary was not Truman's second wife however, there was a wife named Sylvia, then Mary. It was about this time that Truman and Harry began to develop a project that will occupy over two years of their lives. It has to do with something I have mentioned in former episodes, the buried cash along the Mississippi River that law enforcement had never reclaimed and only Truman and Harry knew about. Even the former members of their gang did not know that they had hidden these caches away for future recovery and use.

Both Truman and Harry knew that they would be watched by law enforcement very closely in the months ahead because they were aware that a lot of the money had never been recovered. If either of the former robbers made an attempt to regain the money, and was caught, it could be seized and they could be sent back to prison. So any effort to retrieve the loot and use it was going to have to be done very carefully if at all.

Truman did not tell Harry about his promise to God and decided he would not make any attempt to find out what God might want of him. As time elapsed, he began to think that God was not going to require anything of him but he did not know what to expect nor how to deal with the Lord so he just put it aside and went on with life without God. He still had his New Testament but stored it away and did not read it for many months. Occasionally he would think of doing so and of his promise but always found other things to occupy his time and energy.

He and Harry agreed that they could not touch the hidden money any time soon so they decided to occupy themselves with finding employment and trying to make honest livings. They both had educated themselves while in prison and had no difficulty getting good jobs. Truman had studied radiology and several professions related to the medical field. Both men were able to get jobs and settle down in Terre Haute, Indiana on the banks of the Wabash River. There they began to save money and spread a tale that they had all their lives wanted to travel down the Ohio River to the Mississippi River and on down the Mississippi to New Orleans. According to their story, they had plans to build two large houseboats and spend a year floating down these rivers.

They began to accumulate the materials to build these two highly specialized watercraft and embarked on the project on some property rented from some folks who lived on the banks of Wabash River. The construction was soon a major topic of discussion around the area and people would come by to see how their project was going and often offer help. The two boats were completed eventually and launched into the river in a highly publicized christening event.

It was about this time that Truman was injured while working and spent some time in the hospital in Terre Haute. While in the hospital, he met Sylvia Newman, who worked in the unit Truman was confined in. They became friends and dated and soon married.

During all this time plans for the trip developed. Truman

and his wife Sylvia would travel in one houseboat and Harry and his wife Lillian in the other. They saved every dime they could spare for the trip and eventually were ready to begin the trip. Which they did with great publicity in the newspapers and some local radio stations began picking up the story.

The plan was to be so open with the trip, and so public in what they were doing, that no one would suspect their real reason for the trip. Which was, of course, to collect the hidden caches of money along the way as they floated down the Mississippi. They felt sure that by the time they made it down the Wabash and then down the Ohio it would be evident whether they were being watched by law enforcement and if so, they could alter their plans accordingly after reaching the Mississippi.

Sure enough, they found that they were being watched by many people for the first leg of the trip. Every day would find lines of folks at the river's shoreline watching and calling out to them. Many offered to join the excursion and small boats were put out to join them for hours on end as well wishers and the curious came along side to chat. They felt sure that there were observers in the crowds from law enforcement and often were able to pick out individuals that everyone agreed upon as obviously a part of such. By the time they reached the Mississippi however, the watch seemed to be called off and they found themselves going through days with no sign of observance by anyone but news reporters and occasional well wishers.

Their plan was working. The plan allowed for prearranged stops along the way where the news media would publicize their progress and they would be welcomed and often toasted by local officials and interviewed by the local press and radio.

Anyone looking at their actions would soon decide that

they were truly living out a life-long dream and had become modern day Huckleberry Finns. It was a grand trip. They were very leisurely taking their time and would often throw out an anchor and stay in one place for days at a time. Many stops were made in towns where they might also remain several days enjoying local culture and food and seeing the countryside. They would, more often than not, find the local citizens willing to loan them the use of cars or more often be escorted by local folks who had read of their adventure and wanted to meet them and share the limelight as well as their area with them. They were even asked to stay in the homes of many people in these towns. Often they were given lodging at local hotels because they were becoming celebrities. So much so that it was the expected routine. The vagabonds were living it up and enjoying the special treatment but never lost sight that all of this had a purpose. This was a cover up for the stops to recover their loot at designated places along the banks of the mighty Mississippi unobserved.

When they had completed the journey down the Wabash River to the Ohio River and then on down to the Mississippi River, they were confronted with a major obstacle that made them realize they had made a serious miscalculation. They needed to turn upstream on the Mississippi for a few days toward the city of Cape Girardeau, Missouri. Their first attempt at recovering a large portion of their share of the proceeds from several bank robberies would take place near there.

The little outboard motors that they had equipped the boats with had to struggle against the current and the going was very slow. They had not wanted to spend the money necessary to install large engines in the boats because their money was in short supply until they could regain some of the cached loot. The engines were purchased from a friend who let them have them for next to nothing and the best advice they could get said they would be sufficient for their needs. In addition, they knew that almost all of the trip would be downstream and they felt that they could manage very well with the small inexpensive motors. It was assumed that they would mostly just float along with the current and only use the motors in going across the current.

They discussed the difficulty and since they were not on any kind of time schedule, it really did not matter that the going was slow. The little motors strove mightily against the current and were admired by the two men for their untiring effort.

After struggling with the current for three days they had hardly traveled more than a few miles and they were beginning to worry that they would burn the little motors up and be left stranded with no power at all. They decided to anchor and evaluate the options open to them.

They discussed leaving the women to care for the houseboats and transferring an outboard motor to one of the little dinghies that they pulled behind to make the journey faster upstream but this was ruled out. It would be impossible for them to face the task they had to do without the tools and equipment stored on the houseboats. And then there was the risk of being discovered with loot on the return trip back to the houseboats.

Their reason for going all the way to Cape Girardeau was something that they were cursing themselves for. They had used several landmarks traveling downstream form that city which, when passed in order, would lead them back to the spot where the money was hidden. They had prided themselves back in the old days in the planning they had put into hiding it and remembering how to get back to it. They had made up little nonsense jingles as memory tools, which called off each landmark in order, so they had felt secure in their ability to return to the exact spot. So it was imperative that they get to Cape Girardeau to start the count down to the spot.

After being in the same spot for two days, they were passed by many boats of various shapes and sizes going both up and down the river. Many tugboats were moving large barges up and down the stream and they decided to try and contact one of them and ask if it were possible to attach towing ropes to it for the short trip upstream. They put one of the dinghies to work to use as a shuttle in contacting the tugboats.

After several discussions with some of the tugboat captains, they found one who was willing to accommodate them. So with very little work, they made the rest of the trip upstream and were dropped off at the city docks of Cape Girardeau. They were warmly received by the local folks there and decided to rest for a few days before attempting to turn back down the river.

They did not wish to arouse suspicion by being towed in and then simply leaving with no apparent reason for being there. They had made up a story to cover for their having come upstream this far. They told the local folks they were looking for long lost relatives. Of course they found none. They spent a few idle days in the city and then turned again down the river.

So it was with great anticipation that the two brothers began to sing their little jingles to one another as they slipped steadily downstream. Finally they arrived at the place where they would make their first attempt to locate and secure the recovery of a cache of money. It was buried between two large trees, which had been marked with a series of cuts in their trunks in a heavily forested area. The exact measurements were committed to memory and had been repeated to themselves for years. So there was no doubt they would be able to take a long tape rule for measuring distances and dig up the loot at night, cover their tracks carefully, and store the money in built-in hiding places in the hulls of their houseboats.

The money placed in this cache was totaled at one hundred and one thousand dollars. The location of the place had not been too difficult to find and they were almost beside themselves with excitement at how easy it was going to be.

The designated bend in the river was found. The anchors were lowered. The small skiffs that were towed behind each houseboat were loaded and they shoved off to go ashore for a picnic. They would scout the area and locate the two trees and make certain no one would be able to observe their actions. Their heads were filled with plans to return at night and execute the plan. Their money shortage days were over.

As it turned out, it was glaringly evident almost immediately upon going ashore that they had problems. As they looked the area over, they found that it no longer looked the same as it had so many years ago. Most of the trees in the area had been cut down and except for a narrow margin left along the riverbank there was now a huge open field in their place. Someone had cleared the area and now there were cows and horses grazing over the area where their money was hidden. They were totally dumbfounded and exasperated. Surely there must be some way to locate the cache if it was still there.

They knew they had buried the money five feet deep and as they considered, they felt that whoever had cleared the land probably did not uncover it.

They studied the lay of the land and tried to remember the spot in relation to the river bend. They would walk off what they thought to be the proper direction and distance and mark the spot. At night they would then return and dig up that area. They repeated this from several different approach angles to no avail. The only way the money could be found was for the whole field to be dug up.

They spent several days attempting to locate the spot and finally had to face the fact that it was an impossible task. Their tree-marking plan was a total loss. Too many years had passed and they would have to give this cache up for lost.

Extremely disappointed and now a little worried about the rest of the money, they proceeded on their leisure journey. The next attempt at recovery would be easy because they were confident that time would not be a problem with the spot where the next cache was secured. It was a much more delicate matter however and would require very special care. It would take a several days for them to reach the second hiding place.

They forced discouragement out of their conversations with one another but Truman was having some serious nightmares. He kept dreaming of weird sea monsters rising up out of the murky waters of the Mississippi and biting off great hunks of the shoreline. He fought with them to prevent their eating away enough soil to discover his money and devour it. The dreams became so violent that he decided to give up sleeping till they reached and recovered the cache next in line. After several nights of drinking coffee all night to stay awake he found himself falling asleep while trying to steer his boat. Three times he rammed into Harry's boat and nearly crashed into a tugboat before turning toward shore and throwing out an anchor. He had to get some sleep. Harry laughed at him and said that was fine because he wanted to fish awhile anyway.

Well Kenny, I am going to have to call it a night so we will pick up with the vagabonds on the trip down the Mississippi in higher spirits after several days rest but not without a new awareness that problems could lie ahead.

Bless you my brother,
Clifford

CHAPTER 14
PAY DIRT

Kenny,
I'm back and ready for another episode of Truman's Story:

As we left Truman and Harry floating down river toward their next encounter with a recovery procedure, they were somewhat fearful that this too could be filled with difficulty and danger as they had seen how a landscape could change so drastically over a period of many years.

As they drew near the small village where they had hidden a $75,000.00 cache of money and jewelry of unknown value taken from safe deposit boxes, they began to really know just how much change was possible. What had been a small sleepy village of perhaps 75 people 25 miles from the nearest large city was now a thriving bedroom community with thousands of people living in the immediate area surrounding the location where the loot was buried. The area had changed so drastically that they had to check several maps and go to a library to consult with older maps and development progress by spending 3 days reading before they were able to locate the place they were looking for.

The place was a cemetery. When they were last here they had selected the sight after a long session of brainstorming about the best places to store the stolen goods. The plan had been to find a suitable old settled and stable community cemetery and watch for funeral notices that would tell them when a new grave was going to be dug. They would then wait for the funeral to be completed and during the night they would go out to the cemetery and dig up the newly turned soil over the casket and bury their loot in a stolen casket placed on top of the casket with a body in it.

They would then re-close the grave and keep a record of the headstone identification for use in relocating the spot at a future time. They could then return at their convenience and, under cover of night, dig up the grave and remove the loot and put the soil back in place and no one would ever be the wiser. The chosen cemetery had been a considerable distance outside the small village and they could easily do this totally unobserved.

Well, the best laid plans of mice and men, as they say.

The new community had swallowed up their cemetery and there were now 4 cemeteries in the area.

The problem was that they had forgotten to write down the name of it because at the time, it was the only cemetery in the village. Even if they had, it was now an expanded cemetery and only after much research, did they learn that the old cemetery was still there but deep inside the new one that surrounded it. To make matters worse, there was now a funeral chapel on the grounds and office buildings for the Mortuary as well. How to proceed?

They decided to visit the cemetery in the early morning before the mortuary staff came in for work and attempt to located the grave. This proved to be a relatively simple thing to accomplish but when they considered how to proceed with the digging up of the loot, they realized they stood an excellent chance of being discovered. The cemetery was lighted at night and the grave could easily be seen from two directions by nearby residents of housing developments.

They could not bring themselves to make an attempt at digging up the grave with all that light shining in the area. After long study, they decided to find a way to short out the lighting circuit to the lights in the cemetery and make it look like it was not deliberate. They would then watch to see if anyone would respond to restore the lights immediately the first night. If no one repaired the lines for two nights in a row, they thought it would be safe to venture out in the dark and not be detected on the third night. They had no idea how hard the ground might be and how long they might need to accomplish the task so they figured to wait until after midnight to enter the cemetery and proceed as rapidly as possible in hopes of finishing before daybreak and getting their tracks covered.

The only thing they could think of that would not look suspicious in cutting the power was to climb a pole and disconnect a fuse and replace it with a bad one. Truman and Harry knew how to do this but they did not have the gear needed to climb the pole. Harry made a trip to a neighboring city and purchased the things they would need and they proceeded to complete the task that very night at a place that seemed safe enough. It worked beautifully.

Three nights later, the lights were still out so the plan was implemented. They arrived at the cemetery around midnight and began to dig. The turf was carefully preserved by removing the grass in a section to itself which could be put back in place after the loot was out of the ground

They worked carefully and after about 30 minutes, had the section of grass set aside and began to dig in earnest. They had brought a canvass tarp to put on the ground to put the loose soil on so as to cover the fact that the grave had been opened. They would be able to restore the grave back to a relatively untouched appearance. They congratulated themselves that the progress went well as they dug.

They did not want to risk the grave being discovered as having been opened because if such a mystery were reported in the papers, the people who had been watching them might see it and put their presence in the town at the same time together. That could lead someone to them and that would mean, BACK TO JAIL.

When they had dug far enough to reach their stolen casket, they found that it was in excellent condition. But not so much so that they could open it. They had been very careful to steal a very expensive casket that had a water seal guaranteed for 50 years not to leak. They had stolen the tool to screw the lid down tight and had buried the tool with the casket. The tool was so rusted and corroded that it broke when they tried to use it to turn the screwed down locking device. They could not beat on the casket for fear of making too much noise and arousing the neighbors. They tried prying it open and it would not budge, it was made of very strong material. They did not want to take it with them because this would leave them with not enough soil to cover the grave properly. That would alert cemetery workers that someone had tampered with the grave and they might fall under suspicion and be tracked down.

What to do? They remembered that the Mortuary offices were at the entrance of the cemetery and that there was storage sheds near by. They decided to explore and see what could be found to help them out. They had to utilize skills they had learned in prison to pick locks to the office area and sure enough, they discovered 3 tools for opening caskets in a drawer. They returned to the grave and tried the tools. The locking device was some type of long screw that had apparently rusted and when pressure was exerted to force it open, the device broke inside the casket and now there was no way to open it.

Back to the office to explore. They found a set of keys that opened a warehouse out behind the offices and there discovered many unused caskets. Some of them were in boxes that had not been opened and they were standing end on end.

Harry had an idea. If they could open one of the boxes and remove a casket and then replace the box in place with the opened end toward the ground, it might be a long time before anyone discovered the box was empty. They could take the casket down to the grave and install it in place of the one filled with loot. They could take the loot filled coffin with them and hide it in one of the boats and work at getting it open while under way then sink it in the river.

It was a workable plan and they set out to do it. The next problem arose when they tried to lift the coffin out of the ground. It would not come loose from some roots and when it finally did, they could not lift it out. They managed to get some ropes around it and were able to get it lifted out. Checking their watches, they saw that they were running out of time. Dawn would soon be upon them.

With all the strength they could muster and already dog tired, they put the new casket in the grave, covered it up and found a new problem. The loosened soil would not tamp down enough so that they could return the grass in a way to make it look untouched. What to do? They decided to restore the grave as best they could and take the excess soil on the tarp and drag it over to a new grave in the new section of the cemetery and deposit it on the new grave. This took time and dawn was drawing close. They still had to get that heavy coffin out of the cemetery and to the boat. There was not enough time. What to do?

Truman had an idea. The only thing to do was to take the casket up to the warehouse and put it in the empty box and re-stack it as if unopened. If all went well, they could return the next night and get it out. This was reluctantly decided as the only possibility. They did it.

They finished just in time enough to slip out of the cemetery and make their way back to the boat before full daylight. They slept almost all day as they were worn completely out.

They waited for nightfall with great anticipation and when it came, they returned to the cemetery but what did they find but that the lights had been repaired and everything was flooded in bright light. They returned to the boat and got their climbing gear, returned to the area and climbed the pole again and pulled the fuse. They waited a while to see if anyone would come and investigate. No one did so they reentered the warehouse. They took the loot filled casket out, put the box back in place and lugged the casket out to a trailer they had rented. They loaded it and ran it to the boat. They got the thing hidden away in the boat and Truman returned to the pole and replaced the fuse and restored the lights. He turned to the cemetery with a sharp stance of attention and a military salute of respect, gratitude and farewell. He drove back to the boat tapping his fingers on the steering wheel and singing to himself in joyous celebration. He was so excited that it was all he could do to keep from wetting his pants.

They had to remain in the town long enough to return the rented car and trailer and then they were on their leisure trip once more down the Mississippi.

The job of opening the casket proved to be very difficult. They had to literally cut the lid open like a can of peas. But sure enough, when the thing was opened, there was the cash and a large box of jewelry of still unknown value. The loot was placed in its prepared hiding spot on the boat and the casket was filled with rocks and pushed overboard to sink to the bottom of the muddy Mississippi.

Truman and Harry sat down and congratulated themselves but swore that bank robbing was nowhere near as hard a job as digging graves. The problem was, three more of their caches were in graves as well. The circumstances were different and they now knew that they should not expect anything to go as they had originally planned those long years ago. Everything about life was different. The simple elements that made up life as they had known it no longer existed. Everything about life had become complicated to the extreme, or so it seemed to them. It was confusing to say the least.

Kenny, when I think about the circumstances that Truman and Harry found themselves in, I remember how simple life was for me as a child and how our world has changed so drastically in our own lifetime. Sometimes I find myself looking back and longing for those wonderful carefree days of a life that can never be again and almost weep for the loss. Listening to Truman talk about his feelings, I could really sympathize with him and could not help but reflect upon what it would be like for us today to jump back two generations in life. We would, no doubt, be totally lost.

Saying so, I must confess that life today is hard at times but it is still very good in many ways. We are truly blessed.

Till next time,

God bless you my brother,

Clifford

CHAPTER 15
DOWN THE RIVER

Kenny,

We left Truman and Harry headed toward their next attempt of recovering money with considerable anxiety, which had been created by the difficulties they encountered with the last cache.

They continued to be amazed at the changes that had taken place during their long stay in jail. In their wildest dreams they would never have believed that it was even possible for such physical changes to be made to the face of the land they had left behind upon entering prison.

They had given great thought and planning to the hiding of their loot all those years ago and felt certain at the time that the money was safer in the places they had put it than it would have been in a bank vault. They knew how easily money could be taken from a bank vault better than almost anyone around.

They discussed and remembered how they had progressively come to the conclusion that cemeteries would most likely be the safest hiding place of all those they had examined those many years ago. Graves would have been the last place to be molested and would remain unchanged to the point that they should not have to worry about not being able to find the spot when the time came to retrieve the caches. But they were going to find out that they were very, very wrong and that the funeral industry in the future would become very corrupt in some places. What a sad commentary on humanity that even graveyards could become objects of fraud.

But I am getting ahead of my story.

When Truman and Harry came to the town where the next cache was to be retrieved, they felt very encouraged because the task was relatively simple this time. They had no difficulty in locating the cemetery and after the money was safe on board the boat they began to celebrate their good sense and ability to reason things out as they had progressed in learning where to place the money within a cemetery.

They remembered how they had begun to study burial traditions and had come to the conclusion that they might have trouble with decay by placing the money below ground. They knew that if enough moisture were to be constantly around a buried cache, even one in a water sealed casket, it was possible for it to begin to leak into the money and it would rot and be useless to them. The difficulty they had encountered with the last casket had confirmed that their future cache placement was indeed wise.

You see they had come upon a funeral in progress back in their days of scouting out locations for use that they thought would suit their plans. They had watched the funeral with great interest because they noticed that the body was to be buried above ground in a sealed chamber within an enclosed mausoleum. Neither of them had ever attended a funeral in their entire lives. Even as children, where their father had conducted funerals in connection with the church, they were too young to be involved except for services held in the church. They knew about cemeteries mostly from reading and simply observing them in various places. Neither had ever had a relative close enough to them to die while they were involved in their criminal enterprises so they were ignorant to large extent. They had lost all contact with family while in orphanages and in jail and did not even know if their parents were still alive at the time of their release from prison.

So it was with great interest that they observed the burial above ground. They left the cemetery that day and began to try to learn all they could about mausoleums. What a perfect place to hide their money. They came up with what seemed to be the best of all possibilities. They would take a parcel of money to a carefully chosen mausoleum, carefully en-seal the individual crypt they had chosen, open the casket and remove the body inside and replace it with the money. They would then carefully re-seal the crypt. This could easily be done at night inside a mausoleum completely unobserved and they could then take the body and dispose of it and no one would ever be the wiser. When time came to retrieve the money, it would be an easy matter to return to the crypt and once again carefully unseal it and retrieve the money and then reseal the crypt and go on their merry way.

This was the case for the second cemetery retrieval. The plan went flawlessly. Even though there had been a tremendous growth in the area of the cemetery, it proved to be an easy task to locate and remove the cash. In this case the amount they had placed in the crypt was $125,000.00. In addition to the cash, there was a box of jewelry and some rare gold coins along with some false identity documents that they had secured for themselves. These documents were a part of the overall plan of contingencies that had come to their enterprising young minds. They were very surprised at the condition of these items. They looked as if they had just come off the press. This had certainly been a stroke of genius in placing the cache in a dry sealed place where the temperature was probably fairly constant over the years as well.

Their fortunes were indeed looking bright as they sailed down the Mississippi rejoicing in their genius. They had only spent four days in the community and had aroused absolutely no suspicions whatsoever. Happy days were here again. They decided to celebrate their success by stopping at the next large city and spending some time ashore. They felt that they could safely spend a couple of weeks doing so and gain a much needed break in the tension they had both been experiencing. There was a small concern that they had to deal with. They needed to use some of the cash that they had reclaimed and as they looked at it, they realized it could be dangerous in two different ways.

First off, the money was old but most of it looked new. The bank vaults they had taken money from had mostly been stocked with stacks of unused bills. They did not know whether these bills could be identified by the serial numbers on them or not. One of the things they had not been able to find out during their days in prison was whether all banks recorded those numbers back in the days of their withdrawal practices. They did not know if the banks today might still have a list of the bills that were taken so long ago and might be alerted to what they were doing if some of the money began to appear in circulation. If so, they could be putting their whole plan in great jeopardy. Not only could attention be drawn to them by the banks, but also there could be some of their shadows still making random checks on their progress down the river. If so and they found them suddenly spending money that seemed to have no source, the jig could be up here also.

Harry, who was the mastermind at getting the money and other items laundered to usable cash, was certain that he could make a couple of telephone calls and line up someone to purchase a part of what they now had. He knew that they would lose a great deal on the transaction because the exchange rate in this market was very steep. The question was, did they want to risk exposure by spending a small amount of the cash or was the vacation needed badly enough to pay the necessary cost? After all, they did not know for sure that the people who might purchase the money would not give them away by putting it in circulation and thus alerting a bank somewhere that cash stolen by the Mahoney gang many years ago was appearing again. That would drop a net around them by those watchdogs who were certain to still be on their trail somewhere. They did not want to go back to jail under any circumstances.

They finally decided to make a couple of telephone calls and discuss the matter with Harry's contacts. If they could be assured that the money would go overseas somewhere and not be traceable to them, then they would risk it. If not, then they would stick with the plans to the letter as they had been laid out.

Harry's contacts assured him that the money could be, and would be sent to places where it would be years away from general circulation. Their organization had been in operation for generations and had never been even under the least suspicion by the law. They could handle any amount he wanted to dispose of. The costs of such transactions were fifty cents on the dollar. This was outrageous by Truman's measure but they did need operating capital so a deal was struck for twenty thousand dollars to be exchanged for ten thousand clean dollars that they could spend. Even at that they would have to be very frugal and very careful not to draw attention to cash being spent with no apparent source.

They reluctantly made the exchange and, a few days later, docked the boats and left them in the care of a commercial marina. They rented a car and took a two-week long hiatus. It proved to be a wonderfully pleasant two weeks and they made plans to repeat the experience further down the river when the time seemed right

As far as they could ascertain, there were no longer any representatives of the law watching or trailing them but they discussed it carefully and decided to not let down their guard. They would continue to present themselves to the news media as being involved in a great adventure but keep a constant vigilance.

So we find the master planners in a high state of excitement and anticipation as they floated along toward the next cache. The disappointment of having lost the money buried between the two trees was still there but was now beginning to be regarded as a necessary expense of doing business in their chosen professions.

They were beginning to discuss plans for life at the end of the journey down the river. They knew there would be great difficulty in using the money for they were certain that they would again fall under surveillance by the law and would have to live with this the rest of their lives. They had always known this and had discussed it at lengths but come to no hard plans for the long run as yet. But the closer they came to New Orleans, the more they knew they had to have a very good plan in effect or they would be caught and returned to prison. They had already secured some help from a couple of trusted sources but the final plans would have to remain a little flexible for the time being.

Was it possible for them to handle this much cash at one time by themselves or would they have to involve other people? Time would tell.

So we will leave the happy travelers to ponder their future and join them downstream.

Kenny, I keep reminding myself that this part of the story has never been told and I am aware that there are people possibly still alive who could be adversely affected by the telling of it. If you find me being somewhat vague in details, you will know that I am trying to prevent any such problems.

Between the writing of chapters, as you know, I am doing various kinds of research to safeguard exposing innocent people and disturbing long dead and buried histories that must be taken into serious consideration.

I have had some assistance from some wonderful friends in doing so. I should like you to one day meet some of them. Howard and Barbara Lee of Sam Rayburn, Texas come to mind as a good example. These two wonderful people took part of their vacation and went to considerable expense to travel to Lafayette, Indiana for me. There they attempted to locate relatives of one of the characters named in this story and see if the named individual was still alive.

Some very co-operative and helpful employees of the National Archives and Angola Prison have aided me and saved me many hours of digging through records. Sometime furnishing leads to additional sources that proved invaluable.

The last thing I want to do is cause harm to anyone. As you know, my calling in life is to bring peace, joy and wholeness to those whom my life touches and I do take that calling very seriously.

So be patient with me if all the details you would like are not available. I will do the best I can with what I have to work.

Have a good day my brother,
Clifford

CHAPTER 16
THE HIGH COST OF FUNERALS

Kenny, Truman and Harry were now approaching the fourth place where money had been cached and had every expectation that the job of retrieval here would be as easy as the last because it was in a crypt located in a mausoleum like the last one. But they were very wrong.

After docking at a commercial marina just off the main channel of the river, Truman and Harry rented a car and began an inspection under cover of sightseeing. They had little difficulty locating the cemetery here and drove through the area to check on the condition of the mausoleum. They found that it had undergone a considerable expansion and now was much larger than when they had been there many years ago. The fact that changes had been made to the structure caused them some alarm but after some discussion they reassured themselves that all would be well.

A closer nighttime inspection was called for and so, after 2 AM that night, they carefully entered the cemetery and found that the expansion of the structure had included the placing of a stoutly reinforced metal door at the entrance. This door was going to require them to either pick the lock or cut their way through it. This presented a problem because the entrance was placed where it could be seen from the street. They would need to work in the dark and the moon was at a stage that it was full. There was too much light for safety.

They knew that they could not destroy the door because it would be discovered and investigated with the opening of the crypt being found as well. This would almost certainly be reported in the news and someone could possibly connect the timing to their presence in the city. They decided to wait for a moon change, which was still a few days away. This would give them time to examine the door lock and determine if it could be picked.

Both Truman and Harry had studied lock picking with some of the best teachers in the land in the prisons where they had spent many idle years. The problem was that they knew the techniques needed but neither of them had practiced on anything but doors in the prisons. The rest was learned from verbal instruction and explanations of the various types of locks that one could expect to see in America.

After a discussion of the possible approaches, they went once more to the cemetery and did the best they could to identify the make and manufacturer of the lock on the door. This proved to be much more difficult that they had expected. After several days of intense work they were not able to be sure that they could get it open. They had considerable resources on the boats to manufacture lock-picking devices so they set to work and produced several that might do the job. They knew they did not want to leave any trace that the lock had been picked so great care was called for.

They finally felt confident enough to make the attempt at getting the lock open and in the small hours of the next morning, they worked for over two hours at trying to pick the lock. They failed.

They considered the alternatives and decided there was no way that they wanted to break the door open and possibly bring attention to themselves. Doing any real work on the door at all would be ruled out by the simple fact that it was in a place that was too visible. This was not foreseen on the day the place had been selected. The area had been developed and houses and businesses were far too close for comfort.

They discussed passing this cache by and perhaps returning at some time in the future after any connection with them in a break-in would be less probable. If they could come back by land, say in a year from now, then perhaps it would be safe to break in but they could not pick the lock at the time. It seemed the best course to follow.

As they considered the amount of money that was hidden in this mausoleum, they were reluctant to take a chance on never being able to return. They decided to stay around for a while and look for another approach. There was $200,000.00 in that crypt plus a pretty large box of gold coins. They were beginning to be concerned about staying so long that people would begin to pay too much attention to them. They were very nervous.

At a breakfast that they had been invited to, Truman suddenly remembered the office of the mortuary they had broken into and gotten the opening devices to open the casket they had dug up and could not open. He suddenly saw in his mind's eye, a key in some funeral home that would open that door. All they had to do was find the correct funeral home and steal the key. He felt his pulse begin to race with excitement and could not wait for the breakfast to be over so he could share the idea with Harry.

As soon as they were alone the idea was given a long consideration and they discussed the possibilities and various scenarios that were presented by following up on the idea. It was decided that they would do some research and find out who had keys to the mausoleum and, if possible, lay out a plan to steal one. If they found one available close enough to the cemetery to take it, use it for the job and return it the same night that is what they would do. If they found that a key was available but too far away for a single night of borrowing it, they would steal it and make a wax impression from which they could make their own key. This would not even involve taking the key from wherever they might find it. Just a simple break in, *a piece of cake.*

The job of locating a key was not as difficult as it might have been. Truman and Harry went to a motel and rented a room where they could use a telephone and have a place to meet people if need be. They began to make calls to the Funeral Homes in the area and express an interest in a pre-arranged funeral and found that they were all very co-operative in discussing all the possibilities. They found that only one funeral home handled arrangements for the mausoleum in question and yes they would be willing to sit down and discuss their various plans of interment.

Harry was the best actor of the two and Truman the best make-up artist so Harry was chosen to wear a disguise. He would appear at the funeral home and discuss the possibility of purchasing a crypt in the mausoleum and then ask to see the place in question.

It was a piece of cake. Harry was able to ask whether his family would have a key to the door should they ever wish to visit the gravesite or whether they would have to come to the funeral home to gain access to the crypt for visiting the deceased. He was told that the key was kept at the funeral home but was made available to families who had loved ones entombed in the mausoleum upon request. All they had to do was come by and ask for it and return it after its use.

Harry asked to see the available crypts and watched

carefully as the funeral salesperson went into an office and returned with the key. He now knew where the key was kept. Harry and the salesman got into their respective cars and drove to the cemetery, which was across town from the office. Upon inspection of the crypts, Harry was very pleased and thought that his aged mother would be very happy with a particular one that suited Harry very well.

Harry decided to try a long shot. He asked the salesman if it would be possible for him to borrow the key long enough to go and pick up his mother and bring her out to make a final approval of the crypt. With no hesitation, the salesman agreed and drove off and left Harry standing with the key in his hand. Harry could not believe how easy this had turned out to be. He had already seen the inside of the structure and had even made a mental note that the crypt containing their money was intact. And here he was standing in the street with the key in his hot little hand.

Harry and Truman took the key to a locksmith in a neighboring town and asked if a duplicate could be made. They were told that it could be done only by ordering one from the manufacturer of that particular lock. It was a large key and no blanks of that type were even available locally.

This was a small setback but nothing that a couple of professionals like them could not handle. Their planning had allowed for enough contingencies that they knew this obstacle could be overcome. They were men of considerable resource.

They did some shopping and purchased the materials from a ceramic shop to make an impression and mold. It would then be an easy job to melt down some metal and make the key themselves. This took longer than they had planned so Harry called the funeral home and reported that his mother was napping and asked if it would be alright to keep the key a little longer than he had planned. Permission was given but the key must be returned before the office closed at 6:00 PM.

Frantically the two men worked to copy the key and were successful in doing so and making it back to the funeral home by 5:30 PM. Harry told the salesman that his mother wanted to look at a couple of other locations and that he would get back to him if she agreed to purchase this crypt. All was well.

All preparations had been made beforehand to enter the mausoleum after midnight that very night and it was accomplished with no problem whatsoever. The key worked smoothly in the lock. The work of setting up and opening the correct crypt went smoothly as well but when it was open, the two of them were taken aback at what they found. The crypt was empty. Completely empty. No coffin, no corpse, nothing was in it at all. They rechecked their memory codes and were certain they had the correct crypt. Could the names have been switched someway? That did not matter because they had a little rhyme that they had committed to memory that identified the second row from the ground and third from the end as well as the name. This was the correct crypt. Somehow and in someway, someone had taken their loot.

No one could have known it was there. Only Truman and Harry knew. What had happened? Could it have been opened when the expansion project was undertaken? They decided to open the four crypts adjoining this one. One above, one below, one on each side. One by one they did so and found them to contain bodies in wooden boxes but no coffins. Dumbfounded, they resealed the crypts and made an exit.

They went back to the boats and discussed the possibilities. Harry had been told the procedure for interment by the salesman at the funeral home and the routine called for the body to be sealed in a coffin of choice and placed in the crypt and the crypt sealed forever.

It slowly dawned upon the two bank robbers that they had been robbed. They came to the conclusion that the funeral home was not doing exactly as they were supposed to. They must be going back to the mausoleum after the families were gone and removing the bodies from the caskets and placing them in wooden boxes, resealing the tombs and then reselling the caskets. What a racket!!! Who would ever know? Well they could not help but laugh at the surprise someone had received upon recovering one particular casket so many years ago.

They remembered that they had taken the body that had occupied the crypt when they opened it originally and put it in with the one next to it. When they had opened the one next to it this time, there was only one body there. What did they do with the extra body? It was not in the place that was originally designed for it. A small unsolved mystery that Truman wondered about but decided in the end that the Lord was the only one who could keep up with corpses properly.

What could they do? NOTHING. Harry suggested that they threaten the funeral home with exposing their racket unless they returned the money but this seemed too dangerous to them for the present. After all, they did not know who was involved nor when the money had actually been taken from the crypt. The idea would have to be given great consideration and all the inherent dangers dealt with but perhaps they would revisit the situation some time in the future.

But for now, It was time to head down the river. The idea of using the mausoleums as bank vaults had turned out to be nowhere near as good as they had believed. Their batting average so far was not too good. There was one more mausoleum to visit downstream and hopefully these two crooks had picked more reputable morticians in the next situation. Who would have thought that you could not trust funeral homes? What is this world coming to?

Kenny, can you imagine what may happen in the inner workings of some mortician's office when this story is finally made known to the public? I can see it now. A mad scramble to put caskets back in crypts before the public begins to check and see if their loved ones are buried in a place that fits the descriptions given here.

It is another of those things that I worry about.

Till next time my brother,

Clifford

CHAPTER 17
BANKING MADE EASY

Kenny,

Hope you are having a good day my friend. It has rained here and turned cold this afternoon. Really messed up my plans for the day. But there is still not all that much to kick about because I used the time to work on sermons for the coming Lord's Day.

I have been without time of late to deal with Truman's Story but am going to attempt another episode for you tonight.

I think I need to go back and clarify a thing or two before going any further. This comes out of a visit with Mary, Truman's widow this past Tuesday.

Mary really helped to bring back and clarify some fuzzy areas for me and in a case or two brought out several things I had forgotten altogether. The facts are that Harry had married Mary's sister Lillian and she was on the riverboat with him but these events took place before Mary and Truman were involved with one another. Truman had his second wife Sylvia with him on his boat.

Mary and Truman were married some time after the river trip. I may deal with that again later. The marriages of Truman and Harry play an important role in the story later. Both Mabel, Truman's first wife, and Bessie, Harry's second wife, had apparently divorced them while they were in prison. I do not know what happened to Mabel but Bessie will resurface later in the story. I remind you that both of those wives had gone to prison themselves for their part in the escape from the Caddo Parish Jail many years ago. We will revisit this subject later.

To pick up our story, Harry and Truman were enjoying the trip down the river in spite of the setbacks they had experienced. The boats could sometimes be difficult when they were in swift water and they did have to watch carefully at times to avoid being run down by tugboats and barges of various stripe. On more than one occasion they had to scramble for safety. This was not as easy as one might imagine because they had not taken the time and expense to install engines in the boats. They were still powered by those small eight horsepower outboard motors. At times when they had to turn upstream, against the current, the little motors could not match the onslaught of the water. They would have to call on skills of seamanship that was seriously lacking but improving as they went.

They had considered the purchase of newer and more powerful motors but knew that such a large purchase could be hard to explain, as they had not worked a single day to earn additional cash since embarking from Terre Haute. If someone were to take note, it could lead to further examination and they did not want that. So they would make do with what they had.

The two of them did enjoy fishing so many days were given to sharpening their skills and matching wits with the various species of fish the river afforded. They were getting good at it. Huck Finn would have been proud of these modern day vagabonds. They were also learning many new ways to cook and eat their catches. Life was good and prison was far behind.

The two brothers had been separated for some time while

in prison because the wardens had learned that when they were together, they plotted various methods of escape. So the experiences of moving from one prison to another had left them much to discuss and conversation was spiced all along the way by recollections.

The courtroom trials they had gone through had educated them in jailhouse law. They had found what they thought to be some serious loopholes in their trial records and made appeals to the federal courts and the state court in Louisiana to have their sentences reconsidered. The appeal failed but the records of those appeals are in the National Archives in Ft. Worth, Texas. They had to serve the federal sentences first and then would be sent back to the State of Louisiana to serve out the remainder of the sentences imposed there.

As I have said, the prison officials were afraid to leave them together so they were sent to separate prisons for some time. At one point when Truman was being moved, he found himself in San Quentin Prison in California. After being there for some time he learned that Harry was there as well. He found out by catching a momentary view of him while he was sitting in the dinning hall. Harry was in a line of men who were being escorted through for a meal.

Truman jumped up and screamed Harry's name at the top of his lungs. Harry turned toward him and broke out of the line only to be clubbed to the floor by a guard. At almost the same time, the men around Truman yanked him down and held him to prevent his being struck by a guard also. As it happened, Harry was just passing through on his way to Alcatraz and would be in San Quentin for only a few days. The two brothers did manage to talk to one another for about five minutes on another day before Harry left for Alcatraz. As it turned out, Truman was not there very long either, as he was transferred to Alcatraz himself a short while later. And so it was that they wound up in Alcatraz together. Harry and Truman are today listed as prisoner numbers 508 and 532 among the Famous Inmates of Alcatraz. This place was considered the one prison from which no escape was possible due to the fact that it was located on an Island. That proved to be questionable. Located in San Francisco Bay, the waters around the island prison seemed an insurmountable obstacle to escape. This did not prevent many attempts however and through the years Truman and Harry explored every possible route that their active minds could conceive.

In the history of Alcatrz there were men who were desperate enough to try anything to get off the island. Of those thirty-six who made the attempt, seven were shot and killed, two drowned for certain, five were unaccounted for and presumed dead. Two made it off the island and were returned, one of them was a man that Truman considered a friend. Three prisoners, one named Morris and the two Anglin brothers made it off the island and it is not known if they survived or not. Some evidence exists that seems to indicate that they could have done so.

Truman and Harry spent many hours discussing the various men they had met and associated with in the prisons that housed them but mostly the ones at Alcatraz. There were only 1545 men who were ever sent to this prison in its years of service as a maximum security unit. At no time were there more than 302 housed there because the capacity was not much greater than that. Some few individuals were returned there for one reason or another after being released or transferred elsewhere

The past had been hard. Prison had hardened and molded both men into sharp witted, crafty, suspicious, selfish, skeptical, scheming, strong willed and evil disposed characters. Harry especially seemed to have no loyalty to anyone other than Truman, at least for the time being anyway. As for Truman, he had never lost faith in Harry as the older and wiser brother and generally yielded to Harry in situations where opinions differed. He trusted Harry to a fault. This will be explored in the future events of Truman's life

But to get back to our subject at hand, the next retrieval of loot proved to be a near brush with discovery. As I have said previously, three of their caches were in mausoleums but before the two had hit upon the idea of cemeteries there were a couple of other schemes as well. This next event was one of them.

Harry had come up with the idea of hiding some of their loot in banks and for a short while they had explored ways and means of doing so. When they had purchased the horse farms in Arkansas, Harry had at first thought to use alias identities and establish themselves in the community in that way. While doing so he had researched the possibility of new names and ways to document themselves in a passable manner that would allow them to do normal things.

He had been successful in establishing an identity for both himself and Truman and this had allowed them to open bank accounts. Under these assumed names they had deposited a total of $63,000.00 in four different banks.

Two of those banks were in the next city they were coming to and they were anticipating a simple withdrawal of the funds.

They had been able to hide the documentation of these false identities in the crypt of the mausoleum from which they were able to recover funds already so they had the necessary credentials to make the withdrawals. This, within itself, was somewhat of a miracle that they had placed these documents in a place that remained unmolested during the years of their absence. They had congratulated themselves soundly when these documents were recovered and in very good condition. Actually they were in too good a condition and the two of them spent considerable time working with them to make them appear dog-eared and timeworn. The assumed identities were, oddly enough, for two brothers but in total different sounding names than their real ones.

They had placed the funds in savings accounts that would draw interest. There were accounts in both of their assumed names so they would both have to make the withdrawals. The problem was that in the matter of banking, both of them had very little experience and did not know that funds left unclaimed and in inactive accounts for extended periods of time could be claimed by the government. These accounts had to be reported to the government by the bank's auditors and a procedure was followed as outlined in the particular state in which the bank did business. For federal banks there was a similar procedure. Both these accounts had been placed in this status.

So, in their ignorance, they walked into a bank together and presented their identification and attempted to withdraw the funds. When the bank teller told them that the accounts no longer existed and that they would have to see a bank officer and make a formal request to the government to reclaim the funds in question, they panicked. Wanting to run out the door but afraid and uncertain, they allowed themselves to be shown into a vice president's office where he wanted to know the details of their having not kept up with the accounts for such a long period of time. They had foreseen the possibility of having to account for the long inactivity of the accounts and they were prepared with answers that they had been living in a foreign country all these years and just assumed that money deposited would be there when they returned. They became indignant with the man and berated the institution for not properly handling funds entrusted to them. I find this particularly funny when you consider that these were stolen bank funds, banked by bank robbers and now they were giving the bank a hard time for not meeting their expectations.

The officer explained in an embarrassed manner that he could do nothing but follow the required procedure and fill out the necessary forms to have their money returned. This would take considerable time, probably several weeks. Truman, being the suspicious person that he was, thought the man was trying to cover up the theft of their money and made the accusation in such a threatening manner that the man called out for his secretary to call the security guard. A red flag was immediately raised in Harry's mind and he calmed Truman down and apologized to the vice president and was able to get the situation in hand by scolding Truman before the security guard arrived. The man then dismissed the guard upon arrival and the discussion took a more cordial tone.

Harry explained that they had worked for many years in the jungles of Africa and had lost some of the skills of civilization and would be happy to co-operate in filling out the necessary forms for the reclaiming of their money. The bank officer assured them that the funds and whatever interest due upon them would be returned as promptly as possible. He further explained that they could return at a later date and withdraw the money or, if they chose, have it forwarded to them or transferred to another account in another bank. They instructed the man to begin the process and that they would contact him with their plans for dealing with the situation after giving the matter some thought and contacting their home bank. They needed the time to truly decide what to do.

They left the bank with an understanding that they would be back in touch within a few days with instructions for final disposition of the matter. They also left with considerable fear and confusion. They would have to study this matter and decide what to do. Could they go to another bank in another city and open new accounts and have the money transferred to them? Was it a safe thing to do? Was this too risky? They had not taken the time to establish these new identities in another city and did not have an address to give the bank officials.

They had taken the precaution to check into a hotel locally so as to have a local address to use with the bank. They had anticipated the possibility of needing that before going to the bank so they decided that they were safe for a short time. Long enough to research the subject and decide what to do anyway.

So back at the hotel they first decided to go to another bank in town and open an account in the false names to see if they could do so without arousing suspicion. They knew they would have to establish some kind of permanent address to use on these accounts so they made a phone call to the only person Harry knew that he might trust, his former wife Bessie. This proved to be a bad decision.

He felt that he could trust her because they had maintained contact and she had remained close to his son Johnny, whom she had raised. He only told her that he wanted her to open a bank account in the city where she was living. When she had done so, he would have some funds transferred to it and that he would give her a part of it if she would let him use her address as his home address. He assured her that all she had to do was open the account in her name and call him back at the hotel and give him the bank name and account number along with the address of the bank and her home address. He told her he did not know when exactly the money would be deposited but that it would probably be several weeks.

She was very suspicious but after he told her that the funds were from an account he had opened before going to jail and that it was a completely legitimate transfer, she agreed to help him. He gave her the phony names that the money would come from and the name of the bank from which the funds would come and hung up feeling the matter was well in hand.

They gave her the time she needed to open the account and share the necessary account information with them. They knew they would have to be very positive and confident in their dealings with the bank officers so they set their minds to be ready and not be surprised by anything that could come out of the next stage of the transaction.

After studying the situation for some time and doing all the research they could, they felt that they could return to the bank. It should not be difficult to make arrangements to have the funds transferred when they were freed up by the local bank.

In the meantime, there was the other bank in town and the other accounts to deal with. They had learned much from this first encounter and the lesson was not wasted on them. They were beginning to feel much more confident that the next withdrawal attempt would go much differently than the first. Considerable time had elapsed since they came to town and they were feeling the need to move along so, just past opening time, they walked into the second bank and approached a teller with requests to inquire of the state of their accounts and the means to transfer their funds.

Were thy ever surprised to find that when they stepped up to the window and presented their credentials, the young man smiled and said warmly, "Good morning gentlemen, we've been expecting you. My supervisor has advised me that you might be paying us a visit and left instructions for me to ask you to please take time to visit with him a few moments. I will be processing the closing of your accounts while you visit, if it is agreeable, of course".

This shot all kinds of alarms off in their minds and they both felt their hearts suddenly beating in their throats. What in the world was happening here? Their first impulse was to run but they were able to hold their composure enough to ask, "And just why might he wish to see us?" The response was just as puzzling, "It is just that he was expecting you and wishes to make your acquaintance, I believe. He does not wish to inconvenience you but he knew that your business here would take several minutes to complete and felt that he would be able to help make your stay in our city a pleasant one." Something was definitely not right here. Were they being mistaken for someone else?

Harry made a stab at exploring that thought and said, "Are you sure you have the right people here? We do not know anyone here and have no reason to expect such and invitation. You must be mistaken". The teller seemed completely at ease and smiling warmly, replied, "I can understand your confusion but my supervisor will explain, please wait here and I will ask him to step out and meet you". What could they do? There seemed to be no alternative that was open. So they agreed to wait for the man. As soon as the teller was out of sight, they looked at one another with a shrug that spoke volumes and Harry whispered under his breath to Truman, "be ready to get out of here in a hurry if this goes wrong."

To their utter surprise, the teller returned with a friendly looking fellow in tow who stepped forward in a lively spirit and warmly extended his hand in greeting, "Well, good morning gentlemen, I am very happy that I was here when you dropped in. I have been expecting you for several days and have looked forward to meeting you. Please step into my office while your business is being taken care of". Having said this, he turned to the teller and called him by name and said, "please see that these gentlemen's accounts are handled personally and with all due speed. Then he turned to the two of them and asked very pleasantly, "could I offer you gentlemen a cup of coffee?". They declined and followed the man to a small office where they were offered comfortable seats and the man sat down behind his desk and smiled so broadly that they were both completely disarmed.

"I know you gentlemen must be a little confused by our reception so please let me explain our strange actions. You see, I have a brother-in-law who works over at one of our other banks here in the city and he was telling me of your unusual experience with his bank". He then gave them the name of the other bank and the Vice President's name with whom they had been dealing there. Quickly he related how that the man had casually related the story of their account being closed as unclaimed and the difficulty and confusion that the unusual occurrence had created at the bank.

He made them at ease by sharing that this exchange had taken place over an evening meal, which was quite common for the two families. They were a close knit family and often talked about their business dealings with one another. It would not however be spoken of outside this circle.

He offered that he was so struck by the incident that he could not help but wonder if the names of these men he was hearing about might appear on his bank's records. Being the curious person that he was, he had checked for the names among their files the very next day after his brother-in-law had told him about it. He was very excited to learn that these same two men, or someone with the same names, had accounts with his bank and that the accounts had also been inactive for many years in the same manner as the other bank.

He felt that the odds of it not being the same two men was just too great not to be true so he had decided to look the accounts over and know before their inquiry what the condition of the accounts were. To his delight he had found that these two accounts had not been confiscated by the government. It seems that the difference lay in the fact that one of the banks was a State Bank and the other was a National Bank. They had differing regulations which governed such accounts and the length of time imposed for action by the auditors in one case was not the norm in the other.

Harry and Truman were warmly told that "HIS" bank would not be as difficult to deal with as the one with which they had been dealing. Their money was safe and sound right where they had left it and it would only take a few minutes to close the accounts or to conduct whatever business they might need. He would be very happy to have them remain active customers of his bank and he wanted to offer them his full co-operation. He indicated that he knew that they were going to have to wait for their funds to be freed up by his competitor and that he would be very glad to assist them in any business they might have here in the city. His bank was a "full service" bank and if they needed a partner that was fully reliable, he would welcome their business.

It was suddenly very clear that this man was hoping to see Truman and Harry deposit their funds from the other bank in his and thus keep the ones they now had as well.

It took Harry a few moments to see where the conversation

was going but when he could finally interrupt the man, he thanked him for his offer of assistance. He quickly and easily applied his story that had been used at the other bank to this situation and informed the man that they were interested only in having the funds transferred to their home bank. He would appreciate it if he would take care of the necessary paperwork to accomplish the task and they would be on their way. He congratulated the bank for their not having given up the trust that had been placed in them and assured the man that he would certainly recommend this fine institution to his friends who lived in the area.

This done, they headed back for the river and on downstream. This banking business was filled with all kind of surprises.

But the last of this transaction is not heard from.

Kenny, I have wondered about this part of the story from time to time and as you will see later, Harry could make some faulty decisions when he was not given time to fully consider all the ramifications of his actions. He was a brilliant man in many ways and Truman's confidence in his abilities was usually well placed. This is not one of his best decisions.

Till next time,

Bless you,

Clifford

CHAPTER 18
HONESTY, A PERSONAL OPINION

Kenny,

Well it has been several days since I have had time to sit down and share with you. I hope and pray that you are doing well, having great weather and getting lots done on your bus.

We have had a very busy schedule for the past several days. Folks in hospitals, funeral, one lady who has no one to care for her has been very ill and so my wife and I have taken her into our home to care for her till she can get back on her feet. Was at the hospital with her in the emergency room about 4 hours today. She seems some better at present but is confined to bed.

I have been trying to get my mind together and dwell on Truman's Story for you tonight but I am having difficulty concentrating. Maybe as I write things will clear up. We will see.

Truman and Harry left their encounter with banking with very mixed feelings. There was tension between the two of them over the manner in which the funds were going to be retrieved. Truman did not like Harry's first wife and did not trust her. They argued about what could happen. Truman felt that they were taking a great risk by involving the woman. He was afraid that she would talk about the affair with her son Johnny and perhaps others as well. He told Harry that the more he thought about it, the more he did not like what they had done. Up to this point, he had felt pretty safe in what they were doing and the plans they had made but this was a serious alteration of their carefully laid plans. He could not sleep for several days.

As I have shared, the boats they were on were seriously underpowered. They had planned to simply allow the current to carry them all the way to New Orleans and use the little motors only when necessary. This was a very slow means of travel but that was fine with Truman because he felt that he needed all the time he could manage to re-acclimate himself to the changes that had taken place in the world in his absence. They listened to the radio, read newspapers and took every opportunity to normalize themselves as they were in contact with folks in the towns and cities along their route. On more than one occasion, they made brief excursions up tributaries and into cities and towns of interest to them. It was exhilarating to be able to go where they chose and not have to ask anyone's permission.

At times Truman would find himself waking up from dreams terror stricken. Nightmares of prison and being sent back there haunted him and when the worst of them occurred, he would remember his promise to God and could not keep himself from alternating between fear, rage, and guilt. When he dwelt on it, he would have to say to God, "Yes, I remember" and fear that God would send him back to prison for not attempting to remain true to his promise to serve the Lord of heaven and earth. He could not bring himself to discuss this with anyone. Down deep he knew that God had not forgotten and an accounting lay somewhere down the line. He found himself using a phrase to himself so much that it began to creep into his audible expressions almost unbidden. The phrase was, "We'll see, yes we'll just see'.

In spite of all the unlawful things Truman had involved himself in thus far in life, he prided himself in believing that he was an honest person. He never lied unless he had to. He always lived up to his word if he gave it. He never cheated anyone in personal exchanges. He paid his debts. He felt that he had never hurt anyone who did not deserve to be hurt or who had not forced him to do so. The fact that he had been a thief was not a thing that he condemned himself for. It was just that circumstances in life had left him no other avenue as he saw it. He had to make a living just like everyone else and the only people who had ever been kind to him and shown compassion for him had been thieves. These people, among whom he had been thrust by circumstance, had been his teachers and his idols. There was honor among thieves and he saw himself as an honorable man among his peers. Surely God knew and understood all this and would deal with him accordingly. "We'll see, yes we'll see."

The recovery of the money that they were involved in at the present time was certainly a thing that God would understand. They had paid for the crime of stealing it so, in Truman's twisted reasoning process they had earned the right to it. At least this was what he kept telling himself.

Probably the original owners of the money they had stolen would have been reimbursed by the banks or the government. Or, more probably, they were dead by now. The government certainly did not need the money and would just waste it if it were returned to them so it made no sense to him not to try and reclaim every penny of it. Harry often reminded him that they had worked hard for that money and had fully paid for the right to enjoy it. Maybe he was right, "we'll see, yes we'll see".

The two of them had spent considerable time discussing

how to deal with the money once they had it all in their possession. They knew they could not just start spending it because they would be under some degree of surveillance for many years. Probably the rest of their lives. They knew that there were bounty hunters of sorts who would be watching them even when the government gave up. They would have to find some ways to launder the money. This was especially true of this money because it was old money and yet it was still new looking for the most part. Some great part of it was probably going to be of considerable value as collector's items.

Both of them had tried to keep abreast of changes in printed money during their years in the prisons. Both of them had spent much time talking with master thieves about how to launder money and where to make contact with people who would help them in the effort, for a fee of course. Harry was the mastermind here. He had made contacts.

The jewelry that they would have to deal with was another matter. They had gotten all kinds of advice while in prison about how to turn the best dollar value in the underworld jewelry market.

Harry however had some ideas of his own in that particular area. He was convinced that the best way to deal with it was to learn how to evaluate the stones and metals on their own. In this way they would not depend on others who could cheat them. So, Harry had spent many hours studying the subject of the jewelry business. There had been a couple of excellent teachers in prison cells. He thought that they should spend part of the time drifting down the river preparing the jewelry for exchange.

He wanted to take all the mounted stones out of the settings and do the best job he could of placing a value on them by grading and separating them into proper categories.

He had bought the tools and equipment and books he thought he would need and had them stored on his boat. He also wanted to melt down all the castings and sell the gold and silver in that manner. To do this he had, once again, purchased the needed supplies and had them aboard his boat.

They were finding this to be a very difficult thing to accomplish. They did not trust their abilities and knew they would have to find someone to help them with the final sale of these commodities. They were certainly in unfamiliar waters in dealing with this problem. It would demand great care and probably much time to finally dispose of this part of the loot. One thing they had learned back in their pre-prison days was that the underworld of middlemen took all the profit out of bank robbery for most of those who were in the trade. They had suffered badly at the hands of those they had dealt with. This fact alone had led them to hide so much of the money and loot from their work and plan to dispose of it in better ways than they had been forced into as kids learning the hard way. They had vowed to be wiser and now they felt that they were just that.

Many hours were spent working and speculating on the end of the line procedures. Plans were formulated for anchoring their boats in a remote area that they had already scouted out near New Orleans. They would take all the cargo off the boats and hide it in a safe but easily accessible location where they could dispose of it in an orderly fashion.

As much as they hated to admit it, they were going to have to trust banks with the most of it. They were going to purchase new identities from some forgers that they knew in Baton Rouge, Louisiana. They were then going to open bank accounts in those new names and rent safety deposit boxes and slowly establish themselves in double existences. The plan was then to travel abroad to different places until they found a place where they could settle down and live out the rest of their lives as new men. Preferably country gentlemen. It was a grand dream.

If they could get all of the rest of the money and clean it up, there would be enough for the dream to become reality. "We'll see, yes we'll just see".

Well Kenny, I am finding myself going into greater detail in the telling of the story than I have ever done before. This is all uncharted water for me. I don't know if I have told you or not but the story of the trip down the Mississippi has never been told. I have shared that the trip was made but never the underlying reason for it. I was always aware of the fact that there were people alive somewhere who would take an interest in it in a way that I did not want to get involved with. Some danger may yet be involved in the telling of some of the information that Truman shared with me.

I discussed this with Mary, Truman's widow, the other day and she says that she believes most all those who would try to cause any problem are now dead. So I am moving into uncertain territory here. I am also trying to be very careful in what I say.

Pray that if God wants this to be a book, He will guide me to hurt no one in the process.

Bless You,

Clifford

CHAPTER 19
CONTAGIOUS ENTHUSIASM

Kenny,

It has been many days now since I have been able to continue our story and events seem to be working against me in some of the documentation process that I feel is essential to the story being given the kind of reception it deserves. I am finding that there was an effort on the part of the government to expunge Truman's records in some ways that are difficult to overcome.

Mary told me that the F.B.I. had sent a man to talk to her and Truman at one time who told them that a part of his prison and conviction record would be expunged. They did not believe him. I have found that he was actually telling them the truth.

So far, I have been able to get into a small portion of the record but mostly from newspaper accounts instead of prison records. I think that this will soon be overcome however and I want to include some of that official record within the book. In Truman's words, "we'll see, yes we'll just see".

But on with the story:

Let me jump ahead and back at the same time for some information that will help us to put in perspective some of the actions of our two enterprising riverboat captains. By jumping ahead, I mean that I want to tell you in advance about some of the planning that Harry and Truman have embarked upon for disposing of the money at the end of the trip. By jumping back, I mean that we need to go back in time several months and look at some time spent in southern Louisiana before the construction of the boats began.

Harry and Truman were hard at work in Terre Haute, Indiana planning and saving money to purchase materials for the construction of their houseboats. Truman was given the responsibility of designing the two craft and took the job very much to heart. He researched the subject extensively and made several trips to get a look at boats where ever he could find an owner willing to allow inspection. He made notes and took photographs and made dozens of drawings before settling on a set of plans that both of them approved of fully.

While this was under way and the seeking of materials as well, Harry was taking trips to southern Louisiana to meet with some contacts he had developed through former prison acquaintances. He had known that if he ever got out of prison, he would try to recover the hidden money and that he would probably need help in laundering it. These trips were attempts to determine if the contacts were on the up and up and whether they could indeed be depended upon completely. Being the cautious person that he was and not automatically trusting anyone, he had to satisfy himself that this was the way to deal with the problem.

He did make the contacts and gave them the opportunity to prove themselves to him as capable and reliable. His best judgement was coming to be that this was the wisest and safest way to handle the funds. It was this or take several years learning to do the job totally by himself and this he was not prepared to do. Time was getting away from him and he wanted to live to enjoy the fruit of his labor. So he began to examine how he should proceed to handle the actual job of storing the funds after recovery and the means of making exchanges.

He decided that he would not make a onetime exchange but would instead explore the process by making a series of deals over several months and stopping to weigh the results and dangers as he went along. This meant he had to have a safe place to hide the money, jewels and metals where he could get to it easily as needed.

Everything he looked at seemed to have serious drawbacks involved. Rented houses were not a good place for several reasons that ranged from possible fires to being sold if rented and losing control of the place. He did not have the money to purchase a place of his own so that was out. He examined several commercial storage units of various types and was afraid to trust that much value to a place that could be broken into or examined by a curious owner. He even considered renting several bank safe deposit boxes but ruled them out because of the size limitations.

He really wanted some place that was accessible but one that did not belong to him. He preferred something not connected to him by records that could lead someone else to it by examining his life. It needed to be near enough to the people whom he would have to deal with that he could make good any commitment he needed to fulfil without delay. It needed to be some place that he could have reason to frequent without raising suspicions. He felt that New Orleans was his best choice for this spot and after considerable time, he decided to continue the usage of the boats as long as possible. The hidden compartments they had planned for in the boats would be good enough that it would take a really close inspection to find them. If they continued to live on the boats for a time, he felt that this afforded the best and safest storage possible for a limited time.

He looked into several commercial marinas that could

accommodate the boats and yet let them continue to live in them for as long as necessary. He found what he wanted and arranged for two places to be reserved for the arrival of the boats. He told the owners of his and Truman's great adventure down the Mississippi and that the arrival date was very uncertain but that he wanted to be sure he had a place whenever it was. He found a way to begin his rental but at the same time for it not to be available for at least eighteen months. He could lease two spots and cover the expense by subleasing them to others. It seemed workable so he filled out the necessary papers and left the area with the understanding that the owner would keep the slips rented for him till needed. When the trip was underway and he could estimate their time of arrival, he would call the owner and make sure the slips were vacated by the folks who were subleasing them.

He did not want to commit to a single plan so he continued to scour the area for other options. He became aware of a hunting lease that was available in an area along the Mississippi several miles north of New Orleans and upon examining it, found it to be very promising as well. It did have a hunting cabin on the property that could be utilized as a place to live for the time needed and the large tract of land could afford a place to bury the money if that were to become necessary. Here again he could lease and turn around and sub-let to cover the expense. He had the necessary documents drafted and signed and another alternative was now open if needed.

And lastly, he found a commercial marina and dry dock arrangement in the city of Baton Rouge right on the banks of the Mississippi and a similar arrangement for this site as well. He thought he had enough options to cover all possibilities so he left and went back to Terre Haute and shared the arrangements with Truman.

Truman was glad to see that these details were worked out and felt very comfortable with them. Now, on to boat building, trip planning and supply lists to be considered and filled. This was getting more and more exciting with each passing hurdle. They both felt that there would be many adjustments to make before the trip was complete but faced the task with an enthusiasm that was contagious. Everyone who knew them became interested in this mad plan of adventure but secretly envied them the experience.

Kenny, I am still amazed at the ingenuity displayed by Truman and Harry and the audacity that characterized their every approach to life. In many ways, they were remarkable individuals.

If they had only had someone to take them under wing at an early age, I believe that they would have been great achievers and would have contributed much to society. I am beginning to understand why God had designs upon Truman's life. It was filled with wasted potential. Only an all-knowing and wise God could envision the redemption of his life.

I will have to close for tonight and will get back to you as soon as possible with a further expansion.

May the Lord bless and keep you,
Clifford

CHAPTER 20
MAKING A DEPOSIT

Kenny,
We are preparing to leave for a few days of vacation in Colorado tomorrow and I wanted to get a chapter of the book out to you before leaving. I have been anxious to hear the results of your tests this week and am praying for great reports. I don't know if I will be where I can check my e-mail while in Colorado but will do so if possible. If not, I will be back in touch around the 17th.

Let's take a look at Truman's Story:

The grossly under qualified riverboat captains were learning all sorts of useful things that they would have been very happy not to know, mostly because of the negative manner in which the information came to them. Neither of them would have ever dreamed it possible for their quest for cash to take so many wild and crazy twists and turns. It seemed that some unseen force was at work making their lives a virtual roller coaster experience.

At this particular juncture, they were on one of the high peaks and the world was looking pretty good from this vantage point. They were congratulating themselves very generously.

Harry had always been a very resourceful individual and continually amazed Truman with his ability to think creatively. It was this sterling characteristic that had been responsible, in that distant past, for engineering the placement of their final cache of loot. This was the next item on the agenda for recovery from its unique location.

As Truman lay in his bed listening to the gentle swishing of the current against the hull of his boat, he felt safe. As they most always did, they had anchored for the night just off the shoreline and the rhythmic swaying of the vessel, as it strained and fought with the anchor line, lulled him into a state of subliminal bliss and reflection.

Almost involuntarily, his thoughts slipped back in time. Images surfaced of a night from the distant past and flooded out before him with such stark realism that it might have taken place only yesterday. In gruesome detail of sound, odor and feelings, he envisioned himself following Harry back and forth from their car as they carried the equipment that was required to meet their purpose. Each trip was made as quietly as possible to prevent anyone in the area from being alerted to their presence. They were in a cemetery and were about to engage themselves in opening a crypt inside a mausoleum.

The structure was of stone construction with two rows of vaults facing one another across a chamber about sixteen feet wide. One end was walled shut leaving the other open. The vaults were in rows four high and the one they were going to open was on the second level from the floor. They had brought along a tarpaulin to hang over the open end of the chamber to shield the light from being detected from outside while they worked. It had required them to use a folding ladder that they brought to get the tarp stretched over the opening from the roof downward and anchored to the ground with some rocks.

They were here to make a deposit in what they jokingly had called their "safe deposit box". They soon had all the necessary supplies and equipment lain out on the floor and began in earnest to get the job done.

After finding it surprisingly easy to remove the polished stone cover that faced the crypt, they then had to remove the inner lining, which was sealed with cement. The outside stone cover had been held in place with large screws but the inside seal was made of some material that broke when they were opening it.

This did not surprise them for they had known it probably would do just that. Their preparation for the task had revealed this possibility so they had come prepared to replace it with a duplicate they had borrowed from a company, which manufactured them. Of course they had borrowed it without having asked permission in a late night visit.

The vault they were working with had only been sealed a couple of days earlier while Harry and Truman had watched from a secluded vantage point a short distance away. It had taken considerable time and effort to be on hand to observe the placement of the casket in the crypt and the process used in sealing the vault. They had pretended to be placing flowers on a grave nearby and had crept close while having their presence hidden by a beautifully trimmed hedge that surrounded the area.

Now, after months of careful planning, they were here to open the vault, remove the casket, empty it of its resident and replace him with the retirement account funds and reseal the crypt.

After chipping away the last of the inner seal material, they carefully pulled the casket out and set it on the chamber floor. This proved to be much harder than they had expected. It was very difficult to do so without leaving marks that might cause someone to notice that the crypt had been disturbed. They managed it but both of them were complaining about straining muscles they could not remember having used before.

With the casket laid out, they used another "borrowed" tool to unscrew the locking device and opened the lid. Steeling themselves against the revulsion that both felt, they lifted the body of the aged man out of what had been intended to be it's final resting place, and placed it aside on the floor.

They were now ready for the deposit to be made. Going back to the car and opening the trunk, they removed three military duffel bags filled with cash amounting to $200,000.00. These bags were taken to the chamber and a second trip was required to return with three more canvas bags containing gold coins.

They first placed the duffel bags in the casket and found that there was not enough room left to add the other bags. They considered what to do. They did not want to just dump the coins inside and spread them around because it was impossible to predict what the circumstances might be that would bring them back to withdraw the funds. It could call for a rapid process and they did not want to leave the materials in such a condition that could unnecessarily delay the job of recovery.

In looking around, they decided to utilize a metal toolbox that might allow a different arrangement in the enclosure they had to work with. They put the coins in the box and were able to stack bundles of bills in it as well. This reduced the size of one of the duffel bags enough to allow everything to fit in the space. It was finally re-closed and sealed and they found it a daunting task to lift the now heavier casket back into the crypt. Two older or less strong men might not have been able to handle the job but finally it was back in its former position.

They took great care in resealing the crypt and replacing the stone cover. When the job was finished they stood back and minutely examined their work and gave the job a gold star.

But now came the decision over what to do with the corpse

of the old man. Harry wanted to take it with them and bury it at some remote spot in the forest but Truman balked at this proposal. Harry expressed dismay and asked, "What do you think we should do with it? We certainly can't leave it here and we can't eat the thing".

Truman replied, "Let's leave it here in the mausoleum." To which Harry responded, "How do you propose to do that?". Truman was ready with the answer, "We can put it in with the body in the chamber beside or under the one with the money in it".

Harry could not believe what he was hearing, "Why on earth should we go to that much trouble. And if we tried, how do we know it will fit in with another? You saw that the inside of the other casket didn't have much extra space in it".

"Well, we won't know till we try and it will be easier to open and close the crypt than to dig a grave in the woods. After all, I think if a relative comes to visit a grave, there ought to be a body there to visit. I would not want to be responsible for it not being there, that's for sure. We could get God mad at us and then we would really be in the soup".

This brought out the humorous side in Harry and he had to struggle not to laugh so loud as to give away their presence in the cemetery. He knew that Truman had a gentle side to his nature and had found it difficult to deal with on many occasions. So he agreed to give the proposal a try and they set about the task of opening the crypt beneath their deposit box.

The job of removing this casket proved much easier because they now had experience and the fact that the crypt was on the same level as the floor of the vestibule allowed them to slide the casket out much more easily. When they had opened it and attempted to place the second corpse inside with the other, they could not close the lid. It was obvious that they would have to dismember as least one of them to make room for both. How to go about it? They had the necessary tools in the form of both knives and saws but neither of them had the stomach for it.

They examined both corpses and decided that the one that had been there the longest was somewhat dehydrated in appearance and would most likely be less messy to work with. So they lifted it out and took it outside on the lawn where Harry reluctantly carved and sawed it into several pieces.

As he would remove a portion, Truman would take it inside and place it inside the casket with the new resident. After what seemed an eternity to both, the job was completed. The crypt was resealed and they took their leave.

As Truman remembered this gruesome job while lying in his bed, his thoughts jumped forward to a discussion that resulted from the experience some days later. He had told Harry that he did not want to have to handle any more corpses. "There has to be a better way to do this", he said as pitifully as Harry had ever seen him express himself. So, taking pity on him, he replied, "Let's think about the alternatives for a few days, Bud".

That same night, Harry had burst into Truman's room at the hotel they were staying in at the time, and with a big grin on his face, said, "I've got the perfect solution, Bud". Truman was taken off guard and asked, "Solution to What?" "Our mausoleum problem", Harry retorted. "We will buy our own mausoleum. That will leave us with no more bodies to deal with and we will have full use of the darned thing." The two master thieves were still learning and refining their skills.

A few days later they had found a likely looking small town in which they approached a funeral director who operated his business out of a hardware store and made arrangements to have their own personal mausoleum constructed in a secluded corner of the town cemetery. This was going to be the money vault to end all money vaults. It would have a locking mechanism designed by the latest methods. The key would be owned by the two of them and no one else would have one. It was perfect. Eventually they could even move all the other money caches into this one vault and never more worry about anyone else examining the structure. They made it large enough for six family members and told the man their parents and wives would one day be entombed there.

Several months later, after the completion of the tomb, they had returned and placed within it the proceeds of the first robbery to be completed after the structure. They now had their own private bank and over the next several months had made two more deposits there.

Kenny, the time is getting late and I need to get a little sleep as we will be hitting the road in the bus early in the morning so I will close for now and continue this chapter at a more convenient time.

Bless you,

Clifford

CHAPTER 21
WE'LL SEE

Kenny,
It has been several days since I have had time to communicate but I have been extremely excited to hear of the improvement of the brain lesions. A reduction from 5 to 4 is a 20% improvement and in my book seems to indicate a healing process taking place for you. We will continue to pray for a complete recovery.

But let me share a chapter of Truman's story that I have worked on for several days in what spare moments I could find. We pick up where we left off:

As Truman lay there in his bed, he continued to reflect on what he considered to be the saddest days of his life. The events that took place leading up to the end of their bank robbing career flooded out of his memory and he found himself shaking internally as freshly as he had on the day of his and Harry's arrest. He remembered how he had felt certain that this was the beginning of the last days of his life. They would be condemned to die for the things they had done and for the first time in a long time, he was terrified at the thought of having to face the judgement of God. In some way that he did not fully understand, he cared little about the judgement of man and at that particular juncture of time, spent little time even thinking about anything other than standing before his maker. How would he possibly conduct himself with any dignity in that courtroom where all the secrets of his soul would be bared and accounted for.

The memory of those feelings of dread washed over him and once more, as in many times past, he was reduced to drawing himself up in a fetal position and whimpering remorseful little cries toward a God he knew was reading his mind. For several hours he found himself recounting the many clear promises he had uttered to God in the course of his life. His heart seemed at times that it would not remain in his chest as it struggled and pounded in its effort to meet the challenge of the rising fear rushing through his convoluted and convicted brain. A deep sense of shame settled down upon him and he was powerless to move out from under its terrible weight. He wanted to call out to God for deliverance but could not find in himself the strength to face the consequences of such an act. He had promised so much to God and never delivered and had always known that God was watching and waiting at every turn of events in his twisted past. How could he possibly expect anything but rejection from God at this stage of his pathetic life?

Did God still care? Was there a way out of the evil web he had woven about himself?

Words he had read many times over and committed to the deep recesses of his mind began to creep to the forefront of his thinking. "Whosoever shall call upon the name of the Lord shall be saved". "This is a faithful saying, and worthy of all acceptation, that Christ Jesus came into the world to save sinners; of whom I am chief."

Revolving these thoughts round and round in his mind, he struggled to know his own heart and clutched at the possibility that he could change the course of his life and become the person that he somehow knew that God wanted him to be. He could not fully grasp what that person should be but he was certain that it was vastly different than what he knew himself to be at the moment. What would happen if he tried to share his fear and confusion with Harry? Somehow he was certain that Harry would ridicule and laugh him to scorn. He could not bring himself to allow for that possibility. Why did he care this much about what Harry thought and what Harry wanted of him? There seemed to be no answer. Why could he not be completely his own man? What was missing in him and would he ever be any different. Maybe if he waited long enough, the answers would come to him. Surely there would come a time when he would be strong enough in his being to decide the correct pattern for his life and choose to develop that pattern. Other people seemed to do this. If he waited long enough it would come to him. "We'll see. We'll just see."

With a deliberate act of his will, Truman turned his thoughts back to the subject of the recovery attempt that lay ahead of them. With the decision there came a reflection back once more to the preparation they had made for access to the tomb they had paid to have constructed. They both had a keying tool that opened the tomb and the individual crypts that lay within the structure. There had been a third copy of the tool that had been made and had been buried beneath the southwest corner of the mausoleum. Both of the tools that they had in their possession at the time of their arrest had been hidden beneath the floor of one of the horse barns on the farm they had purchased and they had been afraid to go back and attempt to reclaim them. Someone had told them that the barn had burned and so it was probably useless to even go and look. So they were depending upon the one buried beneath the structure itself to still be there. If not, they could break into the tomb or attempt to use their old false identities to get new ones made if that was necessary. For the present however, they would expect the buried tool to be in its place and waiting for their return.

They were yet a couple of months away from their planned stop to deal with this particular cache and after that only the bank savings accounts to complete the trip. Things were beginning to shape up and yet there was this underlying fear that seemed somehow to continue to grow in Truman. In spite of all he did, it just would not go away.

He tied to remember just exactly what all they had placed in the family mausoleum and talked with Harry about this several times. They had come to have such confidence in the safety of the hiding place till they had failed to completely inventory and commit to memory all that they had hurriedly stashed within it. Plans had been that they would do so at a more convenient time but then they had been interrupted so suddenly by the arrests that there had been no clear understanding of just what was there.

The first deposit was clear enough. It had been their share of several robberies after an accounting and division of shares had been completed. But the last two deposits had been made with the intention of getting the gang together for one of their accounting sessions at the farm. This within itself had been an unusual deviation from their normal procedure and had taken place because they had intended to conduct three more robberies in close succession with a schedule that did not allow time for counting and dividing the loot until five jobs had been completed.

The plans for their extended work together had called for a break after these five up-coming jobs to allow every member to develop their lives in other pursuits. Though Truman and Harry were actively working to build legitimate lifestyles in the horse ranching business, this was not their ultimate goal. It was only a means to another end. They had plans to one day own and operate a horse racetrack on a major scale. The other members of their organization had plans of their own and needed time to work them out also. So, they were looking forward to finishing these five robberies and then disappearing from the scene for three years. After that time, they would get together and reassess where they were and how much more capital they all needed to complete their careers in their chosen professions. In the mean time, they considered themselves to be bi-vocational businessmen. The work project they were currently engaged in called for five robberies to be completed in less than four months.

They had completed two in a row and the whole gang had agreed to allow Harry and Truman to safeguard the whole take until all five could be finished. This arrangement came about because Harry had informed the whole group that he and Truman had acquired a foolproof place for storing the proceeds and they had come to trust one another completely in such matters. The rest of the members of the group were not told where this place was or what it consisted of, nor did they ask.

So when the arrests had come and the law had so suddenly fallen upon them, they had the proceeds from two jobs stashed in the vaults that had been uncounted and undivided including the bonds and securities from Minden. This along with the divided portions of the other jobs that were lying in the vault waiting for Truman and Harry to return made for an exciting possibility that loomed before these two river barons.

There had been several discussions concerning whether they owed the rest of the gang members their loyalty to share their original split in these funds or not. Both of them thought that if any of the members were out of prison or going to be out soon, that it would be the right thing to do to set aside their share. They could either leave it hidden in the tomb or launder it for them and put it in a bank for them somewhere. If any of them were dead then they thought it would be acceptable for them to claim that share as their own. They would have to do some research and determine the proper course in this matter. Both of them considered loyalty and fidelity within the group to be an unquestioned fact.

The problem as they saw it was how to find out where the rest of the group was and if they could discover that, there was still the matter of determining their wishes in the matter. If they were out of jail, it would not be such a large problem to know how to get their shares to them. If they were in jail still, well, that was another matter altogether. Communication with inmates could be accomplished but it could take a long time because they would have to go through other people to do so. That within it-self could be very dangerous since most people could not be trusted to remain confidential with the necessary information to be communicated. This seemed too dangerous to seriously accept as feasible.

There had been no communication with the other group members directly concerning whether the proceeds of those jobs had been found and reclaimed by law officials or not. This left the matter up to Harry and Truman as to the proper course to follow. It was a considerable dilemma and they could not come to a firm conclusion to the matter. The time spent traveling toward the cache was filled with discussions of possible courses of action.

Harry and Truman both knew some family members of these other men but not well enough to approach them with this kind of information. That was out. They both knew a lawyer or two who could probably find out where and what circumstances the men were in, but again they did not trust lawyers either.

On the one hand, they could just go ahead and take the money and use it as they wished and could possibly never have any repercussions from it. On the other, they could do this and one of the men could find out in some way that they were out of jail and locate them and give them a really big problem if they thought they were being cheated. Men had died for lesser offenses in this line of work. What was the best outcome for all involved?

They finally came to a tentative conclusion that they would not make up their minds until they found out how much money and other valuables were actually stored there. If there was enough to make a real difference, then they would come to a decision. If not, then they would just leave the other men's shares in the tomb and hope for the best. So down the river they went.

As they continued down the river, they came to Memphis, Tennessee and decided to take a while away from the river once more. This was a pretty large city at this time and there were several places where they could dock their boats. There was the local country club marina and then there were several commercial sport fishing marinas that they could choose from. It was a recurring problem that they were coming to be more and more conscious of and concerned about. There was an awful lot at stake when they left the boats in the hands of other people. The money and other loot was well hidden but they never felt comfortable that someone might get too curious in their absence and stumble upon their fortune. Then there was also the possibility of an accident of some sort that could result in the discovery of their money. Even a fire could feasibly happen in their absence.

This caused them to look for some individual or private company that had a secure dock where they could feel better about the boats being properly cared for. It took them two days of searching to find a place that was satisfactory but they did finally decide upon a small boat repair shop, which seemed to fit their needs, and left the boats in the owner's charge.

The time away was given to seeing the sights of the city and returning at odd intervals to check on the boats. Harry spent considerable time trying to get some information as to the whereabouts of the other members of their old gang. He discovered that at least two of them were still in prison by contacting relatives that he knew. There was no information available concerning the newest member of the gang who had betrayed them, nor the member who had been ousted just prior to their arrest so many years ago. One person had said he thought they were both dead but was not certain about it. This turned out to be of no help to Harry and Truman in the decisions that faced them in the near future.

After some considerable rest and recreation, the boats were once more turned down the river and the final encounter with the last cache loomed near.

The day finally arrived when they were in the town where the mausoleum was located and they discovered there were no commercial docking facilities available that would allow them to tie their boats up. They began to look for a private pier of some sort that would give them access to a street exit for it would be essential that they have a van rented to use in transferring their holdings from the tomb to the safety of the womb of the boats. There was only one such place available and they were uneasy about using it because there was another houseboat docked there and a family was living on the boat. This could cause serious limitations to their actions. As they considered the options, they found that it could not be helped, they would have to make the best of what was here and find a way that suited their purpose.

They arranged to pay for docking privileges and told the owner that they would be making some minor repairs to their boats and would be bringing new supplies aboard from time to time while there. They told him they would need to rent a van and the man was helpful in arranging for one to be brought to the dock for their use.

It was now time to check out their safe deposit vault and figure out how to make an accurate accounting of what was there. It was obvious that they could not spend much time in the mausoleum and they could not bring all that stuff to the boats to work with without risking a discovery of what they were doing. The easiest solution seemed to be to rent a cottage in the area and transfer the funds there in small volumes until they had worked their way through the task.

A day spent looking for a place produced three possibilities and both came to the same conclusion as to which one was best. It was located only four blocks away from the mausoleum and could be reached easily. It had a garage attached to drive the van into. It was secured and the program got under way.

Harry decided that it would be easiest to occupy the house for a couple of days and scout the area for any possible dangers that they should be aware of before entering the cemetery and inspecting the condition of their bank. If there had been any major changes, they needed to know in advance of preparation to enter it. They had learned by now that time could do strange things to the environment and they did not want to rush blindly into anything.

After settling into the cottage and even meeting and being welcomed by the neighbors, they began to take strolls around the area and, in the process, check for danger signs. They found none that seemed to be of any particular concern. Casually expanding their evening strolls they entered the cemetery and found that there had been a considerable amount of change and expansion, which was to be expected after so many years. It took only a few minutes to orient themselves enough to spot their own private final resting place and "real estate investment" as Truman liked to refer to the mausoleum. They observed it from a distance and deliberately avoided showing particular interest in the structure on that first visit. All seemed to be well. They would return for a close inspection in the wee hours before dawn the next morning.

The first thing they did upon checking the cemetery carefully was to try and determine if the structure had been violated in any manner and make plans to dig for the opening devices buried under the corner. They were delighted to learn that the exterior of the mausoleum was in pristine condition. It was made of a high grade of marble and seemed to be far less aged than they would have expected. There was not a mark on it that would indicate anyone had ever touched it except the groundskeepers who obviously manicured the lawn with great delicacy.

This immaculate grooming of the grounds gave them some cause for concern because they knew that they would need to be especially careful in digging for the tools. They must not leave any evidence that they had done so. It would require removal of a section of the lawn with the intent of replacing it in very precise order so as to leave no trace to be questioned by the apparently zealous gardeners. It proved to be much easier than they expected and they could hardly believe the wonderfully fine condition of the tools as they removed them from the two metal boxes they had been secured in when buried so many years ago.

They had originally decided to pack sawdust around the tools inside one small military ammunition box which they had dipped in tar three times to provide a waterproof and rust resistant container. They had then placed that box inside a slightly larger metal box, which they then poured full of melted tar and after closing it up they continued to dip it in melted tar several times as well. The finished product resembled a solid block of tar and the idea was to not only prevent corrosion but to make it appear to be useless leftover and discarded building materials from the construction of the mausoleum. If anyone were to discover it for some reason, they would probably ignore it. They placed the block of tar in a bag and carried it back to the cottage for the tool removal operation. After placing the block in a metal container, it was placed over a small portable heating devise they had purchased and set up in the closed garage. In due time the melted tar allowed them to fish the boxes out and remove the tools. They patted one another on the back and Harry gave forth with one of his favorite expressions, "great planning produces great results".

It was the next night before they returned to the cemetery and crept silently across the lawn in their approach to the portal of the monetary monument. In opening the solid metal door that guarded their treasure house, Truman could not contain the rush of excitement and anticipation that crept up his spine. It was amazing that the interior of the mausoleum was completely untouched. Closing the door behind them as they had done on the last ill-fated entrance to these chilly chambers as young and confident banking executives, Harry and Truman found themselves extremely nervous. The sense of stepping back in time was unsettling to say the least. Even the odor of the place seemed to cause flashbacks that both of them felt and had to acknowledge to one another almost immediately upon entering the chamber. It took them several minutes to settle their nerves down enough to proceed with the task at hand.

Getting a grip on their frazzled nerves, they set about opening the chamber that contained the hauls from the two banks that had never been sorted out and counted. With a low whistle of relief, Harry reached into the crypt and pulled out a large bulging duffel bag and they discussed how much of its contents they should carry to the house at one time. After a brief exchange they decided to take the whole bag. There were four more bags in addition to this one that would have to be gone through before the job was complete and could end up taking several days. It would be best to transport as much as they could in order to keep down the number of trips necessary. It could become dangerous if someone were to take note of traffic around the tomb and they knew they would have to be very careful not to leave traces of their presence.

The entire process of tabulating the contents of the five bags stretched out over twelve days due to the fact that they were required to make several public appearances at gatherings arranged by the news media. The story of their journey was spreading ahead of them as the trip progressed and more and more this was the case with every stop they made along the winding path of the river. In this particular situation, the news coverage was a real danger because reporters could appear at the most unexpected times and make demands upon their time. Twice while they were in the midst of counting cash, a knock at the door sent them scurrying to stuff their work into a closet and wiping away any trace of the evidence of what they were really engaged in. This done, they would then play the cordial host and set about becoming Huckleberry Finn's loyal followers for whatever time was required to keep the press properly employed.

Finally, when the tally was complete, they were faced with the monumental decision of whether to take it all and forget the possible consequences or remain loyal to the men who were paying the price for the right to spend this cash just as they had. The total of the undivided currency was $800,000.00 give or take a thousand or two in cash and a still undetermined value to be placed on a large pile of jewelry and coins of various types, mostly gold and the various bonds and securities.

Added to this were the already divided shares from the other jobs they had first deposited. The total now rose to just over a million bucks in cash and a box of coins and jewelry that came with that collection as well. They had no difficulty transporting the proceeds which they had full claim to down to the boats and stowing it away in the rapidly filling depositories built into the hulls of the boats. What to do with the other funds in question was proving to be something to argue about. Truman had a very strong sense of loyalty to the men who had pledged their lives right along with he and Harry to obtain these goods and he argued that this could not be neglected. Harry, on the other hand, argued that circumstances had changed so much that they were no longer under obligation to the men and that if the roles were reversed, those men would take the cash and think nothing of Truman and Harry.

They were at loggerheads over it almost to the point of blows. When Harry threatened to take all the other men's shares for his own use and shoulder the full blame if Truman was afraid of the men ever making an appearance and demanding to be paid, Truman relented and compromised.

They would take it all with them but they would launder it and keep it set aside for the men until such time that it was obvious there was no reason to continue doing so. At such a juncture, they would split it between the two of them and claim it for themselves.

The boats opened wide their hungry mouths and swallowed the full meal of cash, jewelry and gold and the journey was joined afresh with both boats riding lower in the water.

Kenny, the trip is nearing its end but the story is far from over so we will pick it up on another day my friend.

Blessings be on you,

Clifford

CHAPTER 22
BATON ROUGE LAUNDRY

Kenny,
 I am having some difficulty determining just how to proceed with the rest of the story. My attempt to safeguard innocent people from unwanted publicity is an ongoing concern. I am discovering that there are many extended family members connected with these people who probably know nothing of the events of which I am writing. Whether to consult with them and risk embarrassing someone or to use some means of concealing identities is a matter I must deal with eventually.

I have decided to proceed as best I can until my research on these people is further along. So I will just pick up and move along with our story. This may be cause for rewriting later so if you find the finished product changed from my original version, you will know that this is the underlying motive and reason.

Kenny, I will cease my sending of the rest of the text with this chapter. As we have discussed, I want you to learn the rest of the story by reading the finished product so I will continue to include some of our communication in the text but will not send it to you as part of our communications for the time being . I really appreciate your continued interest and encouragement. That said, we will pick up the story.

Truman and Harry are becoming more and more nervous

as they have now come to the last small venture in salvaging their stored fortunes. The last bank with deposited funds does not present any unexpected problems however, so the arrangement with Harry's former wife is utilized once more and arrangements are made for the last transfers to be placed in her care. It was a piece of cake.

With what seemed to be the last serious obstacles behind them, the liquid roadway that lay before them seemed to smile upon the years of labor and planning that had brought them to travel its winding pathway.

The current seemed to slow perceptively in anticipation of delivering them to the end of their long journey. The city of Baton Rouge, Louisiana loomed on the horizon one afternoon as Truman and Harry were beginning to make preparations for an anchorage for the night.

It had become more and more necessary that they find safety early in the evenings because of the bulging volume of traffic developing daily on the waterway. Barges lashed together in long strings and pushed by large tugboats were a constant danger and they never stopped. Even the darkness of night did not intimidate the captains of these seagoing trains. So the ritual of searching the shoreline for safe harborage became the norm every day now. Sometimes it would be a dock of some sort and others it might be the mouth of a stream that dumped itself into the muddy waters of the Mississippi, which would offer recluse and safe slumbers.

The sight of Baton Rouge brought a rise in blood pressure for both men because this was a place where the beginning of business in a big way would be born. Harry's contacts here would furnish new identities for all four passengers. This would open the doors of nations and broad possibilities. So it was with great excitement that berthing was found and the city opened its doors to these wayfaring strangers. A sense of wellness that defied the situation worked its way into Truman's consciousness as they made their way around the bustling thoroughfares of the capital city. Having defied what seemed to be almost insurmountable odds, they had accomplished almost every goal they had set for themselves. That is if you didn't count the two lost caches. But that was not something that was inside their control so in a way they did not meet the criteria for failure in Truman's eyes.

The task was superhuman by anyone's measurement and he could not resist the temptation to feel well-earned pride swelling up within his breast. Life was beginning to look so bright and promising. The years of pain and suffering were beginning to somehow seem worthwhile. Maybe God was beginning to smile upon him after all. Could God smile upon the efforts of one who was traveling life's road as Truman? At the moment, it seemed so.

Arrangements were completed for the new set of credentials, which included passports and driver's licenses and even Social Security Cards. They would be furnished with the means to open bank accounts and travel abroad with full freedom of movement. They would be able to establish complete new lives and enjoy the years ahead with ease and even some degree of luxury if the proper setting could be found. Costa Rica and Argentina were much in their minds and they had even looked at the possibilities of Ireland and Scotland.

Harry was even now making inquiries about Australia. The possibilities seemed boundless. They would explore them all. There would be several weeks of waiting for the documentation to be completed but what was a few weeks compared to where these tired, old and abused names they now bore had taken them.

Along with the achievement with the forgers of documents, Harry was planning to add the expertise of an old friend from Lafayette, Indiana who had arranged contacts with other craftsmen currently operating in the Capital City. Within a matter of five days, he had met with these shadowy figures and discussed the business of laundering the goods emboweled in the belly of the boats. Of course he said nothing to them as to the location of these goods but he did disclose a measure of the volume to be dealt with. Sharp interest was immediately aroused among these contacts but they were very leery and eyed Harry and Truman carefully in the first encounter with them.

They demanded references to be checked before any real business could be conducted and when Harry gave them a coded name and a telephone number to contact, they seemed to relax almost instantly and became somewhat cordial. A meeting was scheduled for two days later and when Harry arrived for the meeting, he was told that his contact from the north had insisted that no business be conducted before he could make an appearance himself. This did not seem to surprise Harry at all and he readily agreed to await his arrival. They would keep in touch.

Several days passed before a message was sent that the man was now in the city and would meet the next night with these businessmen at a local hotel at 10:00 P.M.. Harry was to come alone. Upon arriving, he found that there were six men seated in the hotel suite's parlor. It was one of the finest establishments afforded by the capital city and the upper floor windows and balcony afforded a beautiful view of the state capital building. Harry was greeted warmly by his old friend and provided a mixed drink, and then was ushered out on the balcony by his host. The man chatted for a few minutes about the past and family and congratulated Harry on his journey down the river. He had kept abreast of the trip through the news coverage and was happy to see that his old friend was looking so well. Harry later related to Truman that one would have thought them to be brothers or at least very close kin.

As they stood gazing upon the beautifully lit Capital Building he asked Harry if he had visited the structure since his arrival in the city. To the man's seeming surprise and pleasure, Harry said that he indeed had. Upon which the man began to engage him in a discussion of the history of the building of the structure and expressed amazement that Harry warmed to the subject. Harry recounted his interest in history and his extensive reading of Huey P. Long's activities in convincing the state legislature to finance the five million dollar construction of the beautiful 34 story building, which was 450 feet tall, back in the 30's. He spoke knowledgeably about the assassination of Long on the grounds of the structure and delighted his friend with his familiarity with the quote that is carved on the entrance doorway. He recounted the occasion of it being spoken by Robert Livingston back in 1803 at the signing of the Louisiana Purchase agreement with France. Harry however made an application of the first half of the quote, which opened the discussion of the subject on both of their minds. He reminded his host of the many different enterprises that the two of them had engaged in from the distant past and then mentioned the current matter at hand by saying, "We have lived long but this is the noblest work of our whole lives." Thus saying, he was making an ancient quote come alive.

Harry's friend kept him on the balcony and away from the other men seated behind them in the parlor until he had spoken at length about what it was that Harry and Truman wanted done. He expressed appreciation that Harry had come to him with the matter and assured him that he could take care of the whole matter. What had to be discussed was not his ability to do the laundering but the percentage of values expected by both in the exchange. He and his business partners behind him would discuss the matter and make Harry a firm offer the very next day. He then asked for some idea of the magnitude of the goods involved and was visibly shaken when Harry handed him a sheet of paper upon which was a description of the various goods in his possession and his own personal evaluation of them. At the bottom of the page, Harry had three lines of handwritten requirements that must be met in order for a deal to be struck.

Eyebrows raised in surprise and almost immediately lowered in a conspiring manner as his friend leaned close and warned Harry, "Let's not be too demanding with these gentlemen." as he turned and led the way inside.

Once inside, the man sat down and asked Harry to do likewise. He then very matter-of-factly told the men that Harry and Truman were old and trusted friends who had a very interesting business proposition to offer them and then briefly outlined the situation. A few questions were asked and it was stated that a sample of the various securities would need to be brought to them for evaluation, the gold and silver tested for level of purity and the gemstones appraised by their experts. As for the cash, a broad sampling of it and the denominations most representative of the lot examined. If Harry would meet these requirements, the group would be glad to consider doing business with him.

Harry agreed but said he would not surrender the whole consignment in one lot. The business would have to be done in stages of his own choosing and timing. After some discussion, these terms were agreed upon and a meeting was set for two days later in the same room at 10:00 P.M.. Harry would bring his samples and they would have their experts present for a consultation. Upon which agreeable terms, Harry bid the gentlemen a warm goodnight and promptly departed. As he walked down the hallway of the Hotel toward the elevator, he considered the fact that the only names that had been mentioned during the course of the meeting had been his own and Truman's. The only person he knew in the group had been his old friend. He must be careful here. These people must not know that only he and Truman were involved on their end of the deal.

Kenny, the situation here was a very critical one and I will need more time than I have today to do justice to it. So I will close and wish you the best.

Blessings,

Clifford

CHAPTER 23
UNDERWORLD LORDS

Kenny,

Back to our story with a little rest and after some considerable time in research, we find:

Harry and Truman spent the next couple of days going over the various possibilities that could arise in the exchanging of the goods they possessed. They picked one another's brains for hours in an attempt to uncover any dangers that could present themselves. They both knew that the people with whom they would be dealing could prove to be very dangerous. They had to be absolutely certain that they did not allow these men to know where the materials were stored and should give every impression that they were not in any one location. There would be nothing to prevent these people from simply overpowering them and taking the goods from them. It was a looming possibility that could not be ignored. Both of them knew the ruthless nature of the men with whom they were dealing and that their lives were of no value to them outside gaining what they possessed. If there should ever arise a time when their prospective buyers felt that they could forcibly take the goods from the brothers, they would attempt it. They should not deceive themselves one whit in this matter. Great care would be absolutely essential. Every move and every stage of the transaction would have to be approached in the most guarded manner available. Their very lives hung upon their ability to stay several steps ahead of the cunning and ruthless minds of what they considered to be their adversaries.

If ever there could be a test of the nerve of both Truman and Harry, it would come now. After exhausting every scenario their brains could conjure up, it was decided that at no time should they allow the men to think that they were alone in what they were doing. They would spin a tale of several fictitious partners who would never be seen by the men who were making the purchases from Harry and Truman. These make believe partners would shuttle the merchandise from its various fictional storage places into Harry and Truman's hands as required for each transaction. The greatest care would be taken to make their buyers believe that heavy security was maintained at all times and that ruthless action would follow any deception. An air of aloofness and superiority would be maintained at all times. No weakness must be visible that could invite the criminal instinct of these predators to give vent to itself.

No longer would Harry deal with the men by himself. Truman would accompany him as a well-armed body guard who would demonstrate how dangerous it could be to attempt to scheme treachery against them.

To offset the possibility that they were being watched, and to give the impression that they were unconcerned about leaving the boats unattended, a hotel suite was rented that offered a good view of the boats where they were docked. Truman and Sylvia would occupy this room and attempt to keep vigilant watch over them. At the same time another suite was taken for Harry and Lillian to use not far from the hotel that had become a meeting place with the buyers. A scheme was constructed to give the appearance of Harry meeting with other fictional members of their organization as was deemed necessary to confuse anyone who might be trying to decipher the location of the funds. The expensive lodging arrangements were a deliberate subterfuge. They went so far as to arrange for salesmen to call upon them so as to give the impression to anyone watching that a certain activity was taking place there. These people were carefully chosen by calling upon expensive shops to send representatives. Real estate companies were contacted and given the story that Harry and Lillian were in the market for an expensive estate. This brought a steady stream of activity to the hotel suite. The fact that they were not staying on the boats would give the clear impression that the funds were not stored there. At least that was the intent of their actions.

So it was that after a careful rehearsal of the two roles they would play and a selection of samples of their merchandise was made, the 10:00 P.M. appointment was kept by a briefcase carrying, well dressed Harry and his tough looking sidekick, Truman. When they arrived at the door of the suite it was obvious that only Harry was expected. A very cold reception by their host as he answered the door made both of them know that the message they intended to convey had gotten across clearly.

After a momentary silence, the man stepped back from the door and waved both men into the suite. The door was closed behind them and the man asked Harry, "You think you need this kind of support?" To which Harry very calmly replied, "No doubt." It was obvious that this did not sit well with their host so Harry turned to Truman and said, "We're probably in the wrong room." and moved toward the door they had just entered. The host quickly recovered his composure and smiling broadly said, "No, you've got the right place, please come in and let me pour you a drink." He stepped aside and waved them forward into the room where three other men were seated in a comfortable grouping around a very ornate game table set to one end of the room. As Harry and Truman stepped forward past the man, Truman paused facing him and looked the man squarely in the eyes with as cold a stare as he could present. It was very clear that a no nonsense message had been conveyed.

Their host, somewhat shaken, moved ahead of them and stopping near the table, turned and matter-of-factly but with a slight nervousness, stated that the men seated at the table were anonymous experts and that his arriving guests were also nameless. Having laid down these simple rules, he quickly motioned Harry toward a chair that obviously had been awaiting his arrival. The host moved across the room to place another chair for Truman and was curtly told by Truman that he would stand. The implications of the statement were not lost on all the occupants of the room and a perceptible flexing of tensions was evident. Their host then sat down himself and poured Harry and Truman a drink and handed it them to them. Harry took his and sat down at the table placing the briefcase on his lap. Truman took the glass offered him and immediately set it aside.

Their host seemed to make a conscious attempt at friendliness. He explained to Harry that the men who were at the last meeting had entrusted him with the responsibility of ascertaining the quality of the merchandise in question and that he had arranged for the gentlemen present to assist in the evaluation process. He asked if this presented any problem and Harry replied with a friendly, "No, none whatsoever." At which point he simply opened the briefcase on his lap and placed it on the table and said, "Help your selves and let me know if I need to provide any clarification." He pushed his chair back from the table a ways, took a swallow of his drink and deliberately savoring the refreshing liquid, offered a warm smile. All the while Truman stood aloof and sharply alert. He made no move to touch the offered drink.

The men around the table gazed at the contents of the briefcase momentarily and then one of them reached into it and began to empty its contents onto the tabletop. After it was emptied, the case was closed and placed on the floor and with an air of certain self-confidence, the various items were examined and discussed among them. One of the men got up and went into another room and returned with two briefcases of his own and placing them on the floor, opened them and removed several items obviously brought for weighing, magnifying and analyzing the merchandise in question. Several notepads appeared on the table and copious notations were scribbled by all three of the experts. Discussions were held among the three and several questions were pointed at Harry concerning the length of time some of the materials had been held out of circulation. In hardly any time at all, the men came to the conclusion that the securities and bonds would have to be given further research but seemed to be authentic and negotiable. The dollar value would have to be determined after the research could be completed. A couple of weeks at least would be needed to make discrete inquiries in the proper places. The cash was totally acceptable and some of it could be valued above the face value as collector's items. The gold and silver seemed to be of a very high quality but would need more careful analysis before a dollar value could be accurately placed. The gemstones were of good quality, some superior, and could be valued in general terms tonight if it was needed on the spot. All agreed that it was a good idea to write down a value for future reference.

The few gold coins offered for examination roused considerable discussion among the three men and they expressed great interest in the quantity of such that were available. Harry looked at his host and stated that an inventory of their merchandise was known to the man and it was up to him as to whether to answer the question. With this unexpected responsibility being thrown into his court, the host thought for a full minute before replying. Finally he looked at the examiners and said, "We will deal with that later." It was obvious that the examiners were not complete insiders and not privy to full disclosure of the volume of the transactions being contemplated. Harry filed this bit of information away in the recesses of his memory for possible use later.

A few other questions were posed by the examination team to Harry and when he had exhausted their need to know, the host dismissed the three of them and asked Harry and Truman to remain for further discussion. Upon the departure of the examiners, their host asked Truman to please come and sit at the table with he and Harry. "After all Truman, haven't we been friends long enough for you to trust me?" he stated more than asked. Harry motioned for Truman to sit and turning to his host said, " Let's get a few things cleared up here. We both know that our association in the past has been a protected one and from our side at least, an honest and valued one. We also both know that there has never been any reason for us not to trust one another, mostly because the business we have conducted has always been on your terms and never along the lines of volume anywhere near as large as we are talking about here. We also both know that neither of us will be in this large of an exchange by ourselves. There are others on both sides who will remain completely unknown to either of us. That is a fact and I have no reason to want to know who is working with you and I will not allow you to have full knowledge of others working with me. Having said that, we also must both understand that the volume of this business can attract the attention of people who would kill us in a heart beat and think nothing of doing so. Particularly if it was thought that what we have to trade with could be taken from us without purchasing it.

It is not that we do not trust you, it is those whom you represent that we cannot trust and I know that you know full well that what I am saying is the Gospel Truth. For this reason, you need to never take personal offence at any action we may take. If we feel at any time that we or those we are working with, are being lied to or threatened in any way, the deal is off. There are others who will be glad to work with us. AM I MAKING MYSELF CLEAR? DO WE UNDERSTAND EACH OTHER?"

Their host sat very still during and after this statement for several minutes as if in deep thought. Clearing his throat he said, "You have spoken for both of us and yes, we do understand one another. Now lets get to the business at hand. I will need a couple of weeks to allow my people to put a value on your securities and bonds. The rest of the stuff can be exchanged anytime you want to do so. I can have an appraisal report from our examiners ready in a couple of days from the list you provided and we will make you a firm offer at that time if it meets with your approval. What I need to know is how much of this merchandise do you want to exchange at a time and how the exchange is to be made. Are you ready to talk in these terms?"

In response Harry said, "You meet us back here two days from now at the same time as tonight with your offer on everything but the securities and I will be ready with an answer from my people at that time. Agreed?" To which the hose said, "Agreed" and stuck out his hand for Harry to shake. "Now that that is settled, Truman let me pour you another drink. The last one I gave you is no longer cold and I want to catch up on what has been happening in your life."

Harry reached across and slapped Truman on the shoulder and said, "I think we can let our hair down a little and enjoy a drink together." After which about an hour was spent reminiscing in a very cordial exchange in which Truman let his host know that life had taken some hard turns but was now better than it had ever been. The session broke up very warmly and yet when the two brothers walked out the door and down the hall together, both of them knew that life was more dangerous at the present for them than it had ever been. The briefcase in Harry's hand could represent great success or total defeat.

Kenny, I am going to have to take some time away here to take care of some personal business and will be back to the story as soon as possible. Keep your attitude the way it is and I know God will be on your side. Better days are ahead my brother.

You are in our prayers,
Clifford

CHAPTER 24
SECURITY

Kenny,
   Things are beginning to allow me to free up enough time today to offer you a further look into our favorite villain's entanglement with organized crime. I hope it is not too difficult to pick up their trail. Let me see......Oh, yes, our boys have finished their late night hotel visit.

Two days later, at the agreed 10:00 P.M., Harry and Truman were again welcomed into the same hotel suite by their friendly host. Truman was once more in his bodyguard mode and Harry presenting himself as the representative of others as well as himself. Harry was somewhat surprised to find two strangers awaiting their arrival in the parlor. These men rose from their seats as the host ushered Harry and Truman into the room and faced them. No move was made to introduce them, and the host, seemingly a little nervous, spoke up, "Gentlemen, if it is agreeable with all of you, there will be no names used in this meeting. For everyone's welfare, it is best that we understand that all of us are representatives of people who are not present and who shall remain unknown. It is assumed that no effort will be made by either party to identify the absent partners in the business we have to conduct. Do I have your permission to proceed along that line?"

Harry did not answer audibly but simply nodded in agreement as did the other two strangers. A stiff handshake was exchanged and everyone except Truman sat down. The host turned to pour drinks for everyone at a bar and carried them to the table and turning to Truman, remarked, "I suppose you are still a te-totaler?" To which, Truman said, "For the duration." The host simply nodded his head and took a seat at the table around which the others were seated.

He reached inside his coat pocket and removed a packet of papers and laid them on the table. Looking at Harry, he handed him two sheets out of the packet and said, "I think this will be the best way for us to proceed, with your permission. Take as long as you need and look this offer over." Harry leaned forward and began to scan the material presented on the two pages. There seemed, to an observant Truman, to be an almost immediate flexing of Harry's jaw that many years of observance had taught him to recognize as severe agitation. The awareness of the condition invoked a heightened vigilance on Truman's part that went completely undetected by the other occupants of the room.

After several minutes of intense scrutiny, Harry looked up at his host and slowly at the other two men seated at the table and said, "Is this the best your people are willing to do?" There was no immediate response but the other three men looked at one another, apparently uncertain as to who should respond. Finally one of the strangers spoke up, "This does not seem fair to you?" he asked. Harry quickly tossed the papers on the table and sharply responded, "Absolutely unacceptable. If this is your only offer, we have nothing else to discuss."

At which point he pushed back from the table and got to his feet causing an obvious confusion among the three other men at the table.

As Harry stepped back away from the table, his host quickly shot a question in his direction, "Just what were you expecting? Do you have a counter proposal in mind?" To which Harry responded by reaching inside his coat pocket and removed a prepared set of papers representing what he would find acceptable and handed them to his host. "My people will consider nothing short of what is stated here." And after a brief moment, Harry asked, "Are you able to give us an answer or do you have to take this up with others?" Their host carefully looked at the papers and then passed them to the man next to him. Another few moments passed as the man very carefully inspected the figures and when he had satisfied himself, passed them to the last of the three for his appraisal. The third man took much longer to digest the information contained in Harry's proposal and after what seemed to Truman to be a good 20 minutes raised his gaze to his partners and shook his head negatively without uttering a single word.

Their host then turned to Harry and said, "Surely we can come to some kind of compromise here, we are willing to be as reasonable as possible but you must show some flexibility for us to get any further with this." Which brought from Harry a stern, "My people believe the offer is very generous and entirely reasonable seeing as how you have almost no risk involved here and we have invested years to see that you will have this kind of freedom. This makes the whole deal very different than most you will ever be faced with. I speak for all my people in saying this is the minimum we will consider. If it is too much for you, we will not be offended but we will exercise the right of ownership of the merchandise and graciously withdraw. No hard feelings." Seeing the darkness falling over the countenances of the three men, Harry added, "We will be in the city a couple of days yet and if you change your minds, you know how to reach us." With which he turned to Truman and walked past him to the door. Opening the door he watched as Truman backed out the door and then Harry turned on his heels and followed him out the door, closing it gently behind him.

Feeling a need to waste no time, the brothers went immediately to the boats and informed the slip owners that they would be departing within 48 hours and would be needing to place supplies aboard periodically over the next several hours. They left instructions that no one should be allowed to board the boats in their absence and if anyone should show up wishing to do so, they were to be notified immediately. Leaving two telephone numbers where they could be reached, they departed to begin preparations for leaving town.

In order to give the buyers an opportunity to change their mind, occupancy of the hotel rooms was maintained to allow for possible contact by telephone or a visit should someone deem that an option. In discussing the situation, both Harry and Truman were in agreement that the offer made by the buyers was totally unfair as they were being offered less than fifty cents on the dollar in the exchange. Both of them knew they could do better with others but felt that this situation might yet be redeemed. It was a matter of showing a firm resolve. But both of them were determined not to be taken advantage of. They would make it seem that there were others standing in line to take them up on their terms. They would give them the full two days and then head on down river to New Orleans.

What developed was a complete surprise to both of them. About three in the afternoon of the second day of waiting for a contact, the telephone rang in Harry's hotel room. The man on the phone gave no name but stated that he was one of the men who had examined the securities and bonds in the hotel room and asked if Harry would meet with him at a restaurant for an evening meal and a little business discussion. With some reservations, Harry agreed to do so and took down the name of the restaurant and time.

Discussing the possibilities, the brothers concluded that the man might be operating on his own, representing the group they had been dealing with or the whole thing might be a ruse to get their attention away from the boats for a search party looking for the funds. It was decided that Truman would go down and stay with the boats while Harry met with the man.

The evening meal turned out to be a very pleasant one at a very fashionable establishment where Harry found himself being offered an opportunity to meet with a new group of people who were interested only in the securities and bonds. The man explained that when he saw certain of the materials, he immediately recognized a value that would probably not be very well received by the men he was representing at the time of the examination. He further had this confirmed in an after meeting and since he now knew that the buyers whom Harry had been dealing with cared much more for the other merchandise, he saw another possibility. It was possibility for himself, and for Harry's people. He would draw a commission from his contacts and not from Harry.

He went on to share that he had certain contacts in South America whom he had taken the liberty to approach with information that these items were on the market. The things he was most interested in were the Peruvian and Bolivian Bonds taken from the Minden Bank. He explained that, in the right hands, in South America a very nice arrangement could be made. If Harry would meet with one representative in two weeks, he would personally guarantee a very attractive exchange on the face dollar for the bonds and a slightly less offer on the dollar for the other securities. He explained that he could do this because the bonds had increased in value over the years and in the right hands, a handsome profit was possible. Harry agreed to talk to the man in two weeks and said that he would give the man a telephone call stating where the meeting could take place in ten days. The man gave Harry a telephone number and said he was to ask to speak to "Tom" when he called. They parted with a sense of satisfaction warming Harry's heart and stomach.

Leaving the restaurant, Harry made his way to the boat slips and shared the evening's developments with Truman. All had been quiet on the boats but Truman decided to spend the rest of the night on board. Since everything was loaded and ready to cast off, Harry would check them out of the hotels in the morning and bring the women aboard and they would depart on the next day.

Slipping out on the river in the early hours of the morning the boats seemed to instinctively know to point their noses downstream. Truman took the lead and not wanting to waste any time, pushed his little engine to full throttle and the spirit of the tiny thing rose to the challenge of attempting to cover twenty miles a day for the next three days. It was a goal that they had set for themselves in trying to reach the cabin located on the bank of the Mississippi, sheltered and protected by the boundaries of the hunting lease reserved so many months ago. The task that lay ahead would be a daunting one. It was now very evident to the brothers that they could no longer risk keeping all the loot on the boats. Having faced the prospect of being discovered and realizing more clearly than ever before that they were very vulnerable, it was clear that alternate plans must be launched. The cabin now was seen as one of the wisest moves they had made in their planning. The reality of the danger they were in had hit them with earth shattering force. Others now knew what they had. There would be no more leisure till they managed to rid themselves of the burden. It was only a matter of time till someone figured out where the merchandise was stored. They had made a critical strategic miscalculation. Having thought that the offer from their old friend would be the only one they would ever need to consider, they had discounted the possibility of needing to go elsewhere. They cursed themselves for what they now saw as short sighted and stupid.

Arriving in the vicinity of the cabin according to plan, it was near dark when they anchored just outside the mouth of the stream they were going to navigate under cover of darkness. Taking the small boat, Harry swung into the current and explored the far reaches of the stream to make certain no one was there who would be able to report their position. He traveled all the distance up the small stream to where the dock and boathouses were located next to the cabin. Finding nothing out of the way, he quickly entered the cabin and found the keys to the boathouses, went back to the dock and opened the doors to receive the boats as they arrived. Hurrying back down the stream in the darkness, he reported that all was ready and both boats nudged their sluggish carcasses into the mouth of the stream and the little engines chugged mightily to slowly move away from the huge Mississippi.

Fighting the current of the stream proved to be almost an impossible task. Struggling and inching their way along, the two weary and underpowered vessels were eventually wedged into the safety of the boathouses as the sun began to rise in the east with an array of colors that could only gladden one's heart and lift spirits. Closing the doors and locking out any prying eyes, the foursome wearily trudged their way to the cabin, fell into bed and slept 10 hours.

Waking refreshed, the pains of starvation gripping all of them, they merrily prepared a feast of a country breakfast and began to feel greatly relieved to be alone and safe. Jangled nerves began to unwind and they began to assess their situation anew.

The cabin was equipped with a telephone and an old pickup truck, that was a part of the lease agreement, was checked out and found to be in excellent condition and full of gasoline. They had a few days to sort out their next moves carefully. Hours and hours were given to once more updating their situation and evaluating alternatives. One thing was certain. Most of the loot would be stored here on the lease somewhere. A search began in earnest to find the best places. Checking out the water well, it was discovered that it was only about twenty-five feet deep with a thirty-six inch curbing. The water depth inside the curbing was roughly seventeen feet, which left the surface of the water around eight feet below ground level. It was decided that they would remove most of the merchandise that would not be harmed by water from the boats, place it in bags and sink it to the bottom of the well. Truman attached grab ropes to each bag for use in fishing them out later. The electric pump would not be affected so no one would have reason to suspect this hiding place. This was done, leaving enough of the materials aboard one boat for one exchange in the future.

Most of the securities and cash were then hidden in three different locations on the lease. Again leaving enough on board the other boat to bargain with and to make at least one sizeable exchange when the right time came. It seemed that this would help remove the danger they had created for themselves. If someone were to find the riches stashed now on the boats and take it from them in some way, the loss would not be complete. This experience had taught them not to play their whole hand at any given time. The exposure rate had to be adjusted. A deep, unsettled feeling persisted and a gnawing sense of dread plagued both Truman and Harry. Had they set forces in motion that would rise up and destroy what had seemed to be such carefully laid plans? Both of them knew that the underworld of crime was filled with very resourceful people who were bound by no laws except self imposed ones. Once on the scent of easily gotten gain, these forces could be relentless.

Kenny, I will pause here and get back to you with another episode in a few days. Duty calls and I must answer.

Bless you,
Clifford

CHAPTER 25
NEW ORLEANS

Kenny,

The ten days had passed with unbelievable swiftness and Harry's hand shook as he dialed the number that had been given him to contact "Tom". A friendly female voice answered on the third ring and when Harry asked to speak to "Tom", a slight hesitation told him that a consideration was being made as to the proper response. "Tom is not available at the present, could I take a number and have him return your call?"

Recognizing immediately a ploy to get the number where he could be found, for a possible trace, Harry replied, "No, thank you but you may take a message for me. Please tell "Tom" that I will call again in one hour and if he is not available, there will be no further call." Having made this sound as firm as he could, given the situation, he hung up and marked the time.

Exactly one hour later, "Tom" answered the phone on the first ring. The man was apologetic immediately for not having been available earlier but Harry cut him short in a very stern tone and said, "One more try like that will scotch any further business we have with you. Do you understand?" Without hesitation, the man responded, "Yes". It was clear that both of them knew each other's minds very well. "Alright, let's do this right." Harry injected, "Are your people lined up?" To which "Tom" answered very positively, "Yes. How do you want this to play out?" Harry then went into a preplanned speech instructing "Tom" that he should arrive in New Orleans two days from now and check into a particular hotel under an assumed name, which he furnished. The reservation was already made in that name and he could expect to be contacted there by telephone at 8:00 P.M. He was to have with him, at that time one, and only one, of his partners along with full payment for the merchandise. The money was to be packaged according to a predetermined fashion, which he outlined. If this condition could be met with no hitches, the exchange would be made in a way that would be explained at that time. There was no room for error or negotiation. "Tom" quickly agreed and Harry hung up. Turning to Truman, he smiled broadly and said, "This just may work. At least we are in the drivers seat this time."

Two days later Truman and Harry arrived at the hotel early in the day, having driven down to New Orleans during the night in the old pickup truck from the hunting lease. They had made a stop along the way and stolen a set of license plates for temporary use. They had made the switch of plates at a roadside park and then driven on to the hotel. There they entered one of two rooms for which they had made reservations by phone along with the one to be used by "Tom" and his associate. Three suitcases were brought in and placed in the room containing the securities and bonds, which they had gotten all together from their respective hiding places on the boat and lease.

The plan was simple but should be effective. Harry would meet with the buyers in their room and examine the cash to be sure full payment was possible. As soon as this was sure, he would tell the buyers that the merchandise was at another location and that he would step out into the hall with one of them. Once in the hall, he would tell that person to go to the room two floors down where Truman was waiting and examine the bonds and securities. When he was satisfied that everything was in order, he would telephone the room in which Harry and the partner would be waiting and he would then confirm that the materials were in his possession and that he was in another room in the same hotel. The two buyers would remain on the telephone so that they could confirm no trickery. At that time Harry would walk out of the room with the cash and make his way to the third room where he would leave the cash and walk out the front door of the hotel. He would walk across the street and around a corner and enter a building across the street. He would make his way to a point inside the building that afforded a full view of the hotel. Five minutes later, Truman would leave the other room where the merchandise and buyer had remained. Truman would proceed to the third room where the cash was and wait. The two buyers could then proceed as they chose. It seemed a fool proof enough way to safeguard both parties. When Harry was certain that the buyers had left the hotel, he would telephone Truman to meet him at the pickup truck with the cash. They could then feel safe enough to make their retreat.

If the men they were meeting hesitated in any way, before the deal was completed, Harry would simply walk out and leave the hotel. He would call Truman from a place across the street and tell him to remain until Harry could be sure that the men had checked out and departed. He would then return and they would leave town with their merchandise still intact.

As it turned out, the plan went flawlessly. After telephoning the two men that he would arrive shortly, Harry entered the room of the buyers and found them to have the cash in a large suitcase. It was neatly stacked and wrapped in packets of used bills of various large denominations ranging from $20.00 to $100.00 each. Each packet had a hand printed label on it stating the total dollar amount in that particular packet. The suitcase was resting on a table and Harry picked it up and dumped the contents on the bed. He picked up several bundles and examined them quickly. He pulled up a chair and told one of the two men in the room to sit down at the table and write down, in columns, the figures he was going to call out to him. He proceeded to quickly replace the bundles in the suitcase, calling out the totaled numbers on each bundle. One of the men wrote these numbers down in columns until the money was all back in place and the suitcase closed.

Harry then sat down at the table and totaled up the columns of figures and observed that it was exactly correct. At which point he explained to the two men that he would have whichever one of them they chose to step out into the hallway with him where he would give the needed instructions for him to find and examine the merchandise. He would remain here in the room until the man could satisfy himself that all was in order. At which point, he was to use the telephone where the goods were and call the second buyer in the room where Harry and he would be waiting. If both were satisfied at that point, he would leave with the cash and the deal would be complete. This was discussed briefly by the two buyers and agreed to. From that point, every part of the deal unfolded just as planned.

After leaving the building and taking up his position across the street, Harry watched as the two men exited the hotel carrying the three suitcases of securities and bonds. They went directly to a car and drove away. Harry waited almost an hour at his post to see if there was any need to be alarmed or if anything suspicious took place. Satisfied that all was well, he called the room where Truman was waiting and told him to come down and meet him at the pickup truck. Harry walked across the street and got in the truck, started the engine and when Truman arrived, slipped out into the traffic and drove an erratic course through the city and out into the suburbs until he was certain they were not being followed. They then proceeded to the cabin out in the country where they changed the license plates back and threw the stolen ones in the stream near the boathouses. A celebration was in order. They had now disposed of the most difficult commodities and the rest should be much easier.

In the meantime, the suitcase filled with cash was going to need to be hidden away until they could return to Baton Rouge to pick up the completed set of new identities for the four of them. When they were in their new roles, they could then arrange several bank accounts and deposit the funds and begin to make plans to travel abroad. This would take several weeks yet and they still had to work on the rest of the contraband being transferred to ready cash.

The developing plan was to put the boats back on the Mississippi and complete the journey to New Orleans. Since they had removed all the securities and bonds from the one boat, it was decided that they would lift some of the gold, silver, coins and jewels from the well and place about one third of it in the hull of one of the boats. What they considered the most dangerous and difficult to dispose of in the old cash would be placed in the other boat. This amounted to about one half of the total of the cash. They decided that if they were in some way robbed of one or the other contents of the boats, they could live without it.

So, now buoyed up by the successful transaction with the bonds and securities, and several days of rest and relaxation, the boats were swung back into the current of the Mississippi and headed toward New Orleans under cover of dark. They had called ahead to be sure that their leased boat slips were open and ready to receive them and found everything as planned.

Two contacts had been made by Harry with prospective buyers. One of them was a resident of New Orleans with whom he had done business many years ago. The other was a banker from Florida who would meet with them in New Orleans. This second man was a person who had been recommended by one of Harry's prison mates several years ago. It was reported that the man could give the best exchange because he was in the banking business and could very easily put the stolen cash into circulation anywhere in the world.

Upon arriving at the marina where the boats were docked and plugged up to electrical outlets, it was decided that they would live aboard the boats for a while and conduct business from a rented room just a short walk from the marina. Their arrival in New Orleans was duly noted by the press and they were wined and dined for several days by this and that group. A full page of coverage was given to their voyage by a local paper including photos of the group with their boats. It was obvious that it might be difficult to get the goods off the boats safely for some time due to the constant attention of so many of the residents of New Orleans. They would have to be patient.

Three busy days of involvement with the public left the whole group a little edgy and wanting to avoid some of the attention but there seemed to be no way. They would just have to wait till things settled down before they began to conduct business. Early on the fourth day of their residency in New Orleans, Harry decided to call on his old business associate who owned and operated a jewelry store in the downtown area. He casually walked into the store and asked to see the owner and was ushered to a second story office area of the business and was immediately recognized by the man. A considerable part of the morning was given to visiting and at noon, a meal was shared together. It was during the meal that Harry began to feel comfortable enough with what he had learned about the man's current situation that he broached the subject on his mind, the selling of gemstones.

The man was very interested and asked if he could see some of the stones and whether they had been evaluated and appraised. Harry shared that he himself had become somewhat proficient in this area and had placed them in graded groupings. He explained that he had another expert to examine a sampling of the stones and that the two estimates of value were very close. He did allow that the man had a right to examine them and that it could be arranged for him to do so. At which juncture, Harry reached into his pocket and passed a cigarette package sized jeweled box across the table for the man to examine saying, "You don't want to open that here in the restaurant but when you get back to your office, take a look at what is there. I think you will find it interesting and you will also find a paper with my appraisal stated. I will drop by tomorrow and we will discuss the matter if you are still interested. I would want you to know that I represent a group of people who have vested interests in the merchandise and will have to consult with them on any final transactions that we might make. But to show my good faith, I am trusting these samples into your care for the time being, if you are in agreement so far, that is." The man smiled and said he would look forward to a visit tomorrow and the two of them left the restaurant and went their separate ways.

Harry had decided to take the approach that he did for a couple of reasons. One was that he was no longer afraid of losing the whole inventory and secondly, he wanted the man to think that it would be too dangerous for him to attempt to cheat him. He wanted to demonstrate such confidence that the man would have to respect and give much credence to Harry's abilities.

Apparently the plan was working for when the visit was made the next day to the man's office, Harry was ushered into the man's office and the man gave orders to a male clerk that he was not to be disturbed till further notice. A broad smile lit the face of the man as he sat down and invited Harry to a comfortable chair as well. "This is a very impressive sampling you have left with me, my friend." The man said as he reached into a desk drawer and placed the little box on the desk. "I am impressed with not only the quality of the merchandise but with your ability as an appraiser as well. We are very close in the estimations you have furnished, if anything, you have been a bit conservative, I would say." To which Harry replied, "That is a welcome bit of information. Does that indicate that we could do some business together?" "I would certainly be open to doing so." Came the reply. This exchange brought about a lengthy discussion as to prices and quantities to be traded. Harry did not wish to give away too much information so he told the man that he would trade with him in several installments that would allow both of them latitude and opportunity to avoid unnecessary attention to be drawn from unwanted sources. This seemed to please the potential buyer and he agreed to pay Harry for the samples on the desk now, cash of course, and would be glad to process whatever else he might care to bring to him.

Another drawer of the desk was opened and the man produced a cash box and counted out the agreed sum with a jovial grin on his face. Harry pocketed the cash and bid the man good day with a promise to see him again in a day of two.

Arriving back at the boats, Harry came aboard and pitched the cash on a table in front of a seated Truman and said, "This is the way to do this. We should be able to wrap this up in a few days if the cash trades can be carried off as smoothly." That was not to be the case however.

Kenny, I will need to take a few days away so don't be alarmed if I don't contact you. I will get back to our story as soon as time will allow.

We are praying for you and Jackie,
Clifford

CHAPTER 26
FORTUNE SMILES AND FROWNS

Kenny,

The life of a pastor is never his own and I am very weary in attempting to deal with some very sticky and heartbreaking conditions in the lives of some of our people at the present. Perhaps I can turn my mind off for a while and share more of our story with you. I must admit that I find the writing of the adventurous story of Truman to be beneficial in helping me refresh my energy level. A session here seems to allow me to clear my mind and heart of the constant weight of ministry.

It is dangerously tempting at times to allow myself too little personal leeway to refresh my own soul. God knows my heart and the knowledge of that is indeed a wonderful source of encouragement. I suspect that He has been working in the background to bring me to these exchanges with you. It is so like Him to see that our needs are met in spite of our own willfulness in draining our batteries down to the red levels.

I appreciate your prayers and friendship and hope that these little episodes are a respite from the daily pressures you face as they are for me.

Enough of that, on with the story:

Two days later Harry walked into the jeweler's business and asked to see the owner. He was told that the owner was not in and would not be back for three days. Some emergency had arisen that demanded his presence out of town but he had left word to tell Harry to come back in three or four days. Harry thought nothing of this and proceeded to return to the boats and inform Truman.

Perhaps it was just as well for the time had come for their banker from Florida to arrive and so Harry prepared a sample of the old cash to present to the man and went to the rented room to await a call from the banker. As it happened, the wait was less than four hours. The phone rang and the man informed Harry he was in town and would be staying at a hotel down in the French Quarters. He would be available for a meal together at a favorite club in the Quarters and invited both Truman and the wives to join him at 9:00 P.M.. The invitation was accepted.

A very enjoyable evening was spent together that lasted well into the wee hours of the morning. During the course of the outing, many people recognized the brothers from all the recent news coverage. They were toasted by several reporters and their photos would appear in the paper the next day along with the banker. As they were leaving the club, the banker asked Harry if he might not meet with him the next day at 2 P.M. in the hotel bar where he was staying. Harry agreed.

The meeting at the bar was friendly as they met in a semi-private corner and Harry spoke very confidently to the man about having considerable business to conduct with him. He shared that he was a part of a group of people who had in their possession a rather sizeable sum of old cash that would best be spent in another part of the world. The group would be willing to trade the cash for currently circulating currency at a very good rate of exchange. He reached in his coat pocket and handed the banker a gift wrapped box and told him he should open it later and examine the samples enclosed as typical of what they had to offer. If he was interested and a favorable rate was available, there could be three exchanges over a period of 30 days possible. He would expect a telephone call from the man tomorrow afternoon at 4 P.M. with what he hoped would be a pleasant response. Shortly afterward they took leave of one another and both exited the bar in different directions.

Harry was in the rented room waiting for the call from his banker friend the next afternoon, but 4 P.M. came and went and the phone did not ring. Harry began to wonder if he had communicated clearly as to the proper time and so he waited for three hours before deducing that something was amiss. Had the man changed his mind or had something detained him. Harry decided to ring the man's hotel room and in doing so, he was told that the man had checked out. No messages were left at the desk. Alarmed, Harry went immediately to the boats and gave the information to Truman and they sat and discussed the possibilities. Should they be alarmed? Was this some quirk of fate or was there something sinister to be seen in what had developed? What should they do? Wait? Run? They could not decide. Finally they decided to wait till the jeweler returned and see if the banker contacted them in the meantime. A state of great care was to be exercised till they knew what was happening.

No word came from their banker and at the end of the fourth day of the absence of the jeweler, Harry returned to the shop to attempt to see him again. He was in and would see Harry a clerk said. "Please go on up to the office. He was expecting him".

Harry cautiously mounted the stairs and was shown into the jeweler's office where the man was seated behind his desk. He motioned Harry to a seat and it was evident that he was not in a jovial mood. The man was struggling to say something after a few pleasantries were passed and finally blurted out, "Harry, I can't do any further business with you. You need to know that you are in great danger. I would suggest that you disappear as quickly as possible for your own good. I wish I could tell you more but I cannot. Just take my word and leave New Orleans as rapidly as you can."

Harry's mind was spinning. He tried to get the man to be more forthcoming but was met by a stone wall. It was clear that something had really gotten out of hand. After realizing that he would get no further information from the man, Harry thanked him and said he would consider his advice and left the store.

Moving quickly to the boats, he informed Truman of what had happened and they sat and tried to make sense of the events. It was obvious that the jeweler was very frightened. It would be stupid to ignore that the banker probably was tied to this mystery in some way as well. The only thing that could possibly have happened is that some outside source had interfered with the business at hand. The logical question was what force, who could be influencing these men? The only answer had to be that the men from Baton Rouge and points north were behind it. If that were so, then they would either contact them for another offer or were planning to take the merchandise from them. What should they do?

Harry decided to attempt to contact the banker in Florida by telephone. He got through to the man and was told that circumstances had arisen that made it impossible for the two of them to conduct any further business and that the sample Harry had given him would be returned if he ever was able to visit him in Florida. No, he could not explain the reasons for his actions but wished Harry great success with his business and said a very revealing thing, "You need to choose carefully how you conduct business in the near future". With this, he hung up.

Harry and Truman felt certain their old friend from Indiana could answer the riddle but were not yet ready to confront him. They needed time to consider their future actions. A decision was made to go back to the cabin on the lease and give the thing time to cool off. It seemed the only safe refuge available at the moment.

Truman had been engaged in an attempt to sell the boats and had found a buyer for one. It was decided that they would conclude the sale, transfer all the loot on to the other boat, purchase a more powerful motor for the remaining boat and head back upriver. This took two more days to accomplish and they were off and gliding over the water with ease of motion but greatly weighted hearts and troubled minds.

Again, they wanted to enter the stream that would take them to the cabin after dark for sake of trying to keep their location a secret, so they anchored the boat a few miles past the stream in the late evening. By going past the mouth of the stream, they hoped to scrutinize the area and determine if there could be anyone watching for them. They also thought that when they returned after dark, no one would be expecting them to double back downstream. They were beginning to be paranoid about being observed by some enemy yet unidentified. There was always much traffic on the Mississippi and who could tell if the occupants of some of those boats might not be watching their every move.

Reaching the cabin after midnight with no sign detected of the presence of any other humans, they were feeling no small relief. Deciding to sleep and discuss the matter on the following day, they all went off to bed.

Rising early and walking over a rather wide area of the

grounds, Harry and Truman shared their thoughts as they watched for any sign that anyone had been there in their absence. They retraced their whole experience since reaching Baton Rouge earlier in an attempt to discover clues that could shed light on what had gone wrong and who would be able to know of their movements.

It was obvious that the man with whom they had traded the bonds and securities could still be connected in some way with the others they had dealt with in Baton Rouge. For all they knew he may have been sent by them. They did not know the identity of the supposed South American dealer they had met in the exchange. He also could have been a part of the Baton Rouge group. If this were true, then it could have been possible for them to have been followed to the cabin after that exchange but both men thought that a very unlikely thing. They had checked closely for a tail and were reasonably sure there had been none.

It was certainly no secret that they were in New Orleans. With the news coverage, anybody almost anywhere could have read of their arrival there. It would have been very easy for them to be watched by most anyone while in New Orleans. It seemed most likely that the Baton Rouge people were doing just that and had observed their involvement with both the jeweler and the banker. One thing was certain, if Harry and Truman knew these two men to be buyers of stolen merchandise, others would know the same thing. In which case, it did not take a great leap of imagination to see that the larger organization they had crossed swords with in Baton Rouge could send emissaries to rebuff the men from doing business with Harry and Truman. In point of fact, it would be just like them to threaten others off in order to keep the business possibilities closed for the brothers.

They felt that if they simply waited, then whoever was behind their misfortune, would eventually show their hand and approach them. The Million Dollar question was, "when, where and how would they surface"? It would happen sooner or later. The larger issue was, "What should they do in the meantime? Stay put and wait it out or take the initiative and try to regain some kind of control of the situation?" If someone wanted to find them, and had the resources, they would eventually be found. Both of them agreed on this. They knew that it was entirely possible that they had been observed as they came back to the cabin from New Orleans on the boat and should take some kind of preventative action to safeguard their position. But what could they do out here? For that matter, what could they do anywhere? They really had no one to help them and if the people they were up against were to know that, then they were in an untenable position.

One decision was made. The wives needed to be out of harms way. Both of them were beginning to show signs of cracking up under the strain so they would be sent away to safety. Sylvia could be sent back to Terre Haute and Lillian could be sent to some of her folks. A discussion was held as to the possibility of sending them overseas somewhere till this mess could be sorted out but both women refused to agree to that possibility. If they were going anywhere, the first choice was the only choice. So, it was settled, they would put them on buses immediately. Bags were packed and they were driven to New Iberia by Truman to catch busses to Houston and planes from there. Both were given enough cash to keep them living well till the men could get everything organized for overseas travel. They were cautioned not to draw attention to themselves by spending unnecessarily. When things were settled, the men would contact the wives. Just sit tight.

After spending several days sorting out a plan, Harry and Truman decided to get out of the country for a couple of years and establish themselves somewhere in the new identities that were awaiting them in Baton Rouge. The major portion of the merchandise was taken off the boat once more and replaced in the hiding places on the lease. Most of the metal and jewels were placed back in the well and most of the old cash was reburied with the rest of it. They would take the boat to Baton Rouge and sell it and pick up their new identification papers from the forgers. They planned then to come back to the cabin in a rented automobile, spend whatever time was necessary to satisfy themselves that the bulk of their wealth was well hidden and out of danger of discovery till they could return in a couple of years to reclaim it. By that time, it was felt that they could again try to dispose of it permanently in a safer environment. The lease would be extended for a couple of years on the place and sub-leased by their agent. Perhaps a totally new means of disposing of the materials could be found in another country.

They would use the cash they had put together thus far to accomplish this. Harry wanted to take some of the old cash with them and put it in a safe deposit box in a bank in Baton Rouge to be used in case of some unforeseen emergency. The cash they had gotten for the securities and bonds would finance them for several years if necessary so they would establish several bank accounts before leaving the country with that money. The new identities should make this a simple enough thing to accomplish and if necessary, they could place a sizeable portion of it in safety deposit boxes as well.

Realizing that they could be contacted again by the group in Baton Rouge while there, they decided to force a conclusion to that matter by not waiting for such a contact. They would contact their old friend from Lafayette, Indiana and tell him the goods had been disposed of and that if they should ever need to do business with him again, they would insist that any future transaction involve only him and not his organized friends. They would apologize for any inconvenience they may have caused him and offer to cover any expenses he had incurred in dealing with them. It might get them off their backs long enough to disappear overseas.

With a full set of new plans worked out, they boarded the boat in the middle of the night and headed for Baton Rouge.

Kenny, a close is a must here. I will get back to you once again as soon as possible. I will be away for a few days. Death has visited us. Pray for us.

Clifford

CHAPTER 27
BATON ROUGE FEAR

Kenny,
Sorry for the long delay, some lovely people have suffered the visit of the death angel and a very deep pit had to be bridged. God has been victorious. Hope has sustained us once more. Praise our Lord with me.

Returning to our adventure with Truman:

The proprietor of the boat slip in Baton Rouge was glad to see the returning masters of the Mississippi but expressed disappointment when he learned that they had sold one of the boats. The subject led Harry to tell him that he would like to sell the remaining vessel as well and offered him a commission if he would place the boat in dry dock on his property and sell it for him. The man agreed but wanted to leave it in the water for a couple of weeks to see if advertisements would bring a buyer in short order and make it unnecessary to take it out of the water. Harry and Truman agreed and after clearing out all of their personal belongings, turned the vessel over to the man. Harry told him they would be in town for a few days probably and that he would see him before leaving with final instructions. He would arrange for the proceeds of the sale to be deposited in a bank in case he was unavailable when needed.

Checking into a hotel, and wasting no time, Harry promptly called a cab and went to see the people who were manufacturing the new identification papers for the four

Mahoneys. The documents were complete, including bright, new passports, driver's licenses, social security cards, birth certificates and even insurance policies and membership cards for several organizations recognized worldwide and credit cards. The costs were extremely high it seemed to Truman but Harry told him it was worth that and much more. Using these documents, they had a door opened to a complete new start in life.

The remainder of their business in the city included opening a bank account in the new name for Harry and renting a safety deposit box. In the box he placed the old cash he had brought along, a box of diamonds and a selection of gold coins chosen carefully by Harry that could be here in case of future needs. He deposited $5,000.00 in the new account and spoke to an officer of the bank explaining that he would be conducting some business from several foreign countries and wanted to be able to use this account in doing so. He wanted the man to inform him of any difficulties that he might encounter and the means to overcome them. The man was very helpful and acquainted Harry and Truman both with various means of transferring funds between sovereign nations. If they encountered difficulties other than he had covered with them, he advised them as to where to go for help. They left fully armed with the knowledge to deal with other banks where they planned to also open accounts in several different cities.

The second item to be covered was the telephone call to their old friend in Indiana. This they put off until the last day of their stay in Baton Rouge. Having rented a car and with everything else accomplished, Harry nervously dialed the number in Lafayette. He was surprised to be able to connect with the man on the first call and was also surprised that the man was seemingly cordial. Harry spoke of his disappointment that they had not been able to come to terms in the business they had attempted and assured the man that he had no hard feelings about it. He then explained to the man that they had been able to locate a favorable exchange rate and concluded the business deal. He indicated to the man that he could be traveling to Terre Haute before too long and would look forward to perhaps a continued business relationship.

His old friend expressed no bitterness and said he would welcome any future opportunity to work with either Harry or Truman. He encouraged them to keep in touch as needed. The conversation seemed perfectly normal in every way to Harry and he almost began to wish he had not suspected the man of duplicity. He turned to Truman and said, "I sure hope we are wrong about him."

Driving back toward the cabin on the hunting lease, they repeatedly made evasive detours to try and determine whether they were being followed and were never able to spot anything that would lead them to believe a tail was attached. They were less and less sure of the proper diagnosis of their predicament.

A definite plan was firmly in place as they drove onto the lease. They would not unpack a thing. The suitcase containing the cash from the bond and securities sale would be retrieved and they would turn right around and head for Houston, Texas. Once there they would begin to open bank accounts from which they could draw funds from other countries. Accounts were planned for both brothers and would be funded equally from the suitcase. Once finished in Houston, they intended to fly to California and repeat the process there. Duplicating the process in San Francisco, they planned to fly to New York City and finish off the balance of the funds from the suitcase with accounts opened there. From New York they planned to fly back to Houston, pick up another rented car and drive back to the cabin.

Once back at the cabin, they would spend whatever time was needed to secure the remaining merchandise in permanent hiding places till their eventual return. They even discussed the possibility of returning the materials to the tomb that they still owned but chose instead to leave it on the lease. They intended to purchase a couple of heavy plastic barrels with lids that could be sealed to use in burying the merchandise on the way out to the lease.

After all this was finished, they would contact Lillian and Sylvia and arrange for them to meet them in New York. All would then depart for Ireland on the first leg of a two-year journey in search of the perfect permanent home.

Sticking to the plan, they hurriedly drove onto the lease and wasting no time, went straight to the suitcase. It had been secured behind a hidden panel constructed in the bottom of a storage bin in the tack room of the barn. They loaded it in the trunk of the car and drove directly away toward Houston. All went as planned. The trip to Houston was not a long one but they were both tired and decided to stop over in Beaumont, Texas and rest a couple of days before moving on to the task. The weather was beautiful and they enjoyed a couple of days of relaxation then drove on to Houston.

Checking into a motel in Houston, they removed all of the luggage from the car, including the suitcase filled with cash. Houston had been chosen because of the international trade that the area was known for as was San Francisco and New York. If they were setting up bank accounts to be used internationally, they would be less likely to draw any undue attention and if they needed to return for some reason, the airports handled direct international flights to almost anywhere in the world with no difficulty.

So after some research and selecting the banks they would

use, they sat down and opened the suitcase containing the cash with the intention of removing the funds to be deposited in each bank. Stacking the desired amount on the bed beside the opened suitcase Truman proceeded to open a bundle, which would be recounted and relabeled before going to the banks. He was counting out the bills onto the tabletop beside the bed when he was struck by some sense of irregularity and stopped counting and looked closely at the bills. He decided that what had caught his attention was a sense of difference in the feel of some of the bills. Looking closer, he could not see anything different about the bills but was not satisfied so he called to Harry who was in the bathroom shaving.

Harry came into the room and Truman explained what he had felt. Sitting down across the table from Truman, Harry began to examine the bills for himself. Immediately he felt a sinking in his stomach as he thought he recognized some counterfeit bills. Getting up and pulling a lampshade to the side so as to give the best light possible, he re-examined the bills and knew that they were not the same. Sorting out several that seemed irregular, he compared the serial numbers and knew he was looking at bogus money. The numbers were the same. Fear flooded over both of them as they looked at one another in disbelief. There was nothing to do but examine the whole lot of cash and the result revealed that they had been professionally taken for a ride.

Every individual bundle of cash in the suitcase was carefully constructed to appear completely legitimate and legal tender. The first two bills on each side and two in the interior were perfectly good currency but the rest of the bundle contained counterfeits that had been put through some process to wrinkle them just enough to give the appearance of circulated money. How could Harry have been tricked so easily? As he thought about it, he knew it was because he was occupied too much with the other details of the exchange. He knew that this was exactly what the buyers were counting on to fool him. Anger rose up where fear had been and he began to shake in rage, getting up he fell across the bed in full realization of what had happened to them. How could he have fallen for such a simple fraud? But he had.

Taking time to carefully go through the entire suitcase of cash, the brothers saw that they had traded the bonds and securities for only twelve thousand actual dollars. The rest was worthless. They discussed what to do with it. Could it be sold? Neither of them had ever had any experience with counterfeiting but they both knew men who had. They decided to make a couple of inquiries and see if they could find a market for the bills here in Houston.

After meeting with three different people, they found a man whom they had done prison time with who said he would take the whole lot off their hands for $10,000.00. This was better than burning it or getting caught with it, so they sold it to him and left Houston the same day.

The plans were not going exactly right. After considering several options, a bank account for each of them had been opened in the city and $10,000.00 placed in each account. The only thing they could do now was return to the cabin on the lease and regroup. As they drove, they went over and over the details of all the mistakes they had made and came to the conclusion that there was no way they could have done better, all things considered. They had gone up against people who were very accomplished swindlers. They had been woefully unprepared and had gotten a very expensive education in reality. They were just plain old bank robbers. This brand of larceny was out of their league.

The drive from Houston brought them to the cabin in the middle of the night and the two of them went to bed but lay awake most of the night. After a long breakfast, they began to try and decide where to go from here. If there were people who were trying to control them, as seemed to be the case when they left New Orleans, why had they not been contacted in some way? As they reflected on their movements since leaving New Orleans, there was nothing to suggest any further effort on the part of anyone to interfere with their activities in any way. What were they to make of it? It was totally baffling.

There seemed to be nothing left to do but attempt to find a market for at least part of the loot. What part made the most sense? Reason told them that the cash could be spent in small amounts as long as it was done at great distances separating each place where an exchange took place. They could feasibly even take a lot of it across the border to Canada and bank some of it using their new identities. This being so, it was most obvious that the metal and gems needed to be exchanged first. The experience with the jeweler in New Orleans had shown them that it was possible to accomplish this in small amounts rather easily. Experience was teaching them to move much more cautiously so they decided to take about one fourth of the gemstones and head to the western states where they had some contacts to begin with. While there, they could open the planned bank accounts with the proceeds of the sales. This decided, Truman went to the well and began to fish the bags out.

The device they had constructed to accomplish this task had been easy to make. It was constructed of half-inch pipe that could be screwed together to reach the bottom of the well with a hook connected to the bottom end. All they had to do was run the pipe down to the sacks and hook onto the rope loops attached for lifting them to the surface. It was simple. When Truman got the pipe to the bottom, he fished around for the ropes but could not locate them. Becoming panicky, he swung the hook around and around in the bottom of the well and could not get it to hook onto anything. Sinking to his knees, he called out to Harry with such panic that he came running to his side. "What's the matter?" he stammered. "I can't find anything to hook on to down there. Something is wrong. You try it." Harry took the pipe and made several attempts to hook the bags. It was obvious that there was nothing down there to hook.

The realization washed over them that they had been robbed again. The thought brought sudden knowledge that someone might be here with them and it seemed to dawn on both of them at the same time. Dropping the pipe, they both jumped up and ran to the house to get their guns. Storming out of the house armed and at the ready, they began a systematic search of the premises. Nothing was turned up except for the ruts left by some vehicle with tire markings different from the car they were driving and different from the pickup tires. No doubt about it someone had paid them a visit while they were gone.

They sat down and tried to make sense of it. No one knew what was in the well but the two of them and their wives. Could it be possible that they had been betrayed by their own wives, or one of the two? As impossible as that seemed, they had to face the possibility. If this was so, then the other cash buried here might be gone as well. They had to know, so off they went to the three locations where the cash was buried. Arriving at the first location answered the question. An empty hole was all that was left. Further exploration found the same to be true for all the loot. It was all gone. Two totally defeated men slowly walked back to the cabin. Neither of them could utter a single word for over an hour. The silence was finally broken as Truman walked over to Harry and put both hands on his shoulders and looked him squarely in the eyes and said, "Have you ever heard the saying, crime does not pay? I think we are in the wrong profession."

What could be done? Nothing. They could only try to determine if the wives had anything to do with all this. They went immediately into the cabin and called Terre Haute first to see if Sylvia was there. She was not. She had been there but had only stayed two days. No one knew where she was at the present time. The next call was to Lillian's relatives but there was no longer a phone listed for them. They did not know how to contact anyone close enough to find out where she was. This left all sorts of possibilities open.

It was possible that either or both of the women had been kidnapped and forced to talk or even brought back to the cabin to show where the valuables were hidden. It was also possible that Harry and Truman had been followed and a surveillance of some type set up that observed where they had placed the merchandise. This seemed most likely to the brothers.

If the wives were involved and still alive, it was possible that they could track down the persons responsible and get some kind of satisfaction but Truman had completely lost heart and it was obvious to him that Harry was about beaten himself.

Well Kenny, I must shut it off here and return at a more convenient time. Till then, may the Lord watch over you.

Clifford

CHAPTER 28
MYSTERY

Kenny,
We are back and ready to roll with the narration of Truman's saga, so let us begin.

It now seemed pointless, but the Mahoney's were a resilient breed of mankind and after failing to find anything whatsoever in the way of a lead as to who took their goods, they returned to Baton Rouge. The two of them looked up the original contact they had made in the first attempt to do business with their friend from Indianapolis. Harry had a plan developing. He would first locate this contact and then secretly observe him, looking for any evidence that might be apparent in demonstrating that he had anything to do with the theft of their fortune. If there was the slightest reason to believe that this was so, they would capture the man and beat the truth out of him as to who else was involved. From there they would follow the trail to the head of this snake of a plot. Once they found him, they would force payment for the goods. He could not let it drop without doing everything possible.

While they were involved in a covert watch over their target, Truman continued to turn every stone he could in finding Sylvia and Lillian. The efforts paid off in that he did determine that Lillian was reported by a cousin to have been at her brother's home for some time. Sylvia remained a mystery. Repeated efforts failed to locate her. He did learn that two days after arriving in Terre Haute, she seemed to have vanished without a trace. She had received a telephone call from someone and agreed to meet whoever it was for an evening meal. She never returned.

They spent several days watching the people connected with the contacts they had in Baton Rouge to no avail. It occurred to them that the jeweler in New Orleans might give them some place to begin in their search so both of them made a trip there in an attempt to talk with him. When they went to the jewelry store, they were told that the owner was gone and would not return for a month. He was on a buying trip to Amsterdam in Holland and would be in contact with the store periodically during the trip. They left a message with the manager at the store to be relayed to the man when he called. The message consisted of a request for a telephone number where he could be reached. Harry told the manager that he would call the store in a few days to see if the owner had left a number for him.

The next step that seemed logical was to attempt to get further information from the banker in Florida. Rather than travel to Florida, they decided to try a telephone call. After several attempts, they were able to get the man to talk to them but he was not of any real help. He was very reluctant to discuss the matter over the phone and in cryptic language, let them know that his life would be in danger if he tried to help them. He did indicate that he had been threatened by unknown individuals. Two of them had inflicted a rather painful physical warning to leave town and conduct no business with the Mahoneys in New Orleans. This he had done and wanted to have no further involvement, period. It was too dangerous. They could reclaim their sample merchandise at his bank in Florida at their convenience.

All this information seemed to implicate the Baton Rouge connections most possibly. Armed with this information, Harry and Truman returned to Baton Rouge and decided to confront the only contact that they could identify, the original person they had approached in the matter there. Upon arrival, they went to the man's home address and were terrified to see several police cars in the driveway and parked on the street in front of the man's house. They drove on past and went to their hotel room to see if they could make sense of what they had observed.

Listening to the radio for any kind of news, they heard a report of a shooting death in a residential area that was under investigation by the police. No details were available at present but further developments would be reported as they came in. With no alternative left, they sat by the radio and waited for any news. After several hours, they learned that the man they wanted to question was now dead. He had been murdered by gunshot to the back of his head while his hands were bound behind him. Both Harry and Truman knew that this was an execution to prevent their talking to the man and was probably meant as a warning for them to back off. Neither of them took it lightly.

The next move seemed to be dictated by the information they had. The one avenue of contact available in the area was "Tom" to whom they had sold the bonds and securities. They still had the telephone number at which they had contacted him. Knowing it was futile before trying, Harry dialed the number anyway. Sure enough, it was disconnected.

This left no further leads to follow in Baton Rouge so they turned their attention to the next most likely source of information, Sylvia. Where was Sylvia? Truman made another attempt at locating her by telephone, to no avail. It was decided that they would go to Terre Haute and try to trace her from there, so they purchased a car and headed north. Dissecting their situation, magnifying every detail for evidence, following every line of thought that came to light for hours as they traveled toward Terre Haute. Truman was certain that they themselves would be in mortal danger in continuing to search for the people responsible for their newfound poverty. They needed to be on constant vigilant guard. They would need to work together and watch each other's back.

Sylvia's folks were at their wits end with worry over what had become of her. Truman did what he could to comfort them but every effort to locate her produced only dead ends. Eventually a reluctant decision was made by her folks and Truman to contact the police and file a missing person report. Her people had no knowledge of what Truman and Harry had been engaged in for the past several months but did know of their criminal background. They understood Truman's reluctance to involve himself with the police for any reason but his worry finally won out over his fear and the report was filed.

Two days after the report was filed, a call came that a woman matching Sylvia's description had been located in a hospital in Lake Charles, Louisiana. The woman was unconscious and had been found by the roadside in a state near death. A bulletin had been issued by the police in Lake Charles that had found its way to the State Police in Indiana and when the description of Sylvia was seen to resemble the one on the bulletin, the Terre Haute Police were notified. It was not certain that this woman was Sylvia and there was no photograph available. The only way to know for sure would be for some of the family to go to Lake Charles and identify her. If there were any identifying marks borne by Sylvia that could be matched in an attempt to clarify whether it was she, a call to the hospital might be made to rule it out.

A telephone call was made to the hospital and when the situation was explained that the lady could possibly be Sylvia, both Truman and her folks gave the hospital officials a description of three marks on Sylvia's body that were matched on the lady in question. It was almost certainly Sylvia. Truman and her folks left immediately for Lake Charles. Harry remained behind in Terre Haute.

Truman had driven like a madman but still did not arrive until the next day after over 17 hours on the road. Worn out but running on adrenalin, Truman was shocked to the core by the condition he found Sylvia in. She had apparently been beaten and tortured and left for dead on the side of the road several miles out of Lake Charles to the south. She was naked when found and no items of clothing or anything else was recovered from the scene. Her fingerprints had been taken but no matches had been found in police files.

A doctor sat the family down and explained that he did not know if she would live or die. She had a cracked skull and several broken bones. Her brain was swollen and if she lived, she could possibly be brain damaged. Only time would tell. She would almost certainly be scarred from the burn injuries on her body. It appeared that cigarettes had been held against her bare flesh in many places. She had not regained consciousness since arrival at the hospital. Did the family know that she was pregnant? The question took a minute to soak in for Truman but when it did, he almost passed out. He had to have help from the doctor and a nurse to maintain consciousness himself.

The doctor stated that Sylvia was probably about three months along in the pregnancy and the child seemed to be alright for the time being. He could not vouch for the future. He could say that she had been raped.

The local police sent an inspector to the hospital to meet with the family and take statements from them concerning Sylvia's disappearance from Terre Haute. Who was the friend with whom she was to meet for the evening meal? No one knew. There was no explanation for her disappearance. How is it that she was home without Truman?

Truman related how he, Harry, Lillian and Sylvia had made the trip down the Mississippi and the women had been sent back home while the men stayed behind to sell the boats in New Orleans and Baton Rouge. The Inspector had read of the trip and was acquainted with the whole saga. After taking statements from all the family members present, he told them he would be back in touch, and departed.

Sylvia regained consciousness five weeks later and progressed to a nearly complete recovery. Her emotional condition was never the same again. She was at times unstable the rest of her life. The pregnancy turned out to be normal and a daughter was born in all due time and named Karen.

When questioned by the police as to her abduction, rape and transportation to Lake Charles, she had no memory of the events whatsoever. Her last memory before waking up in the hospital was of arriving home in Terre Haute from Houston by airplane through Indianapolis, her first and last flight.

After answering all the questions she could for the police, she was horrified to learn from Truman that all the money was gone. He related the whole chain of events to her and questioned her as to whether she had told her captors where the loot was hidden. She had no such recollection. She did not have any clue as to who had kidnapped her or what she might have or have not told them. All memory was gone as to the whole affair. Truman wanted to believe what she was telling him but Harry did not accept it completely. For years, he would occasionally attempt to get her to remember but with always the same result. There was nothing she could tell him.

Meanwhile, back in Terre Haute, Harry had been apprized of the situation in Lake Charles and told Truman to stay with Sylvia. He would continue to investigate the theft of their funds on his own till Truman could free himself from whatever he was needed for. It turned out that three months would transpire before the two brothers could begin once more to solve this crime perpetrated by criminals upon criminals.

Harry had, in Truman's absence, gone to Lafayette to spy on their friend and former prospective buyer. He had watched the man in an attempt to identify whom he might be involved with. He hoped that one of the people he had seen with the man in Baton Rouge would visit and in this way begin to identify other members of the group. He had accumulated a long list of possible co-conspirators to investigate but all of them had proven useless. He had not been able to identify a single person who had been in the hotel rooms where the evaluation of the merchandise had taken place. He had not been able to identify the two men who ripped them off in the securities debacle. In short, he had absolutely nothing positive to go on. The only possibility left that he had not attempted was to kidnap their friend from Lafayette and beat the truth out of him.

This was the question that he put to Truman after Sylvia's recovery was assured. It seemed the only alternative left open to them. But, what would be the consequences of their doing so. If they kidnapped him, they would probably have to kill him, because he would have them killed if he survived such an assault. Whatever information they could obtain from him might allow them to identify the people they were looking for but would that get the goods back or payment for them? These were the ultimate questions they had to deal with for it was now evident that they had been robbed by people who were professionals at doing so. The kind of professionals who would not hesitate to kill both of them, if they thought they were being threatened by them. What should they do? They often questioned why they were still alive. Why had they been left untouched physically? Was it because the robbers might be afraid of the consequences of killing them? Was it possible that the make believe partners that Truman and Harry had manufactured were now their current protectors? In the underworld they had lived in, fear was always the most powerful motivation available. If their adversaries thought that they had powerful allies, they would be safer than otherwise might be the case. It was all so futile and confusing and complicated. What could they do? What were the limits they could expect?

Truman told Harry that he thought they were going to have to just walk away from it. It was a death trap about to spring on them if they did not. In his opinion, it was not worth the continued risk. He had a child on the way now and he wanted to see it reared. He wanted to take what little they had and attempt to make a life as an ordinary person.

Harry disagreed. He felt it was at least possible that they might force a payment for the loot from those who took it if they worked it right. It was, in his eyes, a matter of finding the head of the snake and putting pressure on him. He wanted to capture their friend from Lafayette and make him talk. Harry thought the man would cave in without having to kill him if they handled everything right. He had developed a plan.

The plan called for snatching the man from his home and taking him to a place where they could threaten him enough to scare him into negotiating with the rest of his group for them. They would not insist on identifying the rest of the group.

They would let him live if he arranged payment for the loot. If he would co-operate with them, they would let him go. If not, they could still let him go if they decided he really was not involved. They would give him a chance to prove himself but they would do so with threats only. They would not physically harm him but only scare the daylights out of him. Truman was skeptical. Harry persisted. Truman balked. Harry pressed him. Truman gave in.

The plan was worked out to take the man to a place Harry had rented out in the countryside about thirty miles from Lafayette. The Mahoneys watched for the proper moment and knocked on the door of the man's house and could immediately see fear in his eyes as he answered the door. They told him they had a business arrangement they wanted him to hear and asked him to join them for a little trip out into the country to meet with some associates. The man balked and said he was not interested as he had more to do at the present time than he could handle. Perhaps another time would be better. Harry insisted with an automatic pistol used as an exclamation point. Reluctantly and threatening retaliation, the man decided to accompany them to the meeting.

Once they had the man sitting in a chair in the country cottage, Harry explained that he knew exactly what the man and his associates had done and that Sylvia had not died. She had told them how they had made her disclose the location of their merchandise and that they now wanted to be paid for the loot. The man was clearly shaken with this knowledge and after a short time of denial, decided to bargain with them.

He said he could not disclose the identity of the group because it would mean the death of Harry and Truman as well as himself. He would pass the proposal to the people and if it was handled properly, he felt he could get the group to make good on the initial offer made back in Baton Rouge. He said, "These men are honorable men and they will honor that offer if I press them with the justice of it. If I express to them that you two will not pursue the matter any further, I am certain they will do what is right. You just need to understand that you insulted them when you refused what they thought was a fair offer. You brought this whole thing on yourself. You know that I have always dealt fairly with you and I will make it right if you will co-operate with me and act like the businessmen you are."

This appealed to Harry and Truman and after a long consultation, they agreed to let the man go with the stern warning that if he failed, he would die. They gave him a set of instructions for payment of the debt and he accepted the terms. He was taken back home and he told them he would meet them at a restaurant with the response from his group in four days at 9:00 P.M.

The man's back disappearing through the front door of his home was the last they ever saw of him. He vanished. They searched for him for over a year before giving up and writing the whole thing off. At least that is what Truman did. Harry really never gave it up. For several years, his life would revolve around revenge and a means of restoration of "his wealth".

Kenny, I must shut down for now. I will return as soon as duty will allow.

Blessings on you,
Clifford

CHAPTER 29
PROVIDENCE

Kenny,
I would like to say that Truman had learned his lesson and removed himself from a life of crime at this juncture of his life, but that would be a lie. He wanted to but he could not find a way to clear Harry out of his life. The web these two had woven around each other was too powerful for him to break. Try as he might, it just seemed impossible for him to face each and every day without some involvement with Harry.

At first, he was just worried about Harry. After finally concluding that they had come to a dead end in their search, Harry had gone into a deep depression and seemed to be losing touch with reality. Truman hung around to protect him until he was back on his feet. This of course called for much sacrifice on Truman's part but he felt that one day he would be free and would go his own way. His Bible reading was picked up once more and he took up reading other literature also. He had memorized large portions of a poem entitled "Rubaiyat" by Omar Khayyam while in prison and in his own twisted soul, he used it as a counterbalance to what he often felt when reading the Bible. He knew that there would be a judgement that he would have to face in God's court. The Bible made it very clear and he believed it was so but that was in the life to come. He was dealing with this life and it was so confusing at times.

Somehow he felt down deep within himself that the losing of what he and Harry had labored for and looked forward to was, in some way, a means of God trying to turn his focus toward a different life here. A life to come? Yes. But a life in the here and now also? How did that section of Omar's poem go?

XXVI
Why, all the Saints and Sages who discuss'd
Of the Two Worlds so wisely—they are thrust
Like foolish Prophets forth; their Words to Scorn
Are scatter'd, and their Mouths are stopt with Dust.
XXVII
Myself when young did eagerly frequent
Doctor and Saint, and heard great argument
About it and about: but evermore
Came out by the same door where in I went.
XXVIII
With them the seed of Wisdom did I sow,
And with mine own hand wrought to make it grow;
And this was all the Harvest that I reap'd—
"I came like Water, and like Wind I go."

God was trying to speak to him. He knew it but could not get past Harry. Could not get past his past. Could God deal with these obstacles? Would He? When? Where? How? He could not tell. In the meantime, he would make the best he could of the hand he had been dealt.

For several years Harry and Truman moved from place to place in whatever job they felt like involving themselves. Harry and Lillian began a family and with the growth, eventually four children, two boys and two girls, they seemed to slip further and further away from Truman. He and Sylvia seemed never to be the same as they had been together before her ordeal in Louisiana. A wall of some kind had grown between them and yet they tried to get along together for Karen's sake.

One day there was a knock on the door at Truman's place in Tennessee and who would be standing there but little Mary, Lillian's younger sister. She was invited in and shared a story with Truman that her aunt had thrown her out because of an accident with a baby that she was supposed to be caring for. She was a long way from home and had been at her aunt's place to help pick cotton for the summer. She had nowhere to go.

Truman and Sylvia took her in and told her she could stay till things could be worked out. Mary was full of life and had come to Truman because she had loved him from the first time she saw him as a little girl and had dreamed of marrying him one day. This was a receipt for trouble in a home where many strains had stretched a marriage to the breaking point. Truman and Mary became intimate and the result was a pregnancy that broke the cords holding things together. A divorce was inevitable and a marriage with a new young pregnant bride was forthcoming. Things were good and bad. More and more jobs, the money was gone. Harry was still trying to keep them going by using the last of the old money, jewels and gold coins from the safe deposit box in Baton Rouge to get them over whatever hump came along.

He would occasionally go down to Baton Rouge and make a withdrawal and attempt to sell small portions of the gold coins or rare bills on the collector's markets. Sometimes doing quite well. He often cursed himself when he remembered how he had trusted $88,0000.00 of their money into the hands of Bessie. The accounts that had been closed and transferred to her were never of any use to he and Truman at all. By the time he had gotten to Bessie to retrieve the funds, she was long gone. She and Johnny both, and by the time he found them, they were stone broke and had spent every cent of it on high living. $63,000.00 plus years of interest had brought the banked funds to the total of $88,000.00 and it was all gone.

Truman had thrown a fit when that was discovered and it was one of the wedges that finally began to unravel the bond that held them together. That and the fact that Mary and Lillian did not get along. So money occasionally became a problem. Sometimes when the pressure was too high for Truman to deal with, he would resort to robbery again.

No banks, but smaller jobs like a J.C. Penny Store or some other place that had practically no security. He had learned how to completely avoid capture and this was child's play to the seasoned criminal that Truman had become. He always hated himself after pulling such a job. Not so much from shame of what was done but that it was work that was below his pride as a master criminal. He often swore to himself and to God, he would not do it again.

There was a time when he and Harry had purchased some acreage side by side in Tennessee and jobs were scarce so Truman and Mary decided to go to Florida and work there for a while. It was during their time there that Truman looked up the old banker who had run out on them in New Orleans with the samples of the old cash. It wasn't all that much, just a few thousand dollars but fair is fair, so Truman paid him a visit and sure enough, and true to his word, the man produced the money. He offered to pay Truman for it and keep it if that suited Truman. It did. They remained in Florida for a while.

A letter came from Harry stating that he wanted to have a pond dug on the property they had in Tennessee and could get it dug free by the government if Truman would sign the title over to him. He needed the extra acreage to qualify for the grant for the pond. He would give it back when Truman returned. Truman signed it over to him.

Some time later, the Floridians returned and Harry went back on his word and would not sign the land title back over to Truman. A real split developed and Truman never told Harry he had gotten the money from the banker. For the first time in his life, Truman had lied to his brother or perhaps a better statement would be, he had deceived him deliberately. They drifted apart.

It was not many years after that Harry was stricken with Hodgkins Disease and after a two- year battle with it, he died a broken man with Lillian and four children left to fend for themselves.

Harry's death left Truman to struggle and search for a new place in life. He went through several years of internal torture in his attempt to locate that place and in so doing dragged his new and growing family through several painful relocations.

Mary and Truman finally came to Beaumont, Texas where Truman went to work for St. Elizabeth Hospital as a Physical Therapist. He had gotten a lot of training while in jail in this field and had even been forced to treat prisoners while in Angola in the infirmary. He was even called "Doc" by the prison guards there.

His expertise was sharpened while working in Beaumont and taking advantage of all possible training, he soon was responsible for opening the first Physical Therapy Unit in Southeast Texas at St. Elizabeth Hospital. He was called upon to direct the opening of the same kind of units in other hospitals in the area, including the Baptist Hospital of Southeast Texas in Beaumont.

It was during this time that he and Mary bought their

little home in Vidor, Texas and not too long after that, the paths of Truman and Jesus Christ crossed in the sweeping of his feet and his home out from under him. He had done so in just the proper timing that a group of caring Baptists could demonstrate the true love of Christ to a beaten, isolated and completely degenerate Truman Mahoney. For the first time in his life, Truman truly came clean with God and set his life on a new course. The Hound of Heaven had found its prey. With no more fight left in him, he surrendered. The chase was at an end.

Life in the last years for Truman was the richest he had ever known. He was accepted completely for who he was. But the person he had been was no longer alive. A new Truman now lived and a total new direction lay before him. He was at peace with God and his fellow man.

Truman Mahoney

Funeral services for Truman R. Mahoney, 66, of 3650 Lakeview Cutoff Road in Pine Forest, will be Friday at 10 a.m. in Pine Forest Baptist Church.

Rev. Don Mitchell, pastor, will officiate and burial will be in Restlawn Memorial Park. He died Tuesday in Baptist Hospital in Beaumont following a long illness.

He was a native of Tarver Hill, Ill. but had lived in Vidor 13 years.

Survivors include his wife, Mrs. Mary Mahoney; two sons, Truman Richard Mahoney Jr. and Joseph Christopher Mahoney; three daughters, Pamala Ruth Mahoney, Jacqueline Marie Mahoney and Trudy Evelyn Mahoney, all of Vidor; and one sister, Mrs. Gladys Hughes of Indiana.

Obituary Notice from June 9, 1977 in The Vidor Vidorian Newspaper

EPILOGUE

Truman had family that I have not included in this narrative. He had three sisters and another baby brother who drowned at age 2 or 3 years. I have not dealt with these siblings because my knowledge of them is too limited and I could find no reliable means of obtaining enough to do them justice. If the sisters are still alive, and read this text, I would want them to know that I loved their brother and would welcome any contact with them. It is my earnest wish that they know that this story is not complete. Truman wanted it to be told but was unable to get it done. I have probably not done it the way he would have but I have tried to share it in the spirit that he shared it with me.

I wish I had been able to have access to the box of documentation that Truman had collected but it seems to have been lost. I have spent many hours and expended considerable funds in researching the National Archives and Newspaper Archives in trying to recreate that documentation. It was too great a task for my resources to complete. It is my intention to complete this task during my retirement years, which may begin very soon. If God will allow me the grace for the task, I will one day publish an amended version of the story with full documentation included. As for now, this is the best I can do.

I did find that the Bureau of Prisons or the courts or possibly the F.B.I. or some such agency has been responsible for expunging some of Truman and Harry's prison records in connection with his pardon conditions. I had to work around this difficulty in my research but I want to thank those who tried to assist me in every way they could and still remain true to their employers. I was able to obtain a photocopy of Truman's pardon and it will be a treasure I will cherish. It came from the files in Washington D.C. Department of Justice and was furnished by the Attorney General's Office.

One interesting highlight may be worth mentioning here and that is that the ex wife of Harry's who made off with their bank account funds could possibly have been another lady. The reason I say that is that the records from Alcatraz indicated that he had been married to Johnny's mother at the time of his birth and either left her or she him. A reference is made to this and it is not completely clear whether Johnny was living with her or Harry's second wife, Bessie, at the time the funds were transferred to one of his former wives. Some things were not crystal clear after all the years have passed.

Truman Mahoney had lived his life in a way that had probably set some world records that he never set out to post in the record books. And sure enough, they were never recorded there. It is not a record that he was proud of and probably never recognized that he was responsible for setting. I never discussed it with him in that way but it has occurred to me that the record was undoubtedly set.

He and Harry, along with their gang, were responsible for robbing more banks than any person who ever existed. **That is one record**. In addition to that, they set the record for the most banks robbed for which they were never even accused of having robbed. According to Truman, there were many bank robberies for which they were responsible that never were solved. Many other people were accused of committing the crimes and went to jail for having done so but The Mahoney Gang actually did the work. Their ability to mask who they were and throw suspicion onto others had worked. So in reality, these robberies truly were never solved. They had been convicted of only one and had confessed to several more for personal gain while in prison, which makes the total so large that I have decided not to give a number until further research can verify them. I have no reason to disbelieve what Truman told me in this regard but the number he gave me was so large that I felt that others might reject the whole book in my being unable to independently verify what he said. There were several people killed in connection with the years of evil activities of the Mahoney brothers that I wish I could identify and clear some others who were wrongly accused and convicted of having done. Regretfully I found no way to accomplish this task.

I do not wish to in any way glorify what the Mahoney brothers did but I do want to say that God saw the great potential in Truman and no doubt is saddened because most of it was wasted due to many influences. His last days were a blessing to human kind and it is a great loss that he was not set on the right path while a young man. I suppose Harry will share in some of the blame for the failure of Truman's life, his parents also and society as a whole perhaps should be included. The church certainly failed him in the early years of his life. Truman himself, in the end, placed most of the blame on Truman. I think the day he did so was the day he became a man.

It had been Truman's aim to one day list all the banks and give the details to all that he could remember so as to set the record straight. He was deeply troubled that he might be able get some few people's name cleared of false convictions he was responsible for. He did not live to do so. I think that God may have had something to do with preventing that from actually happening. I am not sure just why but one day I hope to be with Truman when he asks our Lord about it and I will have my ear turned eagerly toward the unfolding of the **last chapter.**

DEDICATION
A LAST NOTE FOR KENNY

Kenny,
I realize that I have been a long time in sharing the end of Truman's story with you. You have been a wonderful encouragement to me in completing the work.

I want to thank you for your friendship and interest but most of all for your faithful service to our Lord. Your wonderful attitude of servanthood has been an inspiration to me.

I hope and pray that in some small way, the exchanges we have shared were as much a blessing to you as they have been to me. I also hope that your burden has been lightened in some way. If so then I will be happy to have ministered to you and Jackie in perhaps lifting your hearts and minds even if only momentarily.

I continue to pray daily for the complete recovery of your health and look forward to meeting the two of you face to face.

It is to you and the memory of Truman and for the glory of Christ that I dedicate this work.

Your brother in Jesus,
Clifford

A LAST NOTE AMMENDED

During the week that arrangements had been clearly made for the publishing of this work, I sent Kenny and

Jackie Cole an e-mail to tell them the news. We had gone through a year of dealing with publishers and my literary agent had found no buyers for it. Kenny had struggled with me and was so very supportive in believing it should and would get published. We knew that the cancer in his body was quickly pulling him toward a blessed face-to-face meeting with our Lord.

On July 16, 2005 that meeting took place. In his sleep, at his home in Merced, California, he slipped away for the appointment. Jackie was with him as she had been for several months after leaving her job to spend all her time with him. No man ever had a more faithful and devoted wife.

In speaking with her that day by telephone, I learned that she had not yet read the note I had sent them sharing that the book was finally going to be published. Kenny left without having read the conclusion of the work but fully expected to learn the final state of Truman Mahoney.

Somehow I think he is going to get more of the details than I have to publish and may do so before it comes off the press. I suspect that he and Truman will share a good laugh over my feeble attempt to share a story that needs to be told. One thing I am sure about, Truman will receive one of Kenny's famous and coveted hugs.

Clifford Neal

Kenny & Jackie Cole at home in 2004

DOCUMENTATION

In my concern that some would think Truman's story to be a fabrication of my mind, I returned to Vidor, Texas and reestablished contact with Mary Mahoney in preparing to write the book. She is now known by another last name from a subsequent remarriage. I do not have her permission to print that name at this time. She entered a new life with a new husband some time after Truman's death and bore other children., all of whom are now grown up.

Truman and Mary's children are all adults and most of them have children of their own. Mary informed me that she had discussed the book being published with them and that none objected to being identified. I have decided to go no further in doing so than what I have already included in the text of the book. My reasons for this lie in the fact that I offered to meet with and discuss the book with the children and none of them responded to the offer. I took this to be a reluctance to be clearly identified in such a public way. It had been my hope to utilize some of the photographs possessed by the family of the boats, which were manufactured by Truman and Harry and in which they made the trip down the Mississippi River.

I met with some reluctance to allow their usage here, so I decided to rely upon the records that are available to me in the public files. The following materials are portions of rather large volumes of materials from several sources.

The National Archives provided photographs of both

Truman and Harry Mahoney and I am including what was available. Other documentation included is from court records, Federal Bureau of Investigation Files and prison files that survive as historical documents. Many prison records have been destroyed, particularly those from Angola Prison in Louisiana. I am led to believe that this was done in the expunging of records agreed to as part of the conditions of the Presidential Pardon. It may be that they exist but are sealed. An Assistant Warden there did all she could to find them for me but wrote that it was not possible at the present.

A (reduced size) copy of the Pardon is posted here and it will be evident that a portion of this document has been erased as well for probably the same reason. The copy presented here came from the files in Washington, D.C. in the exact form you see here.

The Obituary notice of Truman's death and funeral came from the archives of The Vidor Vidorian, a newspaper of Vidor, Texas.

The newspaper archives of several cities along the Mississippi River will document the progress of the boat trip and particularly the files of the New Orleans papers. I am in the process of obtaining those records and do not have them in my possession at the moment. I hope to soon correct that deficiency. For the present, I have chosen several documents that I feel will give the reader some insight into the reality of this story.

These materials will be presented to the publisher for inclusion in the book.

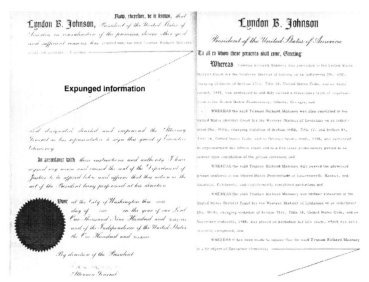

On June 9, 1966 President Lyndon Johnson issued a full pardon to Truman after he had completed all of his probationary sentence. It is noted tht a portion of the text is removed as a part of the expunging of his record. The original contained the reason for the pardon, which was his undercover work in Leavenworth.